History of the
Catholic Diocese of Belleville

Illinois

125th anniversary

Publisher

Éditions du Signe - B.P. 94
F-67038 Strasbourg Cedex 2
France
Tel. (33) 03 88 78 91 91
Fax. (33) 03 88 78 91 99

Photography: John Glover
Director of Publication: Christian Riehl
Publication Assistant: Marc de Jong
Layout: Sylvie Tusinski

Printed in China

Table of Contents

■ *Bishop Braxton stands with the newly ordained priests in 2010. From left are Fr. Sean Palas, Fr. Abraham Adejoh, Bishop Braxton, Fr. Dale Maxfield and Fr. Joseph Oganda. Back row, Fr. Jack McEvilly, Vicar General; Fr. John Myler; Bishop Stan Schlarman and the Rev. Mr. Anthony Onyango.*

The Transfiguration of the Lord
Dear Sisters and Brothers in Christ,

Peace be with you!
August 6, 2011

Jesus of Nazareth is the reason why the Diocese of Belleville exists. Jesus, the Messiah, the Anointed One of God, is the reason why the Catholic Church exists in southern Illinois and around the world. Jesus Christ and the Good news of His life, teachings, wondrous signs, suffering, death, resurrection and ascension are the reason why the Catholic faith began to flourish here 125 years ago, when His Holiness, Pope Leo XIII erected this Diocese on January 7, 1887 and appointed the Most Reverend John Janssen, D.D. as the first of eight bishops to lead and guide the People of God.

This book, which provides a brief history of the parishes that have served the Christian Faithful in southern Illinois, is in reality a history of individuals, families, neighborhoods, towns, and farming communities striving to live out their baptismal commitments to "put on Christ." The powerful presence of the Holy Spirit working in the sacraments has renewed and transformed generations of Catholics by Divine grace through the century and a quarter of our history as a Local Church and through the years before that when we were not yet a Diocese.

The history of any Christian community is the history of the struggle of a people to live by the light of Christ when it is much easier to ignore that brilliant and challenging light. But if Christ can be called the sacrament of the encounter with God, then the Church can be called the sacrament of the encounter with Christ, and each of us can be called the sacrament of the encounter with the Church. Therefore, the most important part of our history cannot be recorded in this slim volume. The most important part of our history is the history of tens of thousands of families living out the dramas of their lives each day, nurtured by the Word of God, fed by the Body and Blood of Christ in the Eucharist, and purified of sin in the sacrament of reconciliation. The deeply spiritual history of a pilgrim people living their faith amid so many joys and sorrows is beyond the reach of a narrator's pen. Keep this in mind as you read the names of men and women, places, buildings and projects in the pages that follow. The history of the Diocese of Belleville is not simply the history of bishops and priests buying land and building buildings. It is the history of bishops, priests, deacons, religious, and all of the People of God getting up each morning discovering their faith anew and making a fresh commitment to love God with all of their hearts and to love their neighbor as they love themselves.

Bishop Braxon pours balsam into oil to make the Oil of Chrism at the annual liturgy in 2009.

As we give thanks for 125 years of history and as we strain forward for a glimpse of the unknown future of the next 125 years, we realize that we are putting out into the deep. But as we move into our future, the one think that we know for sure is that our ongoing spiritual growth and renewal must be our foundation. We must all renew our lives of genuine personal prayer. We must pray for the humility we need to heed the call to personal and communal conversion, if we are to grow in holiness in our personal lives at home, at school, at work, and in our parish communities. By this, I mean conversion to an active openness to the presence of God in our lives, conversion to a scripture and liturgy based personal relationship with Jesus Christ as our Savior, conversion to vital and enthusiastic membership in the Church community under the guidance of the Holy Spirit, conversion to moral integrity in our personal lives, which means living by the Beatitudes, the Ten Commandments and the moral teachings of the Church each day of our lives. Jesus Christ, really and truly present in the Eucharist, the source and summit of our ongoing conversion, calls us by name, Sunday after Sunday, to gather around His altar. Keep this Christ-centered vision ever before your eyes as you read our stories.

Our genuine gratitude for the past must be expressed in planning for the future and planning for the future must take into account the realities of the present. As you probably know, a number of factors have been indicating for many years now that we, who are the Diocese of Belleville, like many other dioceses, need to consolidate some of our parishes, if we hope to have strong and vital Catholic communities in the years to come. By the time this Anniversary Book is placed in your hands, I will have announced the beginning of a PASTORAL PLAN FOR PARISH RENEWAL AND RESTRUCTURING in our Diocese.

I know how much you love the Church and your parish. I am confident that this love will sustain and guide all of us as we undertake this important planning process. As members of the Catholic Church, we live out our faith and bear witness to the Gospel of Jesus Christ in our parish communities, which are part of the larger community of our Local Church, the Diocese of Belleville. Our parishes do not stand alone. Ultimately, the strengths and weaknesses of one parish have an impact on the strengths and weaknesses of all of our parishes.

During these past six years, I have reflected and prayed a great deal about the need for a PASTORAL PLAN FOR PARISH RENEWAL AND RESTRUCTURING in our Diocese. I have also heard many of our priests, deacons, religious and Christian Faithful affirm this need during my Parish Pastoral Visitations. We currently have 117 parishes serving about 70,000 active Catholics. I have been very pleased to encounter many strong, vibrant communities of faith. A number of these parishes are very close together. Others are very small. Still others are struggling to keep their schools open. Some are facing very serious financial challenges. Some of you have told me that our Diocese should have begun the process of parish restructuring a long time ago.

We currently have sixty-nine diocesan priests in parish ministry. Five of these are seventy-five or older and three more are seventy and older. Currently, we have an additional twenty-two priests serving here whom I have brought to the Diocese from dioceses and religious communities outside of the country. We hope to have more in the years ahead. Nevertheless, while it is not possible to predetermine the results of this process, it has become clear that we need to reduce the number of our parishes.

We all know that the question of restructuring and consolidating parishes is a sensitive topic. Please keep in mind that the PASTORAL PLAN FOR PARISH RENEWAL AND RESTRUCTURING is a consultation. I have made no prior decisions about the future of any parish. Indeed, it is my hope that you who are the Christian Faithful will study the realities of your faith communities honestly and propose realistic recommendations concerning the future of our parishes. This entire process we are undertaking must be done in an environment of prayer to the Holy Spirit for guidance.

The PASTORAL PLAN FOR PARISH RENEWAL AND RESTRUCTURING will not be focused on a particular geographical area of the Diocese. All parishes and all Catholic schools are participating. The PLAN will unfold in two phases (Phase One: September 2011- February 2012; Phase Two: March 2012- February 2013) giving all of the parishes, schools and parish leaders a sufficient amount of time to participate fully in the process. I am confident that this process will strengthen our Diocese and I urge all of the Christian Faithful and those who serve in Pastoral Ministry to participate actively, making this diocesan-wide effort a high priority.

I am aware that this process will ultimately involve real sacrifices as devoted Catholics consider the prospect of significant changes in their parish life. However, this process will ultimately strengthen the Church in southern Illinois. It will renew our parish communities and give us hope as we look ahead with confidence to the next 125 years. I am deeply grateful to you for your unselfish participation in this work for the long-term good of the Church in southern Illinois. Please work for vocations to the Priesthood in your parish. Please pray the Diocesan Prayer for Vocations at all Masses once a month. Please pray as well for the fruitfulness of the PASTORAL PLAN we are undertaking for the good of the Diocese. If we do not pray, we have already chosen failure. With prayer at the heart of our endeavor, we can truly embrace the future with hope. Pray that, like the Lord Jesus Christ Himself, we may be transfigured by the power of the Holy Spirit.

Prayerfully yours in Christ,

+Edward K. Braxton

The Most Reverend Edward K. Braxton
Bishop of Belleville

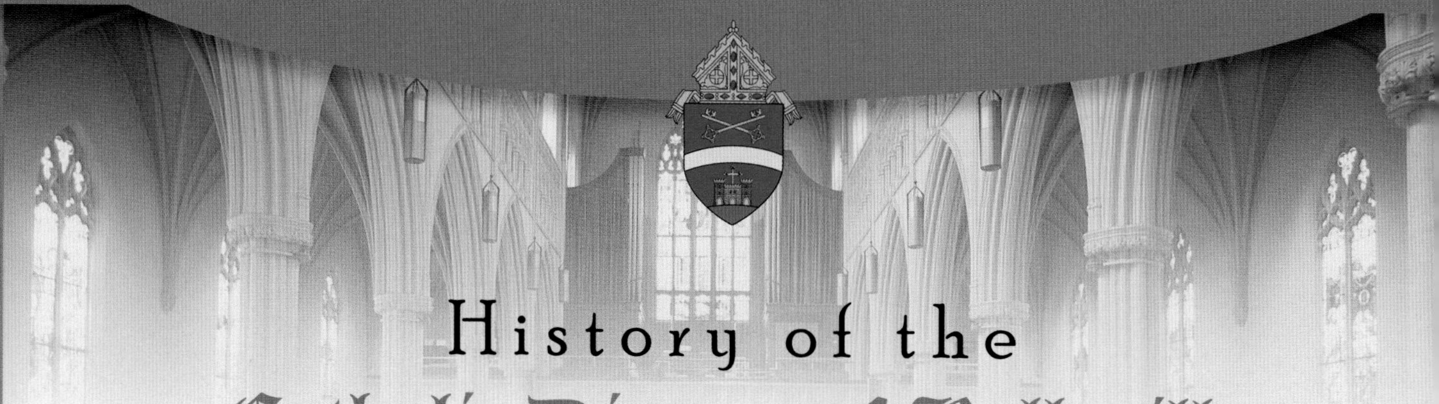

History of the
Catholic Diocese of Belleville

"May I never boast except in the cross of our Lord Jesus Christ through which the world has been crucified to me and I to the world."

(Galatians 6:14)

In the north of France, the landscape is punctuated by wayside shrines, *le calvaire*. Ranging from simple stone crosses to elaborate crucifixion scenes, *le calvaire*, the Cross of Jesus Christ serves as a directional landmark for travelers and as a call to prayer for people of faith. The Belleville Diocese has its own *le calvaire*, three simple wooden crosses atop a small mound just outside of historic Prairie du Rocher, along the road to the restored Fort Chartres.

Our *le calvaire* is the epitome of simplicity: plain wooden beams, nailed together in the Christian sign of hope and victory, rising slightly above the Mississippi River valley. Our *le calvaire* epitomizes the faith of the Church in southern Illinois: strong, humble, rooted in Christ. Our *le calvaire* memorializes all of the ordinary, yet somehow extraordinary, men and women, bishops, priests, religious and laity who worked together to plant the Cross of Jesus Christ in this richly diverse 11,678 square miles that for the past 125 years has been called the Catholic Diocese of Belleville. Our *le calvaire* challenges us to lift our eyes to Christ as our guide for the next 125 years; to replant, to lift up anew the Cross of Christ in southern Illinois in among new generations and in new and exciting ways.

The famed French explorers, Father Jacques Marquette and Louis Joliet, paddled past the Belleville Diocese as they explored the Mississippi River from 1673 to 1674. Illinois Native Americans were open to evangelization, including the Tamarois and Cahokias, who had been dispersed by the Iroquois. These refugee tribes resettled near present day Cahokia. Three priests

Father Marquette preaching ■

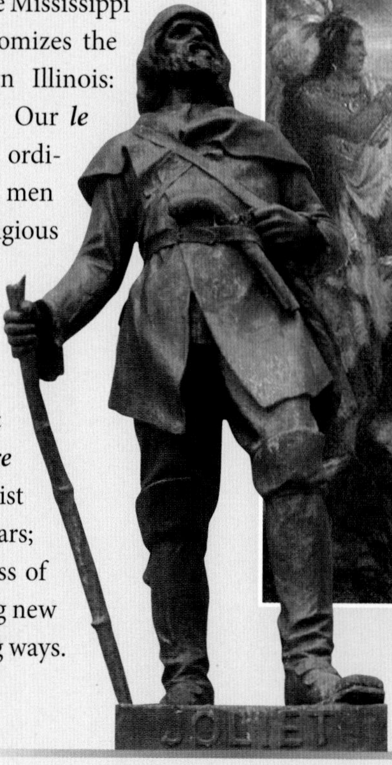

■ *Louis Joliet*

from Quebec came to establish a mission among these people. Fathers Francois Joliet de Montigny, Antoine Davion and Jean Francois Buisson de St. Cosme arrived and celebrated the first Mass at Cahokia on the Feast of the Immaculate Conception, December 8, 1698. Their new mission was dedicated to the Holy Family and became the first permanent Catholic Church in the Illinois country and the first in what would become the interior of the United States.

Holy Family Church was completed on May 14, 1699. "When it was finished, we erected a cross with the greatest possible solemnity," Father Montigny wrote.

Immaculate Conception Mission was established among the Kaskaskias and both Cahokia and Kaskaskia settlements attracted Native Americans and French settlers. The Kaskaskia proved themselves to be very industrious and religious, attending Mass, receiving the sacraments, and participating in catechism classes faithfully. In 1721, the French military assumed administration of the colonies from the missionaries; Fort de Chartres and a nearby town were established. In 1736 a detachment of troops from the fort was massacred and

their chaplain, Father Antonius Senat, SJ, was burned as the stake by the Chickasaw Indians. The settlers chose not to avenge the attack. The fort and its settlement eventually transferred its spiritual care to the log mission of St. Joseph in nearby Prairie du Rocher.

■ *Historial Commemoration at Fort de Chartres, Prairie du Rocher, IL.*

Catholic Immaculate Conception Church in Kaskaskia ■

The fledgling Church in southern Illinois became part of the first American diocese, the Diocese of Baltimore, headed by Bishop John Carroll. Later, new dioceses were created from the Archdiocese of Baltimore, including the Diocese of Bardstown, Kentucky. With Bishop Joseph Flaget as its head, this new diocese encompassed the Illinois country. Bishop Flaget traveled throughout his large diocese often, visiting the French communities along the Mississippi.

After one such tour, Bishop Flaget wrote to Archbishop Carroll, "My visit through the French settlements has been very laborious, but a hundred times more successful than I would have expected. I have confirmed about twelve hundred people, though I confirm none but those who have made their First Communion. At least eight or ten priests are wanting in these immense countries, and if some could be put among the Indians who would be willing to receive them, ten more would scarcely do."

The few Catholics who settled outside the Mississippi River valley found no church to attend, so the Church had to come to them. Several priests became circuit riders, packing their vestments and sacred vessels into saddlebags and seeking out people who needed consolation. The best known of these traveling pastors was Father Elijah "Daddy" Durbin, who road thousands of miles on horseback between 1822 and 1859. He attended the small Catholic communities in Dolan's Settlement (Enfield), Belle Prairie (Piopolis), Pond Settlement, Equality, Carmi, McLeansboro, and Shawneetown, which was a wide-open frontier boomtown at the time.

Illinois' first English-speaking Catholic congregation was formed at O'Hara's Settlement, now called Ruma, in 1818, the year that the state itself was created. In 1824, members of the English settlement at Hecker built a log church, which they placed under the patronage of St. Augustine of Canterbury. It was the first Catholic church built in Illinois in over one hundred years.

DRAWN BY R. RUGER.

1. PUBLIC SQUARE.
2. COURT HOUSE.
3. DISTRICT SCHOOL-HOUSES.
4. TURNER HALL.
5. ENGINE HOUSES.
6. RAIL ROAD DEPOT.
7. MARKET HOUSE
8. COAL MINES
9. GERMAN PROTESTANT CHURCH

BELLEVILLE.

St. Clair Co. Illinois 1867.

CHICAGO LITHOGRAPHING CO.

10. PRESBYTERIAN.
11. BAPTIST.
12. METHODIST.
13. GERMAN METHODIST.   } CHURCHES.
14. CATHOLIC.
15. CONVENT OF THE IMMACULATE CONCEPTION.
16. THOMAS HOUSE.
17. NATIONAL HOUSE.
18. BELLEVILLE HOUSE.

Immigrants from Germany began arriving in Illinois in the 1830s. Most were farmers or merchants and many chose to settle in the area around Belleville. There was still no church in Belleville and the priests who came through were English or French-speaking. In 1839, the first German-speaking priest, Father Joseph Kuenster, arrived as the first resident pastor in the city of Belleville. He immediately organized a congregation, placed under the patronage of St. Peter. The cornerstone for the community's premier Catholic church was laid in April 1843 and the first Mass was celebrated in the sanctuary on Christmas Day, even though the walls were not plastered, the floor was dirt and there was no ceiling. Two candlesticks sat on a plain wooden altar. Yet, the people of St. Peter's had a home.

In 1837, a railroad line was built between the two river towns of East St. Louis and Cairo. Within the next two decades, the face of southern Illinois changed. Towns along rail lines sprang up virtually overnight. The Illinois Central Railroad began recruiting workers from Germany, Ireland, and the American east coast in 1852.

Bishop John Janssen,
First Bishop
of Belleville

The Catholic population of the State of Illinois doubled, redoubled and redoubled again in the years between 1830 and 1860 and churches proliferated. Yet, in 1852 there were only eight priests living and ministering in the future Belleville Diocese at Cahokia, Kaskaskia, Prairie du Rocher, Ruma, St. Francisville, Germantown, Belleville, and Waterloo. With the growth of Catholicism in Illinois, the Chicago Diocese was created in 1843 and fourteen years later, the Alton Diocese was established under the leadership of Bishop Henry Juncker.

Illinois Catholics rallied to the Union cause with the outbreak of the Civil War in 1861. Two priests from southern Illinois served in the Union Army as chaplains, Father Paul Limacher, who in his 38 years in Waterloo built the present Sts. Peter and Paul Church, and Father Louis Lambert of Shawneetown, who was in twenty battles of the Civil War, including the Battle of Shiloh, earning the rank of captain. The most prominent Catholic to serve in the Civil War was another Shawneetown resident, Brigadier General Michael K. Lawler, who led the charge at Vicksburg.

The War Between the States provided many opportunities for Catholics to act with heroic charity. Women religious from various orders worked as nurses during the conflict, including the Sisters of the Holy Cross of Notre Dame, Indiana, who were sent to Cairo, where

Father Augustus Tolton

Shortly after peace was realized at Appomattox Courthouse, Father Augustus Tolton was ordained in Rome on April; 24, 1866, for the Alton Diocese as the first priest of African descent in the United States. Father Tolton began his ministry in Quincy, Illinois, and on February 24, 2011 was declared «Servant of God» in a ceremony in Chicago which opened his cause for canonization. «Father Tolton's life is a triumph of perseverance and faith. He is a model of enormous courage and dedication to the Church, priestly zeal and fidelity in face of the social hostilities endemic to that time... His story reminds us that the United States is a work in progress,» reflected Belleville's Bishop Edward K. Braxton , who participated in the ceremony with Francis Cardinal George of Chicago.

they opened a hospital for the care of fugitive slaves and freedmen. After the war, Cairo residents asked the Sisters to stay and open St. Mary's Infirmary. Decades later during the yellow fever epidemic in Cairo, the Sisters of the Holy Cross were commended for their tireless and fearless care of patients, half of whom would die after contracting the disease.

Burnout walls was all that remained after the deadly 1884 Immaculate Conception Academy fire.

Father Tolton had carried the processional cross that led the clergy and laity through the streets of Belleville to Bishop John Janssen's consecration as the first Bishop of Belleville on April 25, 1888. A statue of Father Tolton stands in front of St. Augustine of Hippo Church, East St. Louis. The artwork was originally installed in front of the former St. Patrick Church, East St. Louis. Pray for the day when we can pray through the intercession of St. Augustus Tolton.

Bishop Juncker died in Alton in 1868 and was succeeded by the pastor of St. Peter Parish, Belleville,

Mother Solana Leczny

(1868-1919)

She stands as an example of the contributions made by southern Illinois immigrants of this era to the Catholic Church. The daughter of Polish immigrants, Martin and Katherine Dominska Leczny, the former Theresa Leczna grew up in St. Michael Parish, Radom, where her religious vocation was nurtured. In 1901, she joined Ernestine Matz and Hilaria Matz in founding the Franciscan Sisters of Our Lady of Perpetual Help at St. Louis. She took the religious name of Sister Solana. In 2011, the congregation includes one novice and 97 Sisters, including three who serve in Belleville and Royalton.

Father Peter Joseph Baltes. The Second Bishop of Alton was remembered by one source who noted, "He established regulations, laws and discipline and demanded indiscriminately obedience and respect for episcopal authority." Bishop Baltes promoted Catholic education, establishing in 1875 the regulations for parish elementary schools including rules for final examinations, textbooks, teacher supervision of pupils, and dress and deportment.

Bishop Baltes also demonstrated great concern for others in need. He welcomed to southern Illinois the Adorers of the Blood of Christ, who had fled the religious persecution of Otto Von Bismarck's *Kulturkampf*, settling first at Piopolis in 1870 and later in their current center at Ruma. He founded St. Agnes Orphanage in Belleville in 1879 in collaboration with the Hospital Sisters of St. Francis, who opened St. Elizabeth Hospital, Belleville, in 1880. Bishop Baltes also welcomed Benedictine monks, who established a monastery at Wetaug, near Anna, where they ministered for several decades.

A great tragedy occurred as fire swept through Immaculate Conception Academy, Belleville, on January 5, 1884, as temperatures dipped to twenty degrees below zero. Fatalities included twenty-two girls boarding at the school and four School Sisters of Notre Dame, including the superior, Mother Jerome, who died making an heroic effort to rescue the young women in her care.

The German and Irish immigrants of the first half of the nineteenth century were joined by other ethnic groups in the course of the 1800's. Hungarian, Czech,

■ *Bird's-eye view of Belleville, Illinois (1910)*

Lithuanian, and Polish communities were formed during the late nineteenth century with the Church at the center of these communities, serving as a safe haven in the frequent storms that beset dislocated people trying to adjust to a new culture, language, and tradition.

An era came to an end with the death of Bishop Peter Joseph Baltes on February 15, 1886. The next year, the Catholic Diocese of Belleville was created.

On January 7, 1887, Pope Leo XIII divided the Alton Diocese and created the Diocese of Belleville and the Diocese of Springfield in Illinois. The new Belleville Diocese covered 11,678 square miles in 28 counties and served about 50,000 Catholics. There were 82 churches, 53 parochial schools, three hospitals, and one orphanage. The Holy Father named His Excellency, the Most Reverend Johannes Janssen, D.D., as the first Bishop of Belleville.

Born March 3, 1835 in Kepplen, Germany, Johannes Janssen was one of eight children of Henry and Mechtilda Peters Janssen. His cousin, St. Arnold Janssen, founded the Society of the Divine Word, a missionary congregation, and the Sister Servants of the Holy Spirit, who are nicknamed the "Pink Sisters" because of the color of their habit. Young Johannes responded to Bishop Henry Juncker's appeal for missionaries to serve in southern Illinois "where there are so many souls to save." Father Janssen was ordained on November 19, 1858 at Alton and served as both a pastor and the chancellor of the Alton Diocese. At Bishop Baltes' death, he became administrator of the Alton Diocese.

The historic *le calvaire* was very much a part of the first years of the Belleville Diocese. Bishop Janssen reflected at the end of his first year, in which he confirmed 4,643 Catholics, "This was the beginning of the new Diocese of Belleville. Although the times were hard, the crops have been in failure for several years and work being scarce, yet all were full of hope for the future."

The Church also had to deal with prejudice and suspicions against the Catholics. In 1889, the Edwards Law passed in Illinois compelling children to attend public school in English. The law was overturned and compulsory education regulations provided for attendance at private or public schools. Bishop Janssen was strongly committed to Catholic education and established a diocesan school board in 1890. Annual Teachers' Institutes were begun. Within twenty years, the Belleville Diocese had 80 schools, with nearly 9,000 students. Adult Catholics were informed through *The Messenger*, then the diocesan quarterly publication, which first appeared in 1907.

Controversy was part of these early years. The Irish parishioners of the former St. Patrick Church in East St. Louis refused to accept a priest of German descent who was appointed their pastor. The crisis continued for two years until the Apostolic Delegate in Washington D. C. intervened. Other crosses came to the diocese in the form of mine strikes, tornadoes, floods and disastrous rail accidents. The Cathedral of St. Peter was lost to a tragic fire in 1912. Yet the fledgling Belleville Diocese met the challenges, prospered and grew.

A letter from Bishop Janssen on Holy Family enrollments, dated February 9, 1897, contained observations which remain timely. "Religion must be the fundamental principle of the Catholic family -- and religion, alas, is vanishing from it more and more. Look at the condition of so many families: instead of piety and holy fervor, we find indifference and coldness; instead of love and obedience, self-will and stubbornness; instead of industrious labor and contentment, indolence and inordinate longing for worldly pleasures," the Bishop observed, adding that many family problems could be addressed in prayer and consecration to Jesus, Mary, and Joseph, the models and patrons of all Christian families.

Following a heart attack in the Spring, Bishop John Janssen died on July 2, 1913 and was buried in the new crypt beneath the Cathedral, which was still under re-construction.

Flooding in Belleville

Yet, faith in Jesus Christ was the foundation for these early years. As Bishop Janssen noted in his pastoral letter marking the 1900 Holy Year, "Gather around Jesus, your divine Savior in the Holy Eucharist, and always show Him due honor."

Bishop Janssen actively promoted devotion to the Holy Family of Nazareth, supporting the efforts of Pope Leo XIII.

Bishop John Janssen ordained Fathers Henry Goosens and Aloysius Wegmann as the first priests of the Belleville Diocese on May 27, 1888. A native of Oeding, Westphalia, Germany, Father Goosens spent almost his entire 40 years as a priest serving as pastor in the West Deanery. Born in Altendorf, Germany, Father Wegmann lived only 21 years after ordination, sixteen of which he spent serving the people of the former St. Philip Parish, East St. Louis.

The first two men ordained for the Church in southern Illinois were German immigrants. In recent years, Bishop Edward K Braxton has ordained three immigrants from Nigeria and Kenya for the Belleville Diocese. The ordination class of 2010 included Fathers Abraham Adejoh and Joseph Oganda along with Fathers Dale Maxfield and Sean Palas, who are natives of southern Illinois parishes. In 2011, ishop Braxton ordained Father Anthony Onyango.

St. Philip School, East Louis, in 1892

The cross loomed on the horizon for the Belleville Diocese and the entire world as the second Bishop of Belleville was consecrated on February 24, 1914. His Excellency, the Most Reverend Henry Althoff, DD, would lead the diocese thirty-three years, marked by *le calvaire*; years of the First World War, the Great Depression and the Second World War. In southern Illinois, these eventful years were also marked by anti-Catholic sentiments and sometimes violence, deadly flu epidemics, race riots, mine disasters, tornadoes and floods. Bishop-elect Althoff seemed to foresee the challenges ahead when he observed, "I know that a difficult task awaits me, but I am encouraged by the thought that the Lord who places a burden upon the weak shoulders of His creatures, will also add sufficient strength to bear it."

A native of St. Francis of Assisi Parish, Aviston, Henry John Althoff was born on August 28, 1873, the oldest of six children. At the time of his appointment as Bishop, the forty-year-old Father Althoff was pastor of St. Barbara Parish, Okawville, and its mission, St. Ann, Nashville. A polyglot, he had learned Polish in order to better minister to the people of Nashville and in his lifetime also mastered the Latin, German, Italian, French, Spanish, Lithuanian, and Croatian languages. This talent served him well as waves of immigrants continued to pour into southern Illinois; this talent for languages revealed the sort of mind that was necessary to navigate the troubled times of his world.

With the outbreak of the First World War, German-Americans and others with foreign names were singled out often for abuse and discrimination. It is reported that 3,259 men of the Diocese served in the armed forces of the United States during World War I and 55 of these soldiers and sailors were killed in action. The violence came closer to home in July 1917 when one of the worst race riots in United States history erupted in East St. Louis, where 48 lives were lost.

Influenza swept the nation. Over 2,000 cases were reported in Belleville alone in two months and 740 southern Illinois coal miners succumbed to the disease. The Poor Handmaids of Jesus Christ opened St. Joseph Hospital in Breese to care for flu patients.

Bishop Henry Althoff sustained the Belleville Diocese through these crises. The Bishop organized the Diocese's six deaneries in order to more effectively administer the Church in southern Illinois. In 1925, he named the first diocesan Superintendent of Schools, Msgr. John J. Fallon, who is credited with modernizing Catholic education in the Belleville Diocese especially through a united course of study. Secondary education flourished as well.

Bishop Althoff promoted the formation of adult Catholics. Over the years, he drafted several series of catechetical homilies meant to instruct parishioners each Sunday on important topics. The first diocesan Eucharistic Congress was held in Mascoutah on September 19, 1937 and laymen's retreats were inaugurated at St. Henry's College in Belleville in 1938. The Diocese assumed ownership of another catechetical tool, the weekly newspaper, *The Messenger*, which had been published originally by Joseph Buechler.

One of the most significant movements in the Belleville Diocese was the formation of the Catholic Rural Life Conference, a national organization which aimed to minister to Catholics living on the land. Msgr. Bernard Hilgenberg of Carlyle was appointed the first diocesan director of the Rural Life Conference in 1923.

During the Great Depression, Bishop Althoff secured investments from financially secure Catholics in order to make low interest loans to struggling parishes. The Church responded to the needs of those who were financially oppressed during the world-wide economic crisis. St. Vincent de Paul Societies were organized in parishes to address the needs of the new poor. The Poor Handmaids of Jesus Christ at the former St. Mary Hospital, East St. Louis treated the indigent at no charge and daily fed the hungry people who came to their door in search of a meal.

With the outbreak of the Second World War, parishes offered prayers and devotions for peace. The Church displayed its patriotism through various collections and drives undertaken to aid war refugees. Scott Field outside of Belleville trained thousands of cadets for the Army Air Corps and priests from the Belleville Diocese served as military chaplains at home and abroad. At war's end, troops returned home and veterans' organizations helped them transition back into civilian life. One such group, the Catholic War Veterans, held its first meeting in the Belleville Diocese in July 1946. The Butz-Jobe Post of Catholic War Veterans in Belleville was honored as having the largest membership in the nation in 1959.

After the war, in March 1947, the entire diocese suffered with the people of Centralia where an explosion in Mine #5 of the Centralia Coal Company resulted in the deaths of 111 men. The bishop visited the area the day after the disaster. Within four months, Bishop Henry Althoff died of cancer on July 3, 1947.

Msgr. John J. Fallon (1897-1945) demonstrated a great devotion to Catholic education throughout his 21 years in the priesthood. He grew up in the former Sacred Heart Parish, East St. Louis. For several years, he worked for the L&N Railroad while discerning his vocation. Shortly after his ordination in 1924, he began graduate studies at Catholic University of America, where he specialized in education. When he returned to the diocese, Bishop Althoff named him the first superintendent of schools.

Father Fallon began by surveying teaching methods, textbooks, teachers' qualifications and study plans. Examinations, textbooks and curriculum were standardized by Father Fallon by 1929. To gauge the success of his programs, the priest personally visited each school in the Diocese at a time when automobile travel was not necessarily convenient. His accomplishments were recognized by the National Catholic Education Society and the United States Department of Education. He was also instrumental in 1938 in founding the former Le Clerc College in Belleville, of which he was president until his untimely death in 1945.

St. Joseph, Eldorado in 1951

The Church in southern Illinois enjoyed the same post-war growth that the rest of the nation experienced. The cross was lifted high above new parishes, new churches, new schools, new hospitals. The architect of much of this growth and expansion was the third Bishop of Belleville, His Excellency, the Most Reverend Albert R. Zuroweste, DD, who encountered the cross in *le calvaire* of disagreement and dissension which often accompanies major change. Tensions resulted from the decades of the Cold War and during conflicts on the Korean peninsula and in Vietnam which would take men and women away from their homes in southern Illinois to fight and die in far off lands.

Albert Rudolph Zuroweste was born on April 26, 1901 in East St. Louis. Albert Zuroweste's father would convert to Catholicism later in life. One of four children, he attended grade school in the former St. Joseph Parish. As a seminarian, he worked during summer vacations at the Illinois Coke and Refinery and the Missouri Pacific Railroad. He was ordained on June 8, 1924 and as a young priest was assigned various ministries: administrator of the former St. John's Orphanage, Belleville; editor of *The Messenger*; administrator of the former Central Catholic High School, East St. Louis; founding director of the diocesan Catholic Charities; pastor of his home parish, St. Joseph, East St. Louis. And for a time, he held most of these posts simultaneously. At *The Messenger*, Father Zuroweste collaborated with a young Catholic journalist, Robert Welzbacher, whose nearly fifty years in the Catholic press paralleled the future Bishop's service to the Church in southern Illinois. Albert R. Zuroweste was consecrated the third Bishop of Belleville on January 29, 1948. In an interview before the Belleville Diocese's centennial in 1988, Bishop Zuroweste cited growth in Catholic education as his major accomplishment. Four new high schools were constructed in Belleville, Breese, East St. Louis and Waterloo. The Newman Center was opened at Southern Illinois University Carbondale. He also led the rebuilding and expansion of St. John's Orphanage. These projects reflected the "bricks-and-mortar" growth that many parishes throughout the diocese were undertaking at this time. Another important apostolate, which touched the lives of thousands of youths, was the creation of Camp Ondessonk in 1959.

Bishop Zuroweste assisted in a groundbreaking on Fairview Heights

Bishop Zuroweste blessed animals in Farme Blessing at Evansville, IL.

A major contribution of Bishop Zuroweste was the expansion and extensive renovation of the Cathedral of St. Peter to bring it into conformity with the liturgical reforms of the Second Vatican Council. The sanctuary was remodeled completely to allow for concelebrated Masses. A south nave was added with a splendid Tree of Jesse window and remarkable windows highlighting the history of the Church in the United States. A prayerful, intimate Blessed Sacrament Chapel was also.

Adult faith formation was promoted during these years through the Confraternity of Christian Doctrine, which facilitated discussion in small study groups throughout the Diocese. Bishop Zuroweste promoted the formation of a laymen's retreat league, which resulted in the opening of King's House of Retreats in Belleville. Cana Conferences enriched the vocation of married couples and evolved into the Pre-Cana marriage preparation program.

To assure the presence of personnel to staff these parishes and institutions, the diocese promoted the Sister Formation Program, which encouraged women religious to complete their college degrees before entering the field of teaching. The Serra Club was introduced to the diocese in 1948 to enlist the help of the laity in promoting vocations to the priesthood. During these years of heightened devotion to the Virgin Mary, Bishop Zuroweste welcomed a visit of the "pilgrim statue" of Our Lady of Fatima and in 1949 the Bishop consecrated the Belleville Diocese to the Immaculate Heart of Mary, proclaiming her the patroness of the diocese. Bishop Zuroweste served as president of the Catholic Rural Life Conference for most of the 1950s.

The 1960s brought tremendous change. After years of anti-Catholic sentiment, the United States elected the first Roman Catholic president, John F. Kennedy. The new Supreme Pontiff was seen as an interim pope, Blessed Pope John XXIII, opened the windows of the Church to allow the fresh air of the Holy Spirit to blow through and to reanimate the Church. Bishop Zuroweste participated in all the sessions of the Second Vatican Council. The various reforms of the Council, most notably the changes in the liturgy, were implemented in the Church of southern Illinois as they were around the world.

The Diocese of Belleville also turned its attention far south of the confluence of the Ohio and Mississippi Rivers, responding to Blessed Pope John XXIII's 1962 call to send priests to assist the Church in Latin America. Mr. Eugene Verdu left Fairmont City for Honduras to serve as the Diocese's first lay missionary there. Three years later, the Belleville Diocese assumed responsibility for El Progreso Mission in Jalapa, Guatemala and Father Theodore Siekmann was assigned to serve that mission. In 1966, a dental clinic was established at El Progreso through the efforts of Dr. Thomas Prosser II and Dr. and Mrs. Arthur Lenzini.

In 1967, Southern Illinois Catholic youth began the annual tradition of Caroling for Guatemala to support the mission. The Guatemala Mission Society, which was chaired for many years by Miss Winifred Osborn of Carlyle, was organized in 1969. El Progreso was returned to the care of the Diocese of Jalapa in 1972. Through the efforts of Father Vincent Haselhosrst and Mr. Len Daiber of Missions International, a sister-parish program has been established between the United States and Guatemala which involves 39 sponsor parishes from the Belleville Diocese.

Women religious served in Diocese,
here are Sisters of St. Francis at Mt. Vernon

Religious, laity and clergy became more active in social justice issues at home, especially in Cairo and East St. Louis, where racial conflict was deep seated. Many left the priesthood and religious life; among the priests who stayed there were often sharp divisions on important issues across a broad spectrum. Even though Bishop Zuroweste inaugurated a "Priests' Senate," in 1968 some priests formed the Southern Illinois Association of Priests (SIAP), which has continued to raise issues and foster debate in the Church in southern Illinois.

The Church continued to strive to address the needs of the times and the people. New agencies and outreach addressed the needs of the urban poor. Educational services were offered to children with special needs. Ministry to youth expanded. Right to Life organizations responded to the legalization of abortion in the United States.

For nearly three decades, the Belleville Diocese experienced growth and construction in some areas and decline in others. All of this was a source of both great joy and great sorrow for Bishop Zuroweste, who retired in 1976. Fittingly, when he died on March 28, 1987, he was buried in a special crypt next to the Blessed Sacrament Chapel which he had built in the Cathedral.

The Second Vatican Council, in which Bishop Zuroweste participated, encouraged the active apostolate of the laity. Perhaps one husband and wife team represents the dedicated service given by lay Catholics throughout southern Illinois over the past 125 years. Members of Immaculate Conception Parish, Columbia, Mr. Charles W. Gruninger (1912-1999) and Mrs. Ermantine C. Gruninger (1913-2007) lived the spirit of the Second Vatican Council.

Charles Gruninger was a long-time, dedicated employee of The Messenger, serving as an advertising representative past the normal retirement age. He also held offices in the Knights of Columbus at various diocesan and state levels. His wife of 66 years, the former Ermantine Range, was active in the Belleville Diocesan Council of Catholic Women and in promoting retreats at King's House. For 35 years, she was president of the diocesan Newman Auxiliary, which since 1959 has supported the Newman Center at Southern Illinois University, Carbondale.

Her efforts were recognized in 1976 when Pope Paul VI bestowed on her the Pro Ecclesia et Pontifice papal honor. The Newman Auxiliary also established an Ermantine Gruninger Award to memorialize her efforts on behalf of Catholic college students.

Upon Bishop Zuroweste's retirement, the Holy See appointed Cleveland Auxiliary Bishop, His Excellency, the Most Reverend William M. Cosgrove, DD, as the fourth Bishop of Belleville. He set the tone for his relatively brief ministry in southern Illinois during his Installation Mass on October 28, 1976, when he stated, "We must grow in our respect for people no matter who they are; no matter how big they are; no matter how little they are."

Born November 26, 1916, in Canton, Ohio, and raised along with his brother by his widowed mother, William Michael Cosgrove was ordained in the midst of World War II on December 10, 1943. His work for social justice and as a leader in the Cursillo movement highlighted his years as a pastor and auxiliary bishop in Cleveland. He continued to serve the less fortunate in the Belleville Diocese through initiatives like the former East St. Louis Illinois Development Corporation, which he started along with Father John Stallings.

Each Christmas, Bishop Cosgrove called for special collections for home mission dioceses and hosted the Bishop's Christmas Dinner, which continues to offer holiday hospitality to the elderly, shut-ins and others who might otherwise spend the holiday alone.

The Bishop communicated with his people through a weekly column in *The Messenger*, entitled "Hello." The popular feature recounted people and places Bishop Cosgrove visited in his travels throughout southern Illinois.

Bishop Cosgrove centralized diocesan offices into the Catholic Center. He established the diocesan Office of Worship and saw the start of the Hincke Home for Retired Priests. On October 18, 1980, he ordained a class of twenty-three permanent deacons.

Bishop Cosgrove suffered the cross of poor health and in 1979, he was given an auxiliary bishop, His

Excellency, the Most Reverend Stanley G. Schlarman, DD, to assist him. Bishop Cosgrove resigned for health reasons on May 19, 1981. He died in his native Ohio on December 11, 1992, but was laid to rest in the crypt of St. Peter's Cathedral, Belleville.

Bishop Stanley G. Schlarman

The first and only Auxiliary Bishop of the Diocese of Belleville was Bishop Stanley G. Schlarman. Born July 27, 1933, the future bishop grew up in Cathedral Parish and attended St. Henry Preparatory Seminary. He studied for the priesthood in Rome, where he was ordained on July 13, 1958.

Father Schlarman was assigned to teach at Mater Dei High School, Breese, serving as a part-time associate pastor at various Clinton County parishes. After fifteen years at Mater Dei, he was named pastor of St. Patrick Parish, Cairo, and on March 4, 1983, he was ordained Auxiliary Bishop of Belleville. Later, he was named Bishop of Dodge City, Kansas. shepherding that flock for fifteen years. Upon retirement in 1998, Bishop Schlarman served as Vicar for Priests first in the Diocese of Joliet and then back home in the Belleville Diocese. He is actively involved in prison ministry, celebrating Mass regularly at Menard Correctional Center.

On the occasion of his golden jubilee as a priest in 2008, Bishop Schlarman reflected "I realized when I became a bishop, the need to devote more time to prayer. I am convinced that this leads a priest to selfless service for as long as he can do it."

Like his predecessor, His Excellency, the Most Reverend John Nicholas Wurm, Ph.D., S.T.D., came to the Belleville Diocese and met *le calvaire* in both the circumstances of the diocesan Church and in his own personal health. Born in St. Louis on December 6, 1927, the future fifth Bishop of Belleville was one of fourteen children! He began his priesthood studies after graduating from the eighth grade and was ordained a priest of the Archdiocese of St. Louis on April 3, 1954.

The pastor of the Old Cathedral in downtown St. Louis beneath the Gateway Arch and Auxiliary Bishop of St. Louis since 1976, Bishop Wurm was installed as Bishop of Belleville on November 4, 1981. The Belleville Diocese was in the throes of a financial crisis brought about by inflation and the national economic recession. Bishop Wurm enacted an austerity program that, though unpopular with some, restored financial stability to the Church in southern Illinois.

He also restructured the administration of the Diocese and created a Diocesan Pastoral Council in 1983. With a great interest in Catholic education for both children and adults, Bishop Wurm approved a new Catechist Enrichment program.

Bishop Wurm also set out to visit every church, classroom and institution in the Belleville Diocese. As a former high school principal in the Archdiocese of St. Louis, Bishop Wurm paid special attention to those classroom visits. It is reported that in his first eight months in the diocese, he traveled 20,000 miles to realize that goal. And there was much to see since during this time, the Belleville Diocese launched a variety of new ministries.

The St. Vincent de Paul Society opened Cosgrove's Kitchen to help feed the needy in East St. Louis. Daystar Community Program dedicated a new outreach center in Cairo. The Pregnancy Care Center opened in Belleville. A new retreat program for prison inmates, Residents Encounter Christ, was organized in southern Illinois. And a relatively new way of caring for the terminally ill, Hospice Care, was introduced by Sister Mary Simpson, ASC, under the auspices of Belleville Area College Outreach. The diocesan Food for Families Lenten collection was expanded to serve the needy better.

Three Masses of Chrism were held at different locations in the diocese for the first time. The Masses were celebrated at the Cathedral of St. Peter, Belleville; Sacred Heart Church, Du Quoin; and St. Mary Church, Mt. Carmel.

There was a certain hope in this new Bishop who promised through his episcopal motto "to bless, to keep , and to love." The hope was cut short in November 1983 when Bishop John Wurm was diagnosed with liver cancer. Through the Catholic press, he more than graciously shared the story of his final journey, including the details of his declining health and his personal suffering with the Christian Faithful.. Just as his Metropolitan, Cardinal Joseph Bernardin of Chicago would do eleven years later, the Bishop taught his brothers and sisters in Christ to see dying as a part of living and to face death with faith, courage, and inner peace. He lived in his final days the Ignatian prayer which he prayed after each Mass, "Take Lord, receive all my liberty..."

Bishop John Nicholas Wurm celebrated his final Mass on Easter Sunday, April 22, 1984. propped up in his hospital bed. His brief service as the shepherd of the Church in southern Illinois ended on April 27, 1984, the Friday of Easter Week; the triumph of *le calvaire*.

In 1983, the Catholic Extension Society presented its Lumen Christi Award to Mr. Joseph Hubbard, coordinator of Catholic Urban Programs since the East St. Louis outreach began in 1973. Lumen Christi, which is Latin for the Light of Christ, recognizes individuals working to help strengthen communities located in the poorest, most isolated regions of the United States.

Born in East St. Louis on January 8, 1943, Joe Hubbard lost his father at an early age and his family was assisted by the St. Vincent de Paul Society at the former Holy Angels Parish, East St. Louis. He felt inspired to return the favor and he joined their ranks as a teenager, assisting with the corporal works of mercy. He gave all of his free time after work to charitable endeavors until Bishop Albert R. Zuroweste hired Joe to head the newly created CUP. When interviewed over 25 years ago about the Lumen Christi, Joe Hubbard reflected, "Society has a dollar or time value for everything, but you can't put a price tag on love."

Born in Chicago on July 31, 1931, His Excellency, the Most Reverend James Patrick Keleher, S.T.D., was ordained for the Archdiocese of Chicago on April 12, 1958. He continued his studies as a scholar of Dogmatic Theology and went on to serve in the Chicago archdiocesan seminary system. He was the rector of St. Mary of the Lake Seminary, Mundelein, Illinois,

when Blessed Pope John Paul II named him the sixth Bishop of Belleville.

The episcopal ordination of Bishop Keleher took place at Belleville's Cathedral of St. Peter on December 11, 1984. The new bishop cited one of his favorite quotes from the Second Vatican Council, "In exercising his office of father and pastor, the bishop should be with his people as one who serves." He later reported that in his first 240 days as bishop, he had made 235 pastoral visits. The Old Testament reading at Bishop Keleher's ordination was from the Prophet Isaiah in which the prophet sees his mission as ""to announce a year of favor from the Lord." (Isaiah 61:2) And such a "year of favor," the Belleville Diocesan Centennial, was a highlight of Bishop Keleher's nine years in southern Illinois. In fact, the official title of the centennial history by Dr. Betty Burnett, "A Time of Favor," echoes this verse.

The centennial was celebrated with publications, liturgies and gatherings. During this "time of favor," fifteen hundred teens gathered at Carbondale for a youth rally; twelve thousand came to the Du Quoin State Fairgrounds for a Heritage festival; six hundred gathered beneath Bald Knob Cross for the Eucharist. The first diocesan Priests' Convocation was held October 4-7 1987, at French Lick, Indiana. This continues to be an annual event.

Bishop Keleher told the priests gathered for that historic meeting: "We look to our past as a source of wisdom, but we must never be mastered by it nor should we be paralyzed by it nor should we shoulder it like a great burden. We may not face our future with anxiety that paralyzes, but only with hope."

He continued, "So the past is a reason for pride; the past is a source of wisdom; and the past should be a continual cause of joy... It should be the springboard to the future."

In their reflections on the past, participants in the Convocation identified key events which shaped the Church in southern Illinois: the Second Vatican Council, the Great Depression, the exodus from East St. Louis, the parish building projects of the 1950s and 1960s, the Catholic school system, influence of women religious, the decline in vocations.

Other efforts of Bishop Keleher at this time helped position the Belleville Diocese for the future. The diocesan Finance Council was restructured and a diocesan Office of Planning was opened under the direction of Sister Michelle Emmerich, SSND. Collaborating with religious, Bishop Keleher brought the Daughters of Charity from Evansville, Indiana to East St. Louis in 1985, and the next year, brought the contemplative Poor Clare Sisters to Belleville to establish a cloistered monastery.

The cross cast a long cold shadow on the Belleville Diocese in October 1992 as news reached southern Illinois of the violent deaths of five Adorers of the Blood of Christ serving as missionaries in Liberia, West Africa. Sisters Mary Joel Kolmer, Shirley Kolmer, Kathleen McGuire, Agnes Mueller, all natives of the Belleville Diocese, and Sister Barbara Ann Muttra, who grew up in the Diocese of Springfield in Illinois, were serving the People of God as teachers, nurses, and reconcilers. Their outreach was cut short by the violence of the Liberian civil war which had torn the nation apart since 1989. The five were shot to death in and around their mission compound in the course of three days. Blessed Pope John Paul II praised them as "Martyrs of Charity." Fifteen hundred mourners filled the Cathedral of St. Peter for a November 5, 1992 memorial Mass for these southern Illinois Martyrs of Charity and two funeral liturgies were celebrated at the Adorers of the Blood of Christ Ruma Center Chapel as the Sisters' remains were eventually recovered and returned home for burial.

Then-provincial, Sister Mildred Gross, ASC, reflected on the events of 1992 and the aftermath. "The impact of their deaths called forth a non-violent stance of reconciliation and forgiveness which flowed from the charism and spirit of the Adorers. The Sisters took an active leadership role by receiving awards and honorary doctorates in their honor, by appearing twice at congressional hearings for peace in Liberia, by involvement with numerous organizations, by participating in a national peace campaign, by attending numerous Eucharistic liturgies in their parishes and by taking every opportunity to tell their story" she recalled. "Nineteen years after the incident their story is still being told, people ask them to intercede for them in their need, the country of Liberia still seeks peace in the midst of political and economical instability and many are reminded of their lives and deaths when they visit the monument that stands in the front of the Ruma Center – five women cast in bronze depicting the dedication of all women and men who give of their life for God's people."

In August 1993, Bishop Keleher called for a diocesan-wide prayer service for all those affected by sexual misconduct. Twelve priests and one permanent deacon were eventually removed from active ministry and placed on administrative leave in the Belleville Diocese for accusations of sexual misconduct.

Archbishop James P. Keleher was installed as the third Archbishop of Kansas City, Kansas, on September 8, 1993.

One of the many woman religious who have made lasting contributions to the Belleville Diocese is Sister Madeline Dosmann, PHJC (1913-1981) Sister's work with the poor and needy in Cairo, Illinois, led to the creation of one of the Diocese's important outreach: Daystar Community Program. Born in Mishawaka, Indiana, the former Catherine Margaret Dosmann entered the Poor Handmaids of Jesus Christ and upon professing vows in 1932 received the name Sister Madeline.

After forty years in primary and secondary education, Sister Madeline came to Cairo in 1977 as pastoral associate to Father Stanley G. Schlarman at St. Patrick Parish. In addition to her pastoral duties, Sister soon found herself supplying people with food and clothing when needed and available. With the approval of Bishop William M. Cosgrove and the support of Sister Joan Fisher, PHJC, Sister Madeline launched Daystar Community Program to assist residents of Alexander and Pulaski Counties. Shortly after announcing their plans in the press, a knock came to the door of the Sisters' convent and Daystar opened the door to their first clients.

Daystar continues to provide food for the hungry and care for the elderly as well as volunteers opportunities for youth from throughout the Diocese who travel to Cairo to assist those in need and to share in the caring vision of Sister Madeline.

On February 10, 1994, His Excellency, the Most Reverend Bishop Wilton Daniel Gregory, S.L.D., Auxiliary Bishop of Chicago, was installed as the seventh Bishop of Belleville. His journey to southern Illinois began just forty-seven years earlier on December 7, 1947 on the south side of Chicago. As a student at St. Carthage Grade School, he converted to Catholicism in 1959 and later became both Belleville's first African-American bishop and the first convert to head the See. By word and presence, Bishop Gregory promoted racial tolerance in southern Illinois. In his farewell interview with *The Messenger* in January 2005, Bishop Gregory said, "I didn't solve the problem of racism... but I gave people some new facts to deal with."

After his ordination to the priesthood on May 9, 1973, Father Gregory earned his doctorate in sacred liturgy from the Pontifical Liturgical Institute in Rome. He was a member of the faculty of St. Mary of the Lake Seminary, Mundelein, Illinois, when he was ordained auxiliary bishop for the Archdiocese of Chicago on December 13, 1983. Eleven years later, he came to Belleville.

A stated goal of Bishop Gregory was the formation of a Diocesan Pastoral Council, which was commissioned on August 11, 1996. Composed of representatives from throughout the Diocese, the council made recommendation to the Bishop on various issues.

In November 2001, Bishop Gregory brought the national media spotlight to Belleville with his election as President of the United States Conference of Catholic Bishops. At this time, the crisis of sex abuse by Catholic clergy was escalating and under Bishop Gregory's leadership the Bishops of the United States established the "Charter for the Protection of Children and Young People." Sadly, the Diocese of Belleville did not escape the tragedy of this sin and the crime of abuse of minors by clergy. During the tenures of Bishop Keleher and Bishop Gregory, thirteen priests of

Blessed Pope John Paul II used the historic chalice from Holy Family Church, Caholcoa, during 2000 Mass in St. Louis
(Messenger photo by Liz Quinn).

the diocese were removed from ministry because of credible allegations. These cases have had a profound impact on the morale of priests and parishioners. The Diocese of Belleville continues to deal with the staggering spiritual, emotional, legal, and financial consequences of these terrible events.

In 2001, the Diocese of Belleville established the Office of Hispanic Ministry. The purpose of the office has been to foster the diocesan commitment to be a welcoming church to the Hispanic population in southern Illinois, where Mass is celebrated weekly in the Spanish language at parishes in Cobden, Carbondale, Damiansville, Fairmont City, and at the National Shrine of Our Lady of the Snows. The Office of Hispanic Ministry also sponsors Hispanic youth days, health checkups for migrant workers, convocations for continuing education and an annual Spanish supplement to *The Messenger*.

On the occasion of his silver jubilee of priestly ordination in 1998, Bishop Gregory reflected, "I am convinced that the challenge of the next generation will be to teach the Catholic faith in its full dignity -- spiritually, morally, doctrinally, and socially. Each component of our faith deserves its proper place in the catechetical mission of the Church."

Bishop Wilton Gregory was installed as Archbishop of Atlanta, Georgia, on January 17, 2005.

Bishop Wilton Gregory often spoke of being "with the people." One person with whom he collaborated closely was Ms. Irene Dill (1936-2000). A native of Buffalo, New York, Ms. Dill came to the Diocese to develop a Ministry Formation Program. At the time of her sudden death on June 16, 2000, she served as Pastoral Services Director. Many came to see her as teacher and spiritual advisor.

In his funeral homily, Bishop Gregory noted, "Irene called us to be our better selves and she was quick to point out when we behaved as our lesser selves." Irene Dill's contributions were recognized in various ways. Blessed Pope John Paul II awarded her the Ecclesia et Pontifice Award and the library in the Diocesan Pastoral Center has been named in her memory.

On March 15, 2005, Blessed Pope John Paul II named His Excellency, the Most Reverend Edward Kenneth Braxton, Ph.D., S.T.D., the eighth Bishop of Belleville. Bishop Braxton was born on June 28, 1944, in Chicago,, the third of five children of Cullen and Evelyn Braxton Sr. He was ordained a priest for the Archdiocese of Chicago on May 13, 1970 by John Cardinal Cody. Bishop Braxton was ordained a bishop in the Cathedral Basilica of St. Louis by Archbishop (later Cardinal) Justin Rigali on May 17, 1995, the 25th anniversary of his First Mass. He had served as pastor of St. Catherine of Siena Parish in Oak Park, Illinois, for five years prior to his appointment to St. Louis. His parents were resi-

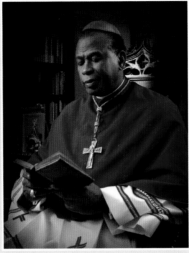

Bishop Braxton

dents of Oak Park and active members of this unique, urban and suburban parish.

The Holy Father appointed Bishop Braxton as Second Bishop of Lake Charles, Louisiana on December 12, 2000. He was installed on February 22, 2001. He was actively and energetically involved in every aspect of the Diocese. At Lake Charles, Bishop Braxton initiated the practice of personally writing and calling families in the Diocese when they experienced a death in the family, a much appreciated practice that he has continued in Belleville.

Bishop Braxton was installed as eighth Bishop of Belleville on June 22, 2005, the feast of St. Thomas More, one of the Bishop's favorite saints. In his installation homily, he said that it was his desire to make his own the words of the English martyr, "I say none harm. I do none harm. I think none harm. If that be not enough to keep a man alive, then, in good faith, I long not to live."

■ *Bishop Braxton blesses a new baptismal font at St. Joseph Parish in Marion with pastor, Msgr. Thomas Flach to the left.*

Bishop Braxton began his ministry by inviting small groups to his home for lunch for informal conversations. These groups included priests, deacons, religious and laity. He also gathered members of the Diocesan Curia for meals, conversation, and prayer. His strong commitment to education led to his frequent visits to every elementary school ant the three high schools in the Diocese. These Pastoral Visits were opportunities for him to encourage the Catholic identity of our schools and to speak about vocations to the priesthood, so urgently needed in southern Illinois.

The Bishop laid out his vision for the Diocese in a major Pastoral Letter, "We Are His Witnesses: Our Spirit-Filled Mission as the Church in Southern Illinois," published on Pentecost Sunday, June 4, 2006. In his letter, he reflected on the abiding presence of the Holy Spirit in the life of the Church and he called upon everyone in the Diocese to be open to the healing power of the Spirit. Commenting on tensions, conflicts, fragmentation and antagonism that are a part of the reality of the Catholic Church in the United States and in the Diocese of Belleville, he spoke of the "Decline of Common Meaning" which leads to the erosion of community at every level, the family, the Parish, the presbyterate and the Diocese. "We Are His Witnesses" has been published in several journals and has been used as a text for courses in theology at the University of Notre Dame.

One of the topics addressed in his Pastoral Letter was that of International "Missionary" Priests. Seeing the urgent need for additional priests to serve in our parishes, the Bishop turned to his brother bishops from other countries which are blessed with vocations and asked for assistance. More than twenty priests from South America, Europe, Asia, and Africa, who are now serving in parishes that might otherwise have no priests.

Bishop Braxton has initiated an annual "All Souls' Day" Mass for the bishops, priests, and deacons who have served this Diocese, an annual "Red Mass" for members of the legal community, and has continued the practice of celebrating a Mass of Thanksgiving for married couples marking silver and golden wedding anniversaries. Four times a year he gathers the missionary priests and the most recently ordained priests at his residence

for lunch, prayer, and theological reflection in "The Wisdom Community." Recently Bishop Braxton has initiated Parish Pastoral Visitations to all of the parishes in the Diocese. While he has been to the parishes already for Confirmations, centennials, funerals, and other major parish celebrations, these Visitations are scheduled for all one hundred seventeen parishes of the Diocese. The Visitations allow him to spend the weekend at a parish, celebrate the Masses, preach the homily, and engage in a dialogue with the parishioners, allowing them to ask any questions they may have about the church and the Catholic faith. He often meets with parish leaders, attends Parish School of Religion activities, visits those who are unable to come to Mass, and visits with the Pastor to learn more about the local life of the parish.

In a letter dated the Feast of the Transfiguration of the Lord (August 6, 2011), Bishop Braxton announce the establishment of the PASTORAL PLAN FOR PARISH RENEWAL AND RESTRUCTURING . The goal of this PLAN is to strengthen our parish communities so that they can be strong and viable for generations to come. The Bishop writes about it in his letter at the beginning of this book. This undertaking is a very important moment in the diocese's history as a community of faith.

As the 125th anniversary of the erection of the Diocese approaches, the Bishop has stressed that the celebration should be modest and the spiritual renewal should be at the center of this celebration for all. In March, 2012, he will lead a pilgrimage to the Holy Land, Rome, and Assisi. Another important part of this renewal is Fanning the Flame. This is a diocesan-wide small group study of the United States Catholic Catechism for Adults in which the Bishop has urged all parishes to participate. Another additional element of spiritual renewal will be the introduction of the new translation of the Roman Missal which will be used in all parishes in the English speaking world beginning the First Sunday of Advent, November 27, 2011.

When the Church is renewed spiritually, that renewal bears good fruit in deeds. There are certainly examples of this in every parish. For example, Catholic Charities USA has named Mr. Michael Schuette of St. Rose Parish in St. Rose, as its 2011 Volunteer of the Year. He has served as chair of Catholic Charities Southern Illinois and its Poverty Services, which addresses the root causes of poverty. Catholic Urban Programs reported a greater demand for assistance as the economy grows more uncertain. It was reported that in December 2010, the diocesan agency gave out 512 food boxes to families and individuals affected by the economic crisis.

Mr. and Mrs. Scott and Karen Seaborn of Sts. Peter and Paul Parish, Waterloo, have been serving as the United States Leadership Team of the Worldwide Marriage Encounter along with Father Tom Griffin, SVD, since October 2009. The Seaborns are the first U.S. Leadership Team for WWE from the Belleville Diocese. During the past thirty-two years, hundreds of couples and dozens of priests have participated in this ministry.

While rejoicing in the many signs of grace in the Church in southern Illinois, the cross of suffering remains ever present. The diocese is mindful of the great suffering of those who have been victims of abuse by clergy. The diocese has been faced with extremely difficult legal challenges as a result of judgments about past instances of abuse. This has led to a variety of appeals, settlements and court decisions requiring the payment of large sums of money. Nevertheless, the Diocese remains committed to preventing incidents of sexual abuse by clergy and assisting those who have been harmed in the past.

In a reflection on the fortieth anniversary of his ordination to the priesthood on May 13, 2010, Bishop Braxton wrote, "While I have had many days in my life as a priest when I was unhappy, I have never had a day when I was unhappy that I was a priest."

Needs and ministries change, but the cross remains constant. *Le calvaire*, the triumphant cross of the Risen Christ still rises above the rich, fertile soil of southern Illinois, the hope and only boast of the People of God of the Catholic Diocese of Belleville!

Sister Thea Bowman
(1937-1990)

One of the most frequently cited names in the parish histories in this anniversary book is Sister Thea Bowman (1937-1990), F.S.P.A. (Franciscan Sister of perpetual Adoration) in whose memory the consolidated Catholic school in East St. Louis is named. Sister Thea Bowman, Ph.D. was a close friend of Bishop Braxton for many years. He spoke to her by phone just hours before her death in Canton Mississippi. She was the first African-American woman to earn a doctorate in theology from Boston College. A gifted educator, evangelist, musician, singer, and spiritual giant she brought many of the U.S. bishops to tears when she addressed them shortly before her death, speaking forthrightly of the sin of racism that endures in American society and in the Catholic Church in this country.

The former Bertha Bowman was born in rural Yazoo City, Mississippi, in 1937, the daughter of a teacher and a physician, both of whom were Protestants. Bertha's mother enrolled her in Catholic school after she failed to learn to read until the fifth grade. In 1953, Bertha decided to enter the convent and devote her life to service. When she entered the Franciscan Sisters of Perpetual Adoration, she took the name of Sister Thea (derived from Theadora, a lover of God) and embarked on a career in education that took her to the front of classrooms of both elementary schools and universities. She used her education to share her African ancestry and spirituality through a variety of media. For many years she served as Consultant for Intercultural Awareness in the Diocese of Jackson, Mississippi. She died March 30, 1990 after living fully and actively for six years after she was diagnosed with breast cancer. Her spirit lives in the heart of everyone who had the privilege to be in her presence. The cause for her beatification has been presented to the Holy See. The Sister Thea Bowman School in East St. Louis appreciates the prayers and financial support that make it possible to continue to serve children in her memory.

Acknowledgments

- Father Frederic Beuckman and Msgr. Christopher Goelz, who compiled and preserved the early history of the Diocese of Belleville;

- Ms. Betty Burnett, who wrote the Diocese's centennial history, *A Time of Favor*, which was a valuable resource for this history;

- All who contributed to the companion volume to that history, *Profiles From Our Heritage*, which also provided material for this text;

- Sister Mary Kenan Wolf, SSND, Diocesan Archivist;

- Ms. Liz Quirin, Editor of *The Messenger*;

- Mrs. Linda Kreher and Mrs. Marilyn Neu of the Chancery Office staff;

- Father John Myler, STD, VF, and Mr. David Spotanski, copy editors;

- Sister Rita Marie Lucash, ASC, and Mrs. Patricia Warner, proofreaders;

- The Most Reverend Edward K. Braxton, who initiated this publication and focused it on spiritual history rather than "bricks and mortar" accounts.

- Father Stanley J. Konieczny, General Editor

Parishes of the
Catholic Diocese of Belleville

Cathedral of St. Peter

BELLEVILLE, ILLINOIS

Founded 1842

The first church in Wabash County, St. Rose Church,
was established and served settlers of French descent for 26 years.

■ High above the main entrance to the Cathedral in Belleville – the "mother church" of our Belleville Diocese – stands a statue of Saint Peter to whom the Risen Christ three times asked, "Do you love Me?" And to the people of the Cathedral the Lord Jesus has also asked "Do you love Me?" for more than a hundred and sixty five years.

"Do you love me?" echoed in the humble beginnings of St. Peter's Parish at a farm near Shiloh where Masses were first offered in 1836. The parish was established in 1842 and, in Spring 1843, after the first pastor arrived, ground was broken for the a wooden frame church, located east of the present Cathedral. Originally, the parish was called "St. Barnabas the Apostle." The name was changed to Saint Peter in 1847 and was dedicated by Bishop William Quarter of Chicago.

St. Peter was a "German" parish staffed by German pastors with Sunday preaching and confessions in German. The School

Sisters of Notre Dame arrived in 1857, starting an educational ministry at St. Peter's that has lasted for over 150 years. In 1863, during the Civil War, the cornerstone was laid for a new Church to accommodate a growing congregation. The stately edifice was dedicated in 1866 by Bishop Henry D. Junker of Alton. Upon the death of Bishop Junker, Father Peter Baltes, pastor of St. Peter Parish, was named his successor and was consecrated a bishop in his own St. Peter's Church on January 23, 1870.

The life of the parish thrived. Young Men's and Young Ladies' Sodalities, as well as an Altar Society were established. A parish library was begun. In 1875, Green Mount Cemetery was purchased. Three Franciscan Sisters arrived in November 1875, and conducted a "provisional hospital" until St. Elizabeth's Hospital opened in 1881. St. Agnes Orphanage was established and later functioned as St. Vincent Home for the Aged, both conducted by the Poor Handmaids of Jesus Christ. A St. Vincent de Paul Society was chartered.

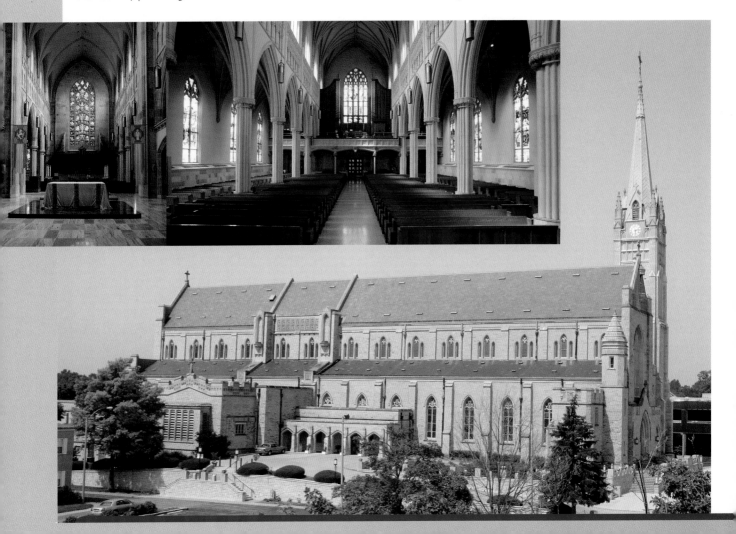

A deadly fire on the night of January 6, 1884 swept through the Academy of the Immaculate Conception and its convent, killing 22 students and four heroic School Sisters of Notre Dame.

There was great joy at the parish when, on January 7, 1887, St. Peter's became the Cathedral of the newly established Belleville Diocese. The Holy See divided the Alton Diocese and the acting diocesan administrator, the Very Rev. John Janssen, was consecrated the first Bishop of Belleville in the new Cathedral of St. Peter on April 25, 1888.

Growth continued as the first high school for boys, St. Peter's Institute, was founded in 1892. Thirteen years later, the Cathedral High School was founded and the Brothers of Mary were entrusted with its direction.

"Do you love me?" echoed hollowly in the charred ruins after the Cathedral was destroyed by fire on January 4, 1912. Frigid temperatures hampered firefighters as many of the fire hoses froze. Only parts of the exterior brick walls remained in place. Within days, Cathedral Rector Father Joseph Schlarman, later Bishop of Peoria, and the parish trustees had visited the homes of all parishioners and sufficient pledges were received to undertake the reconstruction of the Cathedral.

Bishop Janssen died on July 2, 1913, before the rebuilding was complete. Though still under construction, the building was rapidly changed into a suitable temporary setting for the funeral Mass for Bishop Janssen, who was buried in the new crypt. Once the Cathedral was completely rebuilt, the first great event celebrated there was the consecration of the Most Reverend Henry Althoff as the second Bishop of Belleville on February 24, 1914.

After World War I, the high school for girls was moved to Notre Dame Academy and the old Immaculate Conception Academy was remodeled and converted into the Cathedral Grade School. In 1929, the Cathedral Players Guild was founded and is currently in its ninth decade.

Bishop Althoff died in 1947, after thirty-three years as Bishop of Belleville. He guided the Diocese through two World Wars and the Great Depression to the verge of an unprecedented "boom" time in American Catholicism.

On November 29, 1947, Msgr. Albert R. Zuroweste of East St. Louis was appointed the third Bishop of Belleville by Pope Pius XII. At his episcopal consecration on January 29, 1948, two Belleville natives and former Cathedral rectors Bishop Joseph

Schlarman of Peoria and Bishop Joseph Mueller of Sioux City, Iowa served as co-consecrators.

In the 1950's, the number of Cathedral weddings and baptisms reached all-time highs. A new Cathedral Grade School was built to accommodate over 1,000 students; attendance was high at all the Sunday Masses as well as the weeknight Novenas; confession lines were long. As many as four priests at a time were assigned to residence at the Cathedral Rectory. In January 1959, Bishop Zuroweste – and all the Catholic Bishops of the world – received an unexpected call: to an Ecumenical Council convoked by Pope John XXII at the Vatican.

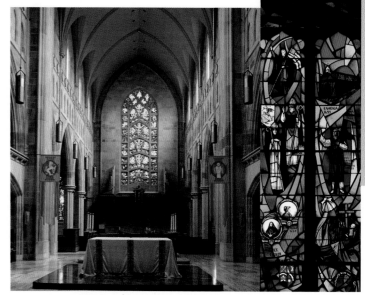

"Do you love me?" rang from the tomb on Vatican Hill to the Cathedral of St. Peter in those early years of the 1960s. Bishop Zuroweste attended every daily session of the Second Vatican Council's four Fall sessions, from 1962 to 1965. It was in Rome, while staying at the Michelangelo Hotel, that Bishop Zuroweste and Italian artisans and architects began drawing plans for the renovation of Belleville's Cathedral, "according to the guidelines of Vatican II." The proposals were not without controversy.

The renovations would make St. Peter's the largest cathedral in Illinois, with a length of 265 feet and width of 65 feet, a height of 90 feet from floor to ceiling – and the bell tower rising to 222 feet. The renovation included plans for a new sanctuary and a new "south" nave, a Blessed Sacrament Chapel, a museum and expanded sacristies. The renovation, which began in January 1966, was completed on December 21, 1968.

An area beneath the South Nave, called the Cathedral "Undercroft", was left unfinished until 2008. It now serves as a meeting room and gathering-dining area.

After twenty-eight years as Ordinary of the Diocese of Belleville, Bishop Zuroweste retired in 1976. Succeeding bishops include the late Bishop William M. Cosgrove from Cleveland; the late Bishop John N. Wurm of St. Louis; Bishop James P. Keleher, now retired Archbishop of Kansas City, Kansas; Bishop Wilton D. Gregory, now Archbishop of Atlanta. Bishop Stanley G. Schlarman, a native son of the Cathedral, was named Auxiliary Bishop of Belleville in 1979, and served as Bishop of Dodge City, Kansas, from 1983 to 1998.

In 2005, the Most Reverend Edward K. Braxton, Bishop of Lake Charles, Louisiana and formerly of Chicago and St. Louis was named the eighth Bishop of Belleville.

Through it all, the people of the Cathedral Parish have continued a three-fold ministry of Worship, Formation, and Outreach:

In Worship, the Cathedral continues to be an example of prayerful, vital liturgical life. Three choirs sing at Sunday Masses; the Sacrament of Reconciliation is available daily; there are weekly devotions to Our Mother of Perpetual Help; a chapel is available for Masses and Eucharistic adoration in the Cathedral School...

In Formation, the Cathedral School, the Parish School of Religion, the Rite of Christian Initiation of Adults, weekly Adult Faith Formation, support for area families who "home school" their children, small Faith communities and a Catholic Book Club all point to growth in the faith for all ages. A Parish Mission is planned for 2012, which will mark the centennial of the Cathedral fire.

In Outreach, the St. Vincent de Paul Society continues its long ministry at Cathedral by operating a Food Pantry and sponsoring Saturday morning breakfasts for the poor and lonely. Cathedral parishioners are key supporters of organizations for Pregnancy Care and pro-life activities. A planned development, "The Cottages at Cathedral Square" will offer affordable housing to senior citizens. Father John T. Myler serves as the current rector of the Cathedral of St. Peter.

Under eight Bishops, through a dozen Rectors, many Associate Pastors, four Permanent Deacons, the Sisters, the choir-masters, teachers, and staff-members ... through the many years, this once "German" parish has welcomed members of all European backgrounds; has become home to military men and women and their families from throughout the United States; welcomed Asians from China and the Philippines; greeted African Americans and Hispanics.

Recognizing this diversity, the weekly Cathedral bulletin reads in part: " You enter this Cathedral ... not as a stranger, but as a guest of God... Be grateful for the strong and faithful ones who built this place of worship, and to all who have beautified and hallowed it by their prayer and praise. ..."

Through every generation, to the people of the Cathedral Parish, Christ asks, every day: **"Do you love Me?"** And, unfailingly, the people of the Cathedral of St. Peter have always answered with Simon Peter: **"Lord, you know that I love You."**

Blessed Sacrament

BELLEVILLE, ILLINOIS

Founded 1926

The first Belleville Diocesan Rural Life Conference
was held in East St. Louis on October 26, 1926.

■ Blessed Sacrament Parish is located in the Signal Hill neighborhood of west Belleville. The name, Signal Hill, is derived in part from the story that Native American communities came to these bluffs on the western edge of the community and lit signal fires to communicate with their tribes throughout the lower Mississippi Valley. With the building of a streetcar line between St. Louis and Belleville, the Signal Hill area began to attract more residents in the years after World War I.

As the west end continued to grow, the Belleville Diocese recognized the need for a new parish in the Signal Hill area. In June 1923, the Signal Hill Catholic Community was formed with the expressed intention of founding a new parish. The group was directed by Msgr. Christopher Goelz, pastor of St. Philip Parish in nearby East St. Louis.

Blessed Sacrament Parish, in Signal Hill, was founded on March 25, 1926 with the appointment of its first pastor, Father Joseph Mueller, who became Bishop of Sioux City, Iowa, in 1947. The parish was named for the Blessed Sacrament to mark the Eucharistic Congress which was held in 1926 in Chicago.

Father Mueller was succeeded as pastor by a young priest from Shawneetown, Father Louis Ell, who would serve Blessed Sacrament Parish from 1930 to 1971. Eventually given the title of "monsignor," Father Ell led the effort to construct the present Blessed Sacrament Church which was dedicated on November 15, 1953 by Bishop Albert R. Zuroweste. In July 2011, Bishop Edward K. Braxton named Father Matthew Elie administrator of the parish.

Throughout the years, Blessed Sacrament Church and School have become a home for a people strong in faith and Catholic identity. Through the daily celebration of the Eucharist and the weekly devotions to Our Lady of Perpetual Help, among other devotions, the faithful of the parish have grown consistently in their belief and have formed a solid, Christian relationship with one another. Blessed Sacrament parishioners reach beyond their parish boundaries through many and varied faith-based initiatives. The parish responds generously to annual drives, donating money, clothing, and toys to those in need.

I AM THE RESURRECTION AND THE LIFE

Our Lady Queen of Peace

BELLEVILLE, ILLINOIS

Founded 1955

Bishop Albert Zuroweste celebrated Confirmation for the first time at Menard State Prison on November 22, 1955

■ In the west end of Belleville beats the generous heart of a faith filled family; Our Lady Queen of Peace Parish. Bishop Albert R. Zuroweste established Queen of Peace on August 10, 1955 "to serve the spiritual and educational needs" of Catholic families, many of whom had moved to the west end of Belleville seeking quiet respite from the more industrial atmosphere of East St. Louis. The once rural edge of Belleville grew quickly.

Initially there were 202 households who made up the parish family with Msgr. Maurice Driscoll as the founding pastor. The young parish immediately responded to Bishop Zuroweste's mandate to serve spiritual and educational needs and on the Feast of the Epiphany, January 6, 1957, the parish celebrated the dedication of its school, which also temporarily housed the parish church.

As the industrial powerhouse in nearby East St. Louis began to experience decline due to the changing needs of the railroad industry, the Belleville area saw a continued increase in population, swelling the parish family at Queen of Peace to over 550 by 1962. Ambitious building projects saw the expansion of Queen of Peace School, the addition of a permanent worship center, a rectory, a convent, and finally a new parish community center. In 1983, Monsignor Driscoll retired and Father John W. McEvilly, VG, became the parish's second pastor and continues to serve in this capacity.

Father McEvilly has led Our Lady Queen of Peace to grow even more aware of their call so that "Guided by the Holy Spirit, we respond to our Baptismal call and celebrate our Roman Catholic faith as a parish family through prayer, education and service to others in communion with our Savior Jesus Christ." This has become the parish's new mission statement, wherein the family recognizes where it has been and where it is called to go. The parish family has always embraced its baptismal call. From

the earliest days, the parish has focused on educating the young people of the community in faith of, in, and through our Lord Jesus Christ.

Until 1985 the Ursuline Sisters were dedicated to instruction of the children of the parish at Our Lady Queen of Peace School. Annually alumni return to share their experience at Queen of Peace with a new generation of parish family members during Catholic Schools Week, giving witness to the value of the education and inspiration fostered through the school's education and religious programs. The parish's education programs also include a Parish School of Religion as well as a Vacation Bible School program in the summer months. The parish sponsors scouting programs for boys and girls from ages six through twenty.

A great many parish members have also embraced adult faith formation over the years, contributing to the success of programs such as "RENEW 2000" and continuing scripture study programs. Many parishioners are involved with preparations for "Fanning the Flame" to mark the Diocese's 125th anniversary in 2012.

Through continual formation the young and old alike are encouraged to recognize the presence of the Lord in their neighbor; in the community at large. The family has found even greater strength through its clustering with Blessed Sacrament and St. Henry's parishes, enabling it to share even deeper bonds with the residents of the west end of Belleville, and to share in ministry to the needs of an even greater area. The parish family at Our Lady Queen of Peace is dedicated today in ever expanding outreach programs, providing ministry to Belleville Christian Center, home, hospital and prison visitation, and has recently chartered it's own chapter of the St. Vincent DePaul Society.

The popularity of the annual Parish Festival illustrates the extent of heartfelt hospitality alive in the parish family.

St. Augustine of Canterbury

BELLEVILLE, ILLINOIS

Founded 1955

St. Gianna Molla, a patron of the pro-life movement, married her husband, Pietro, on September 24, 1955.

■ For over half a century, St. Augustine of Canterbury Church has served as home to Catholics of all ages along the North Belt West corridor of Belleville. Founded in August 1955 with then-Father Urban B. Kuhl as the pastor and organizer, the parish was built upon a ten-acre tract of land obtained from Mr. and Mrs. August Vernier. Bishop Albert R. Zuroweste named the new parish after St. Augustine of Canterbury, the great missionary to England in gratitude for the Verniers' personal donation of land for the church and in honor of both Mrs. Vernier's English heritage and Mr. Vernier's patron saint. St. Augustine's traits of obedience and perseverance were reflected in the parish's first pastor and early parishioners.

Throughout his priestly life, most of which was spent at St. Augustine of Canterbury, Father Kuhl fervently believed that celebrating Mass and receiving Holy Eucharist were the greatest forms of honoring God. And the Eucharist continues to be at the heart of parish community life. In September 1955, St. Augustine celebrated its first Mass in a St. Clair County highway garage, a building that served as "temporary" parish home for over 14 months. With approximately 180 registered families living within parish boundaries, our spiritual foundation started in these humble surroundings.

After a new school was completed in December 1956, Masses, weddings, baptisms, and funerals were celebrated in the school's auditorium until 1969. During this transitional period, St. Augustine's broke ground for a "contemporary designed" church in March 1968. Life-size images of saints, who lived the Beatitudes, are depicted in the stained-glass windows, line the nave of the church. In this holy space certain devotions began and remain key to parishioners' expressions of faith, including ardent devotion to the Blessed Mother, reflected in daily rosary and the Queenship of Mary Sodality group, and fervent devotion to St. Joseph and St. Jude, whose weekly novena is held every Tuesday evening.

Adjacent to the church is St. Mary–St. Augustine Catholic Grade School with Mrs. Sandy Baechle as principal, a multi-functional Community Hall, and athletic fields. Young parishioners grow in Christ through to Youth Ministry activities, scouting programs for boys and girls, and a joint Parish School of Religion with nearby St. Mary Parish. Adults enrich their faith lives by participating in Women's Retreats and Days of Recollection, the monthly Men of St. Joseph fellowship, adult religious education sessions, led by the parish administrator, Father Patrick Okwumuo.

The parish hosts First Friday Eucharistic Adoration and a monthly Healing Mass. Steeped in rich tradition of loving one's neighbor, St. Augustine offers various social outreach programs through its Food Pantry, its Guatemalan sister parish collections, inter-faith collaboration with neighboring Westminster Presbyterian Church, and Advent and Lent gifts to local nursing homes and the Pregnancy Care Center.

Msgr. Ted Baumann is among the vocations from St. Augustine of Canterbury Parish.

Nearing its sixtieth anniversary, St. Augustine of Canterbury Parish stands as "One Parish ... One Body in Union with Christ ... All Dedicated to God, Family, and Community!"

St. Henry

BELLEVILLE, ILLINOIS

Founded 1925

St. Therese of Lisieux was canonized May 17, 1925.

■ Established in 1925, St. Henry Catholic Church was named for the patron saint of Bishop Henry Althoff, Saint Henry II, who even though an emperor, he remained a religious man of deep humility and sense of justice. The parish was originally placed in the care of the Missionary Oblates of Mary Immaculate from the nearby St. Henry Preparatory Seminary. Msgr. Leonard Bauer became the first diocesan priest to serve as the parish's pastor in 1960. Five years later, the current St. Henry Church was built.

The St. Henry Parish mission statement reads "As baptized members of St. Henry Catholic Church, we of all ages have been called to use our God-given gifts and talents to be a community of worship, evangelism, and service to God and our neighbor. We willingly accept the responsibility to worship, to celebrate Eucharist, to further proclaim the Gospel of Faith through evangelism and to provide opportunities for involvement in celebrating the sacraments as well as serving God within and beyond the parish community. We will continually strive to minister to the needs of our parish family and the community within which we live."

This statement is realized through the sacramental life of the church; through the Faith Formation, Worship and Prayer, Social Justice Committees; through religious education of adults and children and the Rite of Christian Initiation of Adults; sacramental preparation; visits to the homebound and those in long-term care.

St. Henry Parish keeps Christ, Eucharist and Scripture at the center of the parish life with the daily Celebration of the Eucharist which is preceded by the recitation of the Rosary. The Eucharist nourishes and strengthens parish life organizations, including the Men's Club, Ladies of St. Henry, the parish quilters, liturgical ministers, the volunteers who provide funeral luncheons and Lenten Fish Fries.

The prayer life of the parish includes a Children's Liturgy of the Word, Adult Choir and Prayer Chain. Scripture study classes are offered as well. Although there have been no vocations from the parish, vocations to the priesthood and religious life remain a topic of prayer and individuals are encouraged to consider such a calling.

Love of neighbor is made visible through the good works of the various groups that are coordinated by the Social Justice and Peace Committee. These include the parish St. Vincent de Paul Council, the preparation of casseroles for Cosgrove's Kitchen in East St. Louis, the Christmas Giving Tree, and pro-life activities. St. Henry Parish also has a Guatemala Sister Parish and provides funding for a scholarship to Althoff Catholic High School.

As St. Henry Parish looks to the 125th anniversary of the Belleville Diocese, the Parish Council, under the leadership of Father Kenneth York, pastor, has begun the process of re-writing the parish ten-year Strategic Plan.

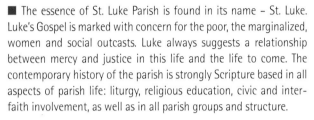

St. Luke

BELLEVILLE, ILLINOIS

Founded 1883

Chester Arthur served as President of the United States.

■ The essence of St. Luke Parish is found in its name – St. Luke. Luke's Gospel is marked with concern for the poor, the marginalized, women and social outcasts. Luke always suggests a relationship between mercy and justice in this life and the life to come. The contemporary history of the parish is strongly Scripture based in all aspects of parish life: liturgy, religious education, civic and inter-faith involvement, as well as in all parish groups and structure.

A move to organize St. Luke Church as the first English speaking congregation in Belleville began as early as 1866. By 1881, the various factions came together long enough to establish the parish. Father James Gough was the first pastor after the congregation separated from St. Peter Church in 1883. A school was held in the basement of the Immaculate Conception convent and taught by the School Sisters of Notre Dame. The present church of Tudor Gothic design was constructed in 1928.

Some insights into life at St. Luke Parish can be gained from the reflections of previous pastors. In the 1997 picture directory Msgr. Jim Margason wrote: "Together we share God's story. Together we share our personal stories...Together, God's People." In the 125 year anniversary booklet, published in 2008, Father Gene Neff reflected: "I believe that spiritual, educational and social growth as a Catholic community will continue because of the intense faith of the people... The challenge of being primarily an older parish in the inner part of the city provides an opportunity to be creative in our ministry."

A unique structural aspect of life at St. Luke's is the fact that through the years the ministry of three deacons-- currently Deacon Bob Lanter, Deacon Peter Cerneka, and the late Deacon Otto Faulbaum -- has enriched parish life. Also in 2004 when the clustering of Belleville parishes was begun, St. Luke was unique in welcoming the liturgical celebrations with many different priests especially through the time of the illness and death of Father John Venegoni. Rather than being limited by that experience, it was an opportunity and challenge to assume more responsibility and awareness of the role of each person in the congregation.

The 125 anniversary publication noted also: "St. Luke Parish is committed to meet future challenges with openness of spirit and a willingness to accept new roles of leadership by taking on the roles given each of us in baptism. Rather than bemoan loss, we renew our pledge to be church to one another, to take to heart the words said as we are sent forth from each liturgy. We will "go forth to love and serve the Lord and one another."

The Gospel of Luke is lived out in an on-going commitment to the poor through a very effective St. Vincent de Paul ministry and through efforts by the Social Justice commission which was instrumental in the formation of the present Ten Church Food Pantry in the area and an unusual generous spirit in the annual diocesan appeal, as well as addressing many issues and concerns that surface during the year.

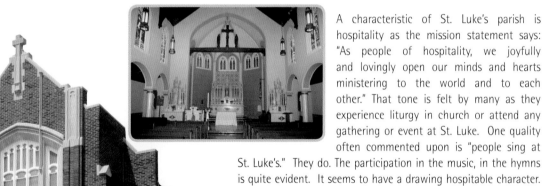

A characteristic of St. Luke's parish is hospitality as the mission statement says: "As people of hospitality, we joyfully and lovingly open our minds and hearts ministering to the world and to each other." That tone is felt by many as they experience liturgy in church or attend any gathering or event at St. Luke. One quality often commented upon is "people sing at St. Luke's." They do. The participation in the music, in the hymns is quite evident. It seems to have a drawing hospitable character. The noon luncheons, funeral planning and luncheons, the Ministry of Care which keeps contact with our homebound, or beginning ministry to the bereaved, the welcoming to groups using the parish center, the acknowledgement of parishioners in the news or personal achievements, the Tuesday Soup project by our retired men for the poor, the homebound, those alone, and participation in the Franklin Neighborhood Association. Sister Grace Mueller, SSND, serves as parish life coordinator of St. Luke Parish.

St. Mary

BELLEVILLE, ILLINOIS

Founded 1893

Blessed Michael Kozal, martyr of Dachau, was born on September 27, 1893, in Poland.

In September 1934, Bishop Althoff appointed Father Joseph J. Orlet as pastor of St. Mary. He would serve the community for 39 years, would later be named a monsignor and would eventually be succeeded as pastor by his nephew, the late Father Raymond Orlet. The current pastor of St. Mary Parish is Msgr. William McGhee, who also serves as one of the three vocation directors of the diocese. That seems especially appropriate since nearly fifty sons and daughters of St. Mary Parish have responded to the call to priesthood and religious life. Deacon Gerry Bach assists Msgr. McGhee with Sacramental preparation. the Thursday evening novena to Our Lady of Perpetual Help, Pro-Life Rosary, First Saturday Adoration and other aspects of life at St. Mary Parish.

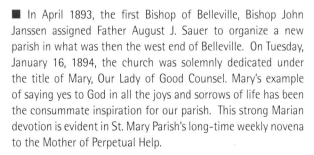

■ In April 1893, the first Bishop of Belleville, Bishop John Janssen assigned Father August J. Sauer to organize a new parish in what was then the west end of Belleville. On Tuesday, January 16, 1894, the church was solemnly dedicated under the title of Mary, Our Lady of Good Counsel. Mary's example of saying yes to God in all the joys and sorrows of life has been the consummate inspiration for our parish. This strong Marian devotion is evident in St. Mary Parish's long-time weekly novena to the Mother of Perpetual Help.

A parish school was opened in 1894 and in August 2008, two neighboring parochial schools were consolidated to form the new St. Mary-St. Augustine Catholic School, offering quality Catholic education to children of both St. Mary and St. Augustine Parishes, as well as others who come seeking a solid education with Catholic values.

Through liturgy, a vibrant choir, life-long faith formation, a spirit of hospitality and service, and a multi-faceted outreach to youth. St. Mary Parish strives to live its mission statement: "We the people of St. Mary's are called to develop a family of faith in the way of Jesus Christ. We seek to create bridges between very active, involved parishioners and those who seek to participate more fully in parish life. Our faith community respects a steadily evolving faith shared in the present community."

St. Teresa of the Child Jesus

BELLEVILLE, ILLINOIS

Founded 1926

The former St. Mary Hospital, east St. Louis,
opened its doors to its first patients on September 10, 1926.

■ Founded in 1926 by Bishop Henry Althoff, St. Teresa of the Child Jesus Parish was formed from Cathedral of St. Peter and St. Luke, and placed under the protection of the young Carmelite nun known as "The Little Flower" less than seven months after her canonization. She promised: "To spend my heaven doing good upon the earth. I will send a shower of roses."

The first pastor, Father William Hoff, and 120 families purchased property located in the 1100 block of Lebanon Avenue for a church, rectory, convent, and school. The church and school were dedicated on August 29, 1926, and the school opened with 135 pupils. The School Sisters of Notre Dame took up residence on September 21, 1926. To accomplish all of this in one year was quite a feat for such a small number of households.

By 1950, the parish had grown to nearly 500 families and a new school was dedicated by Bishop Albert R. Zuroweste on September 7, 1952.

The present church was built under the leadership of the parish's second pastor, Msgr. Joseph Stenger and was dedicated on May 7, 1967. St. Teresa Church stands on the site of the former Star-Peerless Brewery. Wicks Organ Company designed a pipe organ specifically for St. Teresa Church, which also features stained glass windows imported from France depicting the life of St. Teresa, and a distinctive 46 foot bell tower with three bronze bells.

In 1991, the parish realized the shortage of religious vocations, when the School Sisters of Notre Dame left St. Teresa School. Msgr. Donald W. Eichenseer initiated the Belleville Diocesan Perpetual Adoration Chapel at St. Teresa Church. St. Teresa has showered her Belleville parish with many blessing, including vocations. In 85 years, St. Teresa Parish has been blessed with nine sons ordained to the diocesan and religious priesthood and eleven daughters consecrated to the religious life. Two permanent deacons have come from St. Teresa Parish as well.

In July 2007, Bishop Edward K. Braxton named Father David Darin the pastor of St. Teresa's 1,150 families and 316 students. Together, they strive to live the parish mission statement: Through Baptism, we become the Body of Christ. God calls us as a family of faith to gather around the table of the Lord to hear the Word and break the Bread. Enriched by our heritage and moved by the Spirit, we develop our gifts, love and serve one another and reach out to all others with the love of Christ.

St. Pancratius

FAYETTEVILLE, ILLINOIS

Founded 1838

The Martyrs of Vietnam died in a persecution unleashed in 1838.

■ In 1838, Father Casper Ostlangenberg celebrated the first Mass in the log cabin of Frank Buehner, which was located in the vicinity of present day Fayetteville, named for the great hero of the Revolutionary War, Chevalier de Lafayette. Area Catholics built a church in 1849 and the worship space was dedicated to St. Pancratius, a teenaged martyr of the early Roman church. Six years later, Father A. Rustemeyer was named the first resident pastor.

The current parish church was constructed in 1957 and the nearby former rectory has been converted into a parish center, which is described as "the heart of the parish" and is used for parish activities, including the parish school of religion, as well as events sponsored by the village's fire department.

St. Pancratius parishioners host an annual church picnic in addition to being involved in various projects that support diocesan agencies such as Catholic Urban Programs, the

Pregnancy Care Center, and Hispanic Ministry. The parish celebrates the feast of St. Nicholas on December 6 with an annual Mass, dinner and party for the children of the community. On the eve of the diocesan 125th anniversary, the parish has promoted the Right to Life campaign with signage displayed prominently on the parish property.

The Parish Council is guided by the parish administrator, Father Kenneth York. Missionary Oblates of Mary Immaculate have served as sacramental ministers for the parish which does not have a resident priest. Volunteers maintain the church buildings as well as the gardens around the parish property.

St. Pancratius is guided by a mission statement, which states in part: "Our aim is to show Christ-like charity and concern as a faith community. Our parish will attempt to be spiritually challenging and generously welcoming."

St. Joseph

FREEBURG, ILLINOIS

Founded 1856

James Buchanan was elected U.S. President in 1856.

■ In the early 1850s, the Catholic population in the ever growing community of Freeburg began their quest to have their mission established as a parish. Their prayers were answered in 1857, and their Catholic home would be known as St. Joseph Parish.

The first families of the parish purchased a log home, which they converted into a church. This was located on the site of the present St. Joseph Church. For the first several years, Mass was celebrated in this small church whenever a circuit-rider-priest came to town. The parish's first brick church was completed by 1860. The current church building was complete 100 years ago in 1912, and 2012 will be a centennial year for St. Joseph Parish, Freeburg.

One year earlier, Father Bartholomew Bartels was assigned to St. Joseph Parish as the first resident pastor. Following the example of St. Joseph the Carpenter, his parish's patron, Father Bartels began to build. First, he converted the old log church into a schoolhouse and later built a rectory.

Six young men from this parish were called by Jesus to become priests by sharing their faith and guiding other Catholics. These include Father David Kalert, OMI, former provincial of the Missionary Oblates of Mary Immaculate; Dominican Father Gerald Stookey; and the late Father Francis X. Heiligenstein of the Belleville Diocese.

Sixteen women from this parish were called over the years to enter into various religious orders. One St. Joseph family, the Krupps, had four daughters, Hilda, Amelia, Ida and Celestine, who entered the religious life.

Established in 1861, St. Joseph Catholic School has provided quality, faith-based, Catholic education to many students for 142 years and continues today. Formerly staffed by School Sisters of Notre Dame and later the Adorers of the Blood of Christ, the student body at St. Joseph is currently taught by lay faculty.

St. Joseph Parish offers opportunities to serve others through many groups and organizations, ranging from clubs for men and women to activities involving seniors and youths. St. Joseph Church has evolved and remained a powerful Catholic presence in the city of Freeburg. The parish's collection of historic photos from the tiny log cabin chapel to the present beautiful church show the growth of this parish and community.

Since days of Father Bartels, 14 resident pastors have served St. Joseph Church, Freeburg. The current pastor is Father Mark Reyling.

St. Joseph

LEBANON, ILLINOIS

Founded 1862

President Abraham Lincoln signed the Homestead Act on May 20, 1862, to encourage Western migration.

■ There's a German saying "that all good things come in three." The present location of St. Joseph Parish is the third one in Lebanon. In the beginning, Mass was celebrated in the homes of Catholic families. Father August Reineke of Breese had the first church built in 1862 on the east side of what is now known as Pearl Street. This mission chapel, constructed of wool, held about 100 people. At the time we were in the Alton diocese. The first resident pastor, Father Trojan, was appointed in 1879.

In 1982, a second church was built of brick and stone in a Gothic design on Fritz and Schuetz Streets. A minor earthquake did extensive damage to the church in the 1960s and thought was given to buy property that would be adequate for a new church. The land that was purchased was an abandoned cornfield. The old church was dismantled in exchange for the windows. An auction was held for most of the contents. The parish retained the tabernacle, bells and an icon of Our Lady of Perpetual Help, which was given by Father Emile Chuse who was a WWI chaplain. The picture was made at the Redemptorist Church in Rome where the original is enshrined and, like the original, it is painted on wood.

The cornerstone was placed by Bishop William M. Cosgrove on November 5, 1978 and the bells were consecrated on Thanksgiving Day, 1978. The original bell from the first church is named "Joseph." The second bell was purchased from a Catholic church in Cairo and is called "Mary." The smallest bell came from Red Bud, and is named "Jesus." Brother Mel Meyer, SM, designed the artwork in the adoration chapel. The symbol of the Burning Bush from which the voice of God spoke to Moses tells us that

we are on sacred ground. The tabernacle was made to look like a house of cedar like the Ark of the Covenant in the Old Testament.

The art glass was done by Emil Frey of St. Louis. Two windows are of faceted glass and picture two scenes from the life of St. Joseph: the Nativity and the Holy Family. Wood carved statues of Joseph and Mary were carved in Switzerland. The Stations of the Cross were done by an internationally known German artist in St. Louis. The marble of the altar, ambo and font are Travertine marble from Italy. The church was consecrated on the Feast of St. Joseph, March 18, 1979.

Members of St. Joseph Parish are active in all aspects of community life, most notably in outreach and ecumenical relations. A sister relationship with Catholic Urban Programs, established in the late 1980s, continues to be nurtured today, as well as outreach through a chapter of St. Vincent DePaul, which was formed in 1990. St. Joseph Parish was among a small group of local churches to pilot a home health care service for seniors and disabled in 1995. The area churches also work together to operate a community Food Pantry and provide counseling assistance to the needy, offer a community wide Vacation Bible School, and worship together at Thanksgiving and Good Friday Stations of the Cross.

St. Joseph parishioners plan to mark the faith community's 150th anniversary in March 2012. Brenda Pehle serves as Parish Life Coordinator.

St. Anthony of Padua

LIVELY GROVE, ILLINOIS

Founded 1868

May 30, 1868 was the first official observance of Memorial Day in the United States.

■ St. Anthony of Padua Parish, Lively Grove, had a very unlikely start. In 1865, a non-Catholic, Presley Walker, donated ten acres of land to the Bishop of Alton for the construction of a Catholic church. Two years later, seventeen Catholic families living in the vicinity of Lively Grove came together to build a small wooden church on the site over the course of twelve months. Later, a one-room school house was added and was eventually staffed by the Adorers of the Blood of Christ. St. Anthony School eventually closed due to the shortage of women religious.

The present St. Anthony Church was built of brick and dedicated on October 3, 1888, by Bishop John Janssen. The pastor, Father Longinus Quitter, personally donated over half of the construction costs of the building.

Various aspects of parish life in Lively Grove reflects the community's involvement in agriculture, especially dairy farming. Eucharist is celebrated at 7:30 p.m. on Saturday evening in what is called the "Dairy Mass" since the time of the vigil liturgy accommodates milking schedules. Two of the statues, that decorate pillars in the church. depict patron saints of rural life: St. Isidore, twelfth century Spanish farmworker, and St. Wendelin, seventh century Scottish prince turned herder. A recent pastor of St. Anthony Parish, Father Stan Konieczny, revitalized the custom of blessing animals on the Feast of St. Francis of Assisi in October 2010. In addition to a variety of pets, two full cattle trailers were brought to the blessing to acknowledge the parishioners' dependence on God's Providence as they work to feed themselves and others.

St. Anthony of Padua Parish hosted the Diocesan Farm Blessing in Spring 2011. Bishop Edward K. Braxton visited the farm of Gerald and Joan Luechtefeld, blessing fields, equipment, seeds and livestock. "There was a lot of work with the Farm Blessing, but it was not all that bad. Everyone from the parish pitched in and things were done. That's the way we do things out here," Mrs. Luechtefeld explained.

St. Anthony Parish conducts an annual blood drive in cooperation with the American Red Cross. The Women's Sodality social most recently benefitted the retired Adorers of the Blood of Christ at the ASC Ruma Center. Members of the parish assist Deacon Andrew Linkter in a weekly Communion Service at the nearby Coulterville Care Center. For a number of years, St. Anthony Parish and members of St. Peter United Church of Christ in nearby Stone Church held joint Lenten services. These interfaith services have been expanded to include St. Liborius Catholic Church and United Presbyterian Church, Oakdale. The parish's annual Polka Mass and festival draws hundreds of visitors to Lively Grove on the first Saturday of August. St. Anthony Parish has an active Parish Council, Men's Club, Women's Sodality, Youth Ministry and Parish School of Religion.

A display of historic photos in the vestibule of St. Anthony Church pays tribute to parishioners, who long ago responded to God's call to the priesthood or religious life. Included in the display are Father Peter Behrman, OSB, Father Carl Roesner, Sister Josina Behrman, OSB, Sister Rosina Lake, ASC, Sister Valentine Lake, PHJC, Sister Mary Daniel Leadendecker, RC, and Sister Benigna Schmersahl, ASC. Another young woman from Lively Grove, Agnes Lake died at age 14 while a postulant with the Adorers of the Blood of Christ in 1906.

Holy Childhood of Jesus

MASCOUTAH, ILLINOIS

Founded 1857

Abraham Lincoln made a speech against the Dred Scott Decision in Springfield on June 26, 1857.

■ Early settlers from Germany and Alsace-Lorraine settled in the fertile area known as "Looking Glass Prairie" as early as 1837. The first Mass was celebrated in the cabin of Philip Rachrig in what is now known as the town of Mascoutah, which was originally called Mechanicsburg. The Rev. Dr. Francis Bloesinger was named the first resident pastor in 1857.

Named for the early life of Jesus Christ, the Mascoutah parish has demonstrated a special responsibility for the faith formation of children and young people. Holy Childhood School was established in 1859 and continues to focus on bringing Jesus into every aspect of the child's school day. Over 150 students, kindergarten through eighth grade along with 30 preschoolers, learn to pray frequently throughout the school day, to apply the lessons of the Gospel, to reach out to others, and to work together as members of the parish family.

Holy Childhood Parish School of Religion offers religious instruction and spiritual formation for students attending public schools. A Youth Ministry program offers spiritual, social, cultural, and service activities to a large number of high school age youth.

Over more than 150 years, Holy Childhood has fostered vocations in 21 young people called to religious life. Today a Traveling Chalice goes from family to family, who pray for vocations with the sacred vessel as a reminder of the priesthood.

Various Small Christian Communities meet regularly in people's homes for Scripture study and discussion while encouraging one another to grow in faith. The Prayer and Praise Ministry as well as Prayer Chain members offer devotions and sacrifices daily for the sick and for the parish's special needs. A faithful assembly of adults recite the Rosary aloud before daily and Sunday Mass. Eucharistic Adoration is held twice each week. During Lent, parishioners gather for Mass, Stations of the Cross, Soup and Speaker evenings.

Through the parish's Ministry to the Sick and Aged, Mascoutah Catholics care for those in hospital, in nursing facilities and the homebound with phone calls, personal visits, and distribution of Holy Eucharist. The parish also celebrates a quarterly Mass with Anointing of the Sick.

Members of the Social Services Ministry receive special training and make confidential references to helpful services and resources. Holy Childhood Parish sponsors eight Community Blood Drives each year and the St. Vincent de Paul Society provides food, utility bill assistance, prescriptions, and rent to those in need. Parishioners also assist in Meals-on-Wheels deliveries,

hold monthly Shepherd Sunday drives for the local food pantry and volunteer for community-wide services.

Holy Childhood of Jesus with its long-time pastor, Msgr. Jerome Hartlein, proudly welcomes many military families stationed at nearby Scott Air Force Base. With a depth of experience developed by their call to service, they gracefully assimilate into parish life, bringing new energy to school, liturgies and parish ministries. Over time many of these families choose to retire in Mascoutah.

At Mass, Holy Childhood parishioners are called to "Go in peace to love and serve the Lord." They do that by living the parish mission statement which sees the parish a being called "To be a credible sign of God's love and care, our parish needs to be a loving, charitable and caring community that is spiritually challenging, generously welcoming and liturgically alive... We strive to reach out to those in spiritual and material need... With God's help, we endeavor to live out the Gospel message."

45

St. James

MILLSTADT, ILLINOIS

Founded 1851

Jesuit Father Peter Claver, the slave of the slaves, was beatified on September 21, 1851.

■ Catholics settled in the vicinity of Millstadt in the early 1800s and a church was built in the area and dedicated to St. Thomas the Apostle as early as 1837. In 1850, a brick church was constructed in the settlement of Millstadt, which at that time was called Centreville. This church was dedicated in 1851 in honor of St. James the Greater. A Catholic school was also established at this time. In 1886 a storm destroyed the church and a new brick church was built and dedicated in 1887. The school building presently serving St. James was dedicated in 1958 and the Father Stephen Freund Parish Center was dedicated in 1987. The parish has grown steadily and now numbers over 700 families.

Still, St. James Parish retains its hometown atmosphere. Members of the parish interact regularly with the local civic community and with members of the other churches in town.

Throughout its history the parish has provided for the Sacraments and the spiritual needs of its members and has established a tradition of Catholic education that strives to pass on the faith to each succeeding generation. Ministries like the Rite of Christian Initiation for Adults, the Why Catholic discussion groups, Scripture study, the Parish School of Religion and the Parish Stewardship program all work to share the faith with those who are interested in learning more. An Early Childhood Center and an Infant and Toddler Center now also serve the needs of the families of the Millstadt community.

A variety of committees in the parish work to include and encourage active involvement With a very active St. Vincent de Paul Society there has also been a consistent effort to reach out to serve the needs of the poor. The parish at Millstadt has long been known for its many activities throughout the year such as the Parish Festival, the Schlachtfest, and annual Dinner Auction. Church members regularly step forward to demonstrate their sense of stewardship and volunteerism on behalf of the parish.

Over the course of its history St. James Parish has produced a number of religious vocations, including fifteen women religious and three Brothers. More recent vocations from Millstadt include Deacon Ron Karcher and two diocesan priests, Msgr. Kenneth Schaefer and Father Paul Wienhoff. Msgr. Marvin Volk is the pastor of St. James Parish.

St. Agatha

NEW ATHENS, ILLINOIS

Founded 1870

Ladislaus Strattmann, beatified lay physician, was born in 1870.

■ Prior to the establishment of St. Agatha Parish in 1870, Catholics living in New Athens, a town on the Kaskaskia River, were served by priests from St. Joseph, Freeburg and St. Liborius, St. Libory. St. Agatha Church was a mission of the Freeburg parish until 1894 when Father Bernard Hater was appointed the first resident pastor.

The parish was entrusted to diocesan priests until 1901 when Father Anthony Breek, a Carmelite priest was sent to the United States to start a Carmelite community in the Belleville Diocese. Bishop John Janssen designated the parish of St. Agatha as the site of the new community. Unfortunately, the community never established itself and in 1903 the Carmelites left the parish and went to South America. One Carmelite priest, Father Marcarius Walterbosch, remained and joined the diocesan clergy.

St. Agatha has offered religious education to its children by way of St. Agatha Catholic Grade School, which opened in 1910, and the Parish School of Religion. For many years, dedicated lay people have volunteered to educate the children in their faith in the Parish School of Religion. St. Agatha Catholic Grade School continues to offer children a well-rounded education, including Catholic formation in Scripture and Church doctrine. Many area high school valedictorians and salutatorians are alumni of St. Agatha Catholic Grade School.

Over the years, parishioners have practiced their faith at the celebration of Sunday and weekday Eucharist. At present the parish offers weekly Eucharistic Adoration. There is also a miniature statue of Our Lady of Fatima, which goes from home to home on a weekly basis. Father Dean Braun helped to bring about a deeper awareness of spirituality to the parish and introduced Cursillo, an international program of spiritual renewal which many parishioners have attended over the past 30 years.

Two men from St. Agatha Parish studied for the priesthood and were ordained. The late Father Matthew Lehn was ordained in 1952. He was not a "native" son as his family had moved to the parish when he was young. Baptized at St. Agatha and graduated from St. Agatha Catholic Grade School, Rev. Gary Gummersheimer was ordained in 1979 and currently serves as pastor of St. Andrew Catholic Church, Murphysboro.

Ecumenism, stewardship and evangelization are important facets of parish life at St. Agatha. The parish is involved with the other churches of New Athens in ministering to those who need food, clothing and assistance with paying electric bills. St. Agatha Parish has a strong tradition of helping in the parish and the community. From community soup suppers to the annual parish picnic to Lenten fish fries, the parishioners are there in support as good stewards and evangelizers. Father James Nall, JCL, is the pastor of St. Agatha Parish.

Belleville Deanery

47

St. Clare of Assisi

O'FALLON, ILLINOIS

Founded 1867

Blessed Pius IX occupied the Throne of St. Peter in 1867.

■ St. Clare Parish was founded in O'Fallon, nearly 150 years ago to serve the needs of the then-fledgling town's 40 Catholics. Father Anton Rustige, whose residence was in nearby Lebanon, celebrated the first Mass in the parish's earliest church building on December 29, 1867. With the creation of a permanent pastoral residence in 1868, St. Clare Parish was formally established under the care of Father Theodore Kamann, who also established St. Clare School serving as its first teacher.

Through the years, St. Clare Church has stood as a physical and spiritual landmark in the community. The historic red brick structure in downtown O'Fallon, with its soaring steeple and sturdy bell, served as the parish's worship space from 1895 until 2007. It continues to serve the needs of St. Clare School as a chapel for daily Masses and prayer services.

In 2001, Louis Rasp, a long-time parishioner, donated 20 acres of land for the construction of a new church to meet the needs of a growing parish. The new St. Clare of Assisi Church was dedicated in September 2007 by Bishop Edward K. Braxton. Much as our former church, it is a visual landmark which is now seen from Interstate 64 and that witnesses to the strong and faithful Catholic presence in our community.

The new church recalls the design of the Basilica of St. Clare in Assisi, Italy. Inside, parishioners and visitors alike find welcoming spaces for prayer and quiet contemplation as well as lively, joy-filled celebration. Be it hushed Taize prayer or glorious performances by the region's Masterworks Chorale, St. Clare revels in celebrating the beauty of God's creation. And week after week, Sunday liturgies inspire all to lead Christ-centered lives.

St. Clare Parish also honors the Franciscan tradition through dedication to earth-friendly, environmentally respectful practices. From cutting-edge geothermal heating and cooling system to the parishioners' commitment to recycling, St. Clare Parish takes to heart their patroness' call to live simply and mindfully. Parish gardeners enhance our grounds with beautiful blooms and parishioners' tables with bountiful produce all summer long.

In addition to providing a beautiful environment for prayer and fellowship, the parish offers more than 80 ministries for people to grow in their faith. Hundreds of members serve in liturgical and support ministries, volunteer their time in Christian formation and participate in evangelization and social justice activities. For example, St. Clare parishioners help stock O'Fallon's food pantry, feed families in East St. Louis, and partner with other regional congregations to promote just causes.

The words of our Mission Statement best express the journey our founders set upon, and we continue on: "We, the people of St. Clare Parish, in the Diocese of Belleville, are called by God in baptism to be disciples of Jesus Christ. Centered in the Eucharist and strengthened by the gifts of the Holy Spirit, we strive to live the Gospel and further the reign of God. We do this by creating a vibrant faith community, by actively promoting justice and evangelization, and by using our gifts in the service of God's people."

The approximately 1,000 households of St. Clare of Assisi Parish have Father James Deiters as their pastor.

St. Nicholas

O'FALLON, ILLINOIS

Founded 1982

St. Maximilian Kolbe, martyr of charity of Auschwitz,
was canonized by Pope John Paul II on October 10, 1982.

■ Since its establishment on May 16, 1982 under founding and current pastor, Msgr. William Hitpas, St. Nicholas Church strives to be a "school of spirituality" believing that the spiritual journey is a life-long endeavor. St. Nicholas Church, its recently completed Good Shepherd Center and the St. Nicholas Center focus on developing and nurturing the mind, body, and spirit of parishioners and all who wish to participate through liturgy, quality programs and outreach, that touches people in the local and nearby communities. St. Nicholas Parish also provides educational opportunities for children through St. Clare Catholic School, a Parish School of Religion, and a Pre-school for children ages three through five.

St. Nicholas Church is at the center of the parishioners' pilgrim journey of deepening their relationship with God coming together as a community to celebrate the Liturgy of the Word and Liturgy of the Eucharist enriched by meaningful homilies and a vibrant music ministry. Weekdays, parishioners gather for Mass and, on occasion, the Liturgy of the Word with communion in Mary's Chapel preceded by the devotional reciting of the Rosary. The Marian Hour of Devotion on the third Monday of every month focuses on one of the mysteries of the Rosary.

The parish's Good Shepherd Center responds to spiritual hunger through programs and activities that provide for personal growth, healing and peace through prayer, Scripture studies and other programs that focus on following in the ministry of Jesus Christ. Good Shepherd Center works at creating an atmosphere of hospitality and peace.

An active Youth Ministry group provides a nurturing environment for teens to develop and strengthen their spiritual and social lives. St. Vincent DePaul Society members, comprised of St. Nicholas, St. Clare of Assisi, and Corpus Christi parishioners, faithfully carry out the Church's corporal works of mercy to the impoverished while showing fidelity to Christ's command to love our neighbor. St. Nicholas Parish outreach extends from nearby East St. Louis to their sister parish in far away Guatemala.

49

St. Michael

PADERBORN, ILLINOIS

Founded 1843

The Archdiocese of Chicago was established as a diocese on November 28, 1843.

■ St. Michael Parish, Paderborn, traces its origins to a log church, dedicated to St. Thomas, in an area called Prairie Du Long. A cholera epidemic swept this area sometime around 1849. It is claimed that fifty-two persons died and were buried in the "old" parish cemetery. Most of the graves in the west end of the plot were never marked.

Construction began on the present stone church in 1859. Some of the people in the northern portion of the settlement wanted the church built in Floraville and began building a brick structure that same year. In 1861, Father William Busch arrived on the scene. Much evidence indicates that he came from Paderborn, Germany. Father Busch reached an agreement with the people in Floraville and one church was constructed. The new stone church was dedicated and named in honor of St. Michael the Archangel on May 8, 1862. Around this time, the area became known as Paderborn.

Father Busch built first an eight-room rectory and then a parish school was built. The church was reconfigured in 1884 with the addition of a sanctuary and sacristy on the west end, and a bell tower steeple with the main entrance on the east end. This gave the edifice a more church-like appearance as well as more interior room.

St. Michael parishioners have strongly supported Catholic education. At first, the parish funded its own school with their own school from 1863 to 1965. Today, St. Michael Parish has students in neighboring Catholic schools and conducts a strong Parish School of Religion for youths in non-parochial schools.

The people of St. Michael Church keep Christ, the Eucharist, and Scripture at the center of their lives by the way they live in reaching out to those in need either by the giving of material items, money, or just listening and being there. St. Michael Catholic Church and St. Paul United Church of Christ of Floraville join together at various times working and worshiping with each other --- parish picnic, quilting, prayer and special events.

In 1992, a parish council was formed to give direction and vision to the parish. Committees were formed to organize adult education, liturgy, maintenance, social justice and to co-ordinate the social and financial areas of parish life.

Only one son of the parish, Msgr. Joseph J. Orlet, has offered his First Mass at St. Michael. Over the years, the parish claims a number of other priests with roots in Paderborn, including Father Edmund Sense, Father Emil Helfrich, OMI, Father Leo Reinhardt, Msgr. John Fellner, Father Frank Weskamp, Father Dennis Schaefer, Msgr. Kenneth Schaefer, and Father Roger Karban. Women from the parish who entered religious life include Sister Martha Wachtel, ASC, Sister Hedwig Neff, ASC, Sister Dorothy Neff, ASC, and Sister Marilyn Mueth, OSU.

Recently parishioner Cletus Mueth was honored posthumously as one of the recipients of the 2010 Faith in the Marketplace from *The Messenger*. Another parishioner, Bob Wachtel, who teaches at Freeburg High School and at Southwestern Illinois College, received the Emerson Excellence Teachers' Award.

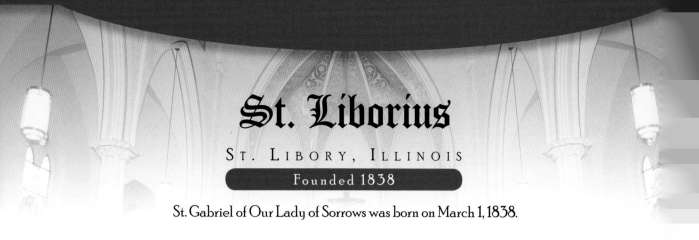

St. Liborius

St. Libory, Illinois

Founded 1838

St. Gabriel of Our Lady of Sorrows was born on March 1, 1838.

■ As you enter St. Liborius Church, St. Libory, you will see a small table to the right, reverently covered with a white embroidered cloth. The table stands beneath a brass sign which reads, "This is the table on which the first Mass in St. Libory was offered in the Harwerth home." In a sense, that table captures the spirit of St. Liborius Parish, a community which is strongly rooted in the Eucharist with strong devotion to its nearly 175-year Catholic heritage.

On August 25, 1838, Father Casper Ostlangenberg celebrated the first Mass at what is now St. Liborius Parish in the log home of William Harwerth. After Mass, the priest met with the settler and urged them to build a chapel. Bernhard Dingwerth donated ground and the community built a small log chapel, where Father Ostlangenberg lived in the sacristy as he visited the circuit of nearby parishes.

The present St. Liborius Church was built under the direction of Father Anthony Brefeld in 1883. Construction materials had to be hauled by farmers of the parish eleven miles from the nearest railroad station. On October 24, 1883, Alton's Bishop Peter J. Baltes consecrated the church, which features a 175-foot bell tower. Illuminated at night, the church steeple is a landmark for travelers along Illinois Route 15.

In the early years of the parish, St. Liborius conducted a parochial grade school and even a short-lived high school, staffed first by the School Sisters of Notre Dame, the Poor Handmaids of Jesus Christ and later the Adorers of the Blood of Christ. St. Liborius Church continues to pass on the faith to the next generation of Catholics through its Parish School of Religion and an active Youth Ministry program. A RENEW group promotes continuing formation of adults. In his remarks at the parish centennial in 1938, Bishop Henry Althoff observed, "It was through the influence of Catholic truth preached in the churches and the ministration of the pastors, that religious life flourished in the homes of the parish."

Religious life continues to flourish in St. Libory homes through the parish's devotion to the Eucharist. Mass is celebrated twice each weekend and Eucharistic adoration takes place every Wednesday from 8 a.m. to 8 p.m. The Rosary is prayed after each weekday liturgy. A funeral tradition unique to St. Liborius is the parish choir accompanying the body and the mourners from the church to the cemetery while singing the Benedictus or Canticle of Zechariah. This is a long-standing custom in the parish, according to Harry Rutter, who has served as organist and later choir director for over 50 years.

St. Liborius Parish responds generously to appeals from food drives to baby items collections for the Pregnancy Care Center to a Christmas collection for Catholic Day Care in East St. Louis to assistance for the victims of recent natural disasters like the tornado in Joplin, Missouri and the tsunami in Japan. A major effort of the parish's Youth Ministry is the annual 5K benefit run/walk. Over the past ten years, "Run for the Son" has raised over $23,000 for local institutions and agencies as well as individuals and families experiencing a crisis, according to Mona Mense, parish Youth Ministry coordinator.

Other groups in the parish reach out to those in need. The parish Council of Catholic Women furnish altar supplies for the church, and also sponsor a child in the Third World. Council 37 of the Catholic Holy Family Society undertakes various projects. Their most recent effort was to refurbish a garden, which was turned into a shrine to St. Francis of Assisi. The site was blessed by Father Stan Konieczny, pastor, after the annual Memorial Day Mass in the cemetery on May 30, 2011.

Corpus Christi

SHILOH, ILLINOIS

Founded 1913

William Howard Taft completed his term as U.S. President in 1913.

The history of the present village of Shiloh began in the year of 1845 when the first house was built. A post office, blacksmith shop, and a store soon followed. In 1912, Father John Grootens became the assistant pastor of St. Peter Cathedral, which included Shiloh within its parish boundaries. Soon, Father Grootens saw the need for a Catholic church in the Shiloh village, because while the farmers of the area had means of transportation to attend the Cathedral, the large number of coal miners from the Shiloh mine did not.

A Catholic parish was organized in Shiloh in January 1913 and Mass was offered in the town hall until the new church could be built.

Bishop John Janssen purchased two lots for $160 on which the church now stands. The cost of the church was approximately $7,000 and a $500 grant was received from the Extension Society with the provision that the church would be named Corpus Christi. The white wood frame church was dedicated on July 30, 1913. Among the furnishings in the church were pews that had been rescued from the Cathedral fire of 1912. Several burn spots are still visible and attest to the fire.

A classroom was built onto the church to be used as a parochial school. The first school for the parish was started in the fall of 1913. There were 41 students in eight grades. The school was operated for only one year because it was too great a financial burden on the young parish. There was also a large sacristy that could serve as a temporary residence for the visiting priest. Due to the large debt, it was decided to build a large chicken barn and use the profits of raising chickens to reduce the parish debt.

The bell that hangs in the tower is the first bell that rang to call Catholics to prayer in the Belleville area. It hung in a small chapel on the Stauder farm located several miles north of Belleville, and Catholics in the area would attend Mass in the chapel. The chapel was closed in 1844 around the time of the completion of the first phase of the future St. Peter's Cathedral. The bell later hung in the St. Agnes Orphanage in Belleville until it closed in 1913 at which time the bell was brought to Corpus Christi.

A new rectory was built in 1974 when the parish had its first resident pastor. A new parish center was erected in 1992. The new Corpus Christi Church will be dedicated in late September 2011. Msgr. James Margason serves as the pastor of the Shiloh parish.

St. John the Baptist

SMITHTON, ILLINOIS

Founded 1867

The State of Nebraska was admitted to the Union in 1867.

■ St. John the Baptist Parish can trace its history to the early days of St. Clair County. While a Catholic mission had been established to serve German and French settlers in the area, the first Catholic Mass, in what is now Smithton, was celebrated at the home of John Rapp in 1852. Sacramental records of these early days of the Church have been preserved at Freeburg and Paderborn.

Eventually, two towns were platted out on either side of the road that lead south of Belleville. Georgetown was established in 1853 and Smithton in 1854. The two were combined to form the Village of Smithton in 1878. A Catholic church was built on land donated by Jacob Fischer on the southeast corner of Lincoln and Stoerger Streets in Georgetown and dedicated to St. John the Baptist on September 30, 1868 by Father John Peter Baltes, who had been delegated by Alton's Bishop Henry Damian Juncker. Later a sanctuary and a belfry were added.

The original parish school was built in 1876 and also served as a rectory. Prior to that time Catholic school classes were held in the current Turner Hall building and in local homes. Adorers of the Blood of Christ from Ruma taught in the parish school from 1888 until 1983. Father Bernard Rossmueller was assigned as the first resident pastor at St. John the Baptist Parish in 1884.

On the bitter cold night of February 5, 1899 the church building was totally destroyed by fire. The only equipment available was a "little giant" fire apparatus hand pump which was used to pour water on the convent and the rectory. Sister Christina and many local residents made several trips to rescue articles from the conflagration. The dedicated Sister had to be dragged out of the flaming church on her last trip and the entire roof collapsed just as she reached the outside. The present Gothic-style church was dedicated on December 3, 1899 by Bishop John Janssen, the first Bishop of Belleville.

Today the parish campus includes buildings from the traditional nineteenth century to the twenty-first century "Munier Center," all of which are used for worship, education, and social activities. On property steeped in history, the parish looks to the future by the parish's strong continued commitment to its grade school, a vital Parish School of Religion and teen youth ministries.

St. John the Baptist Parish is a Eucharistic community. In addition to the regular celebrations of the Mass, weekly Eucharistic Adoration is held from 6:00 a.m. Tuesday until 1:00 a.m. Wednesday. The Chaplet of Divine Mercy is prayed before each weekend Mass during Lent. Lenten Services have included Benediction and Stations of the Cross. Faith Development and Prayer Services are held jointly with the local United Church of Christ. Through Christians United, the local churches worship together during the annual Week of Christian Unity, and also rotate hosting joint services at sunrise on Easter and at Thanksgiving. Devotion to the Blessed Virgin Mary is an important part of parish life, with recitation of the Rosary before Mass in October and May, and a May Crowning is held at the outdoor statue of Our Lady of Grace that was dedicated in 2010 to "All of Our Past, Present, and Future Priests, Deacons, Sisters, and Brothers Who Have Freely Given Their Talent, Time, and Prayer to St. John's Parish."

All parishioners are involved in seasonal social outreach activities, including collections of items for new mothers, babies, and pregnant women, food items to feed the hungry, winter coats to warm those in need, and Christmas gifts for the poor. This outreach calls to mind the words of the parish patron, St. John the Baptist, a herald of charity, who once taught, "Whoever has two cloaks should share with the person who has none. And whoever has food should do likewise." (Luke 3:11)

Immaculate Conception

BRIDGEPORT, ILLINOIS

Founded 1856

Blessed Pope Pius IX occupied the Chair of Peter.

■ Bishop Anthony O'Regan of the Diocese of Chicago acquired a ten-acre tract of land from Menomen O'Donnell in Lawrence County to establish a church and cemetery in 1855. The following year, the first Mass was celebrated in the O'Donnell home in the settlement now known as Bridgeport.

When the first church was built, originally it was placed under the patronage of St. Patrick and was located four miles south of Bridgeport alongside the current parish cemetery. The name of the parish was changed officially to Immaculate Conception in May 1866. Although the church had no resident priest, it was visited periodically by priests from the surrounding areas, sometimes from as far away as Missouri.

The 1871 parish roster showed 200 parishioners. At the request of Bishop John Peter Baltes of the Diocese of Alton the country frame church was abandoned and a new church more convenient was built in town, which became known as Bridgeport in 1872.

Father Jeremiah McCarthy was appointed the first resident pastor of Immaculate Conception Parish in 1909. While originally St. Lawrence Parish, Lawrenceville, was a mission of Immaculate Conception, the situation was reversed in 1971 when pastors began living at St. Lawrence Parish while ministering to both parishes.

Masses are celebrated at Bridgeport each Friday and Sunday and the parish currently has 35 households.

Father Bernardine Nganzi is the administrator of the three parishes in Lawrence County which include Bridgeport, Lawrenceville and Saint Francis Xavier in St. Francisville. While each of the churches maintain their respective Finance Councils, the three parishes currently operate under a common Pastoral Council. This arrangement allows the parishes to join resources in order to build and continually develop the Lawrence County parish community and then to fulfill their mission statement:

"Our Roman Catholic Community of Lawrence County seeks to be educated, inspired and enthused about our faith--sharing with all others the beliefs and practices of our Catholic community. We strive to grow in spirituality and membership through open communication and caring service to all."

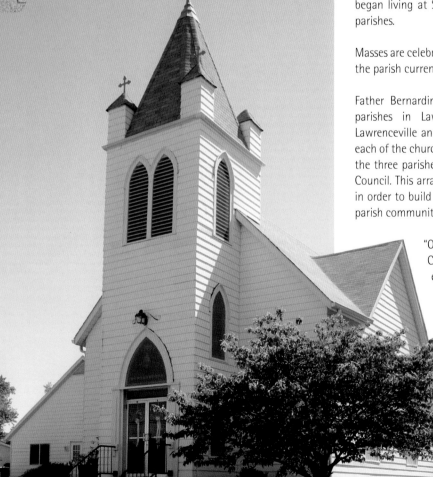

St. Polycarp

CARMI, ILLINOIS

Founded 1847

Blessed John Henry Newman returns to England a Catholic priest.

■ The legendary circuit-riding priest, Father Elisha "Daddy" Durbin celebrated Mass in the home of John Rebstock, shortly after the family settled near Carmi, in 1847. "Daddy" Durbin continued to visit the Rebstocks and their neighbors for the next 12 years. From 1859-1882, this fledgling faith community was served by priests from the surrounding area in several temporary locations until the first St. Polycarp Church was completed in 1877.

In January 1882, Father Joseph Spaeth became the first resident pastor at Carmi and established the parochial school. More than a dozen pastors shepherded St. Polycarp Parish through various stages of growth. The parish centennial was marked in June 1947 with special celebrations and a "new church fund" was established. That dream became a reality 12 years later when Father Clement Dirler oversaw the construction of the present church, with seating for 370. Bishop Albert R. Zuroweste came to Carmi in 1960 for the dedication of the structure.

In 1979, the School Sisters of Notre Dame ended their 97-year presence in Carmi. After their departure, parents assumed responsibility for the religious education of their children.

The present pastor of St. Polycarp Parish, Father Stephen Rudolphi, came to Carmi in 1990. Many more improvements have been made during his over 20 years in this community. He has stated, "Always the greatest challenge is to pass the faith to the next generation."

St. Polycarp Parish has given the Church four vocations to the religious life and the priesthood. Sister Mary Modesta Farney, PHJC, entered the Poor Handmaids of Jesus Christ in September 1910 and worked in healthcare. Sister Therese Mary Rebstock, SSND, has served as a School Sister of Notre Dame for over 60 years with many of those years spent in her congregation's mission in Japan. In June 1972, Father Daniel Friedman was ordained for the Diocese of Belleville and at present, he is the pastor of St. Francis of Assisi, Aviston. Father Stephen Churchwell, a convert to Catholicism in his teen years, was ordained a priest April 1975 for the Atlanta Archdiocese where he continues to serve.

St. John Nepomucene

DAHLGREN, ILLINOIS

Founded 1893

Grover Cleveland began his second term as U.S. President in 1893.

■ An area of Hamilton County called Cottonwood had been a beautiful area when the Louisville and Nashville Railway built a station on the site, which was renamed Dahlgren after Admiral Dahlgren, whose wife was a Catholic. Charles Aydt and his four brothers, Thomas, Joseph, Solomon, and Alphonse moved from Piopolis and were joined by other pioneers, trading farm produce for staples and hardware goods.

Today's St. John Nepomucene was part of the St. John the Baptist Parish, Piopolis, until 1893 when the first church was built on West Main Street in Dahlgren under the direction of Father John N. Enzleberger. Father Henry Keuth became the first resident pastor in 1896.

In 1903, Father Henry Muenster, built a two story brick structure measuring fifty by thirty five feet and providing four classrooms with living quarters in the upper story. The bricks for this building were made in a kiln in Dahlgren and the school itself was constructed by parishioners who were interested in the project. The parish school was opened in 1903 and maintained until 1931 with the Benedictine Sister from Jonesboro, Arkansas. In 1931, the Adorers o the Most Precious Blood took charge of the school until 1965, when a CCD Center was established. This center then moved first to Carmi, then to McLeansboro.

Msgr. Meinrad Dunn broke ground on August 24, 1958 for the present church in a contemporary modified Gothic design, seating 380. The open tower at the southwest corner of the building houses the bell salvaged from the original church. Near the con-

fessional is found a beautiful shrine in honor of the parish patron, St. John Nepomucene. This parish family selected as their patron saint, St. John Nepomucene, martyr and patron of confessors, because he had refused to reveal in 1393, to the King of Prague, Czechoslovakia, the contents of the Queen's sacramental confession. In one hand he holds a cross, the finger of his right hand crossed over his lips, ever a reminder of the secrecy and the unbroken seal of confession.

The spectacular stained glass windows grace the church and had originally been installed in the chapel of St. Elizabeth Hospital, Belleville, in 1914. With color and artistry these windows tell stories St. Francis of Assisi and St. Clare.

The Parish Family is proud of the vocations to the priesthood and religious life, including Father Henry Aydt, ordained June 22, 1920; Sister Colletta Aydt, ASC, Sister M. Irma Aydt, ASC, Sister Irma Ewald, ASC, Sister Mary Rapp, OSB, Sister Mary Louise Degenhart, ASC and Sister Theresa Ann Kiefer, ASC.

In its mission statement, the parish family of St. John Nepomucene remembers and celebrates its beginnings; pledges to continue to respond to present and future goals for Eternal Redemption of all its members as well as new converts; and focuses all efforts to the greater honor and glory of Almighty God.

ST. JOHN NEPOMUCENE CATHOLIC CHURC EST. 1893

St. Mary

ELDORADO, ILLINOIS

Founded 1900

The founder of the Christian Brothers,
St. John Baptist de La Salle was canonized in 1900.

■ St. Mary Church in Eldorado was dedicated to the patronage of Our Lady of Victory by Bishop John Janssen on April 10, 1901. Father J. Bernard Hater was responsible for the organization of the parish. A parish school opened in 1922 with the Sisters of the Incarnate Word and later the School Sisters of Notre Dame on the faculty. St. Mary School formed generations of young Catholics until its closing in 1970. During his 35-year pastorate, Msgr. Wilfrid E. Hanagan supervised the construction of the present church, which was dedicated on May 9, 1954, by Bishop Albert R. Zuroweste, Bishop of Belleville. The church was built with a bequest from former Mayor Thomas Mahoney.

Bishop Wilton D. Gregory created a parish cluster of St. Mary, Eldorado; St. Mary, Harrisburg and St. Joseph, Elizabethtown. Currently, Father Ignatius Okonkwo serves as administrator of the cluster.

The Blessed Virgin Mary, Our Lady of Victory, serves as this faith community's model of faith and hope. St. Mary Parish provides formation through its Parish School of Religion and the Rite of Christian Initiation of Adults. Parishioners are active in the Pastoral Council, Altar Society which is affiliated with the Belleville Diocesan Council of Catholic Women and the Holy Name Men's Club.

A unique ministry in St. Mary Parish is its Rosary Guild, which has made and sent over 10,000 rosaries to Catholic missions. The Eldorado parish contributes to the evangelistic pursuits of the universal church by her participation and sponsors a sister parish, Crucified Jesus, in Guatemala.

Priestly and religious vocations from St. Mary Parish include: Father Michael Podrasky, ordained June 6, 1944; Father Walter Barr, ordained May 23, 1959; Father Thomas Barrett, ordained June 5, 1971, Father Phillip DeVous, ordained May 23, 2004 for the Diocese of Covington, Kentucky; Father Scott Duvall, ordained May 24, 2009, for the Diocese of Rockford, Illinois. Sister Mary Blanche Brown, and Sister Gilda Bruce are the women religious from Eldorado.

St. Joseph of the Woods

ELIZABETHTOWN, ILLINOIS

Founded 1864

Abraham Lincoln was elected to a second term as president on November 8, 1864.

■ Father Killian Schlosser celebrated the first Mass in the area on May 3, 1858 at the Volkert family home with others who sought refuge in southern Illinois from a cholera epidemic in St. Louis, Missouri.

In 1863, Father Weggener, who was assigned to serve the needs of Catholics along the Ohio River, encouraged the construction of a small log church on the Emmanuel Herrmann farm near Elizabethtown. The new Hardin County church was named St. Joseph of the Woods. Father John Henken was appointed first resident pastor in 1897. After a wild fire destroyed St. Joseph Church in 1924, the present brick sanctuary was built and dedicated on November 10, 1925.

Father Henry Reis served the parish for twenty-nine years. Father Donald Abell, the thirty-ninth priest at Elizabethtown, guided St. Joseph in a transition to a cluster parish until 2006 when Fr. Ignatius Okonkwo became the administrator for the three cluster parishes with Catholic communities in Harrisburg and Eldorado.

With a rich, immigrant and illustrious history, St. Joseph has remained steadfast to their parish mission statement to worship God, witness to the Good News of Jesus Christ, and respond to the spiritual and basic material needs of all people through purposeful faith-building, educational and social programs. Youth and adults receive in-depth and on-going religious education through the Parish School of Religion and adult faith study programs.

Other activities include: cluster parishes retreat, annual parish picnics, funeral meals for bereaved families, social activities, food collections for the needy, and coat and clothing giveaways. St. Ann's Council of Catholic Women and the Holy Name Society are active organizations and help provide for the needs of the parish and community.

Four vocations originated from St. Joseph: Carmelite Father Jack Flanery and three women religious: Sister Veronica Hermas, Sister Jerry Schmidt and Sister Christina Eckmans.

St. Patrick

ENFIELD, ILLINOIS

Founded 1839

Blessed Jeanne Jugan founded the Little Sisters of the Poor in 1839.

■ The first Catholic in the Enfield area was Patrick Dolan, from Queen's County, Ireland. He made his claim in White County in 1839 and he paid for his property by working on the Illinois Central Railroad. Dolan served in the Illinois Legislature and conducted the auction of the original lots of Enfield in 1853. In 1841 the Hanagans, Dunns, and Connellys came to the area, and the Millers joined the group when Daniel Hanagan sent for his bride-to-be. Others joining the community were named Bannon, Campbell, Crawford, Connery, Devoy, Driscoll, Erskine, Hayden, McCloskey, McGuire, McMahon, Mitchell, Pierce, Reagan, Shields and Weeks.

The famed circuit-rider, Father Elisha J. Durbin, was the first priest to visit the settlement. Sometime after 1850 a log building on the Dolan farm was dedicated for worship. A wood-frame building replaced the log church between 1862 and 1865 and was located on what is now the new section of St. Patrick Cemetery.

Father William O'Reilly was the first resident pastor in 1871. The newly-ordained Father Baltasar Wittauer was appointed to the parish in 1885 and served St. Patrick until his death in 1914. During his dedicated service, he initiated the construction of a new Gothic style wood-frame church, which was completed in 1890, at a cost of $5,000. Father Wittauer established a motherhouse and boarding school which was home to the Order of the Servants of Mary from 1895 to 1908.

During the final decades of the 19th century several families originally from Belgium and France--Belva, Fyie, Etienne, Douby (Dauby) and Deom--settled near Springerton. Father Wittauer served these families by saying Mass once a month at the home of Narcissus Belva.

Father Fred Halbig was pastor on November 27, 1938, the Sunday after Thanksgiving, when the wood church was destroyed by fire, blamed on a defective flue. With mainly volunteer labor the present St. Meinrad sandstone church and rectory were quickly constructed. One year later, dedication services for the new St. Patrick's were held on Thanksgiving Day, 1939, with Bishop Henry Althoff presiding.

Due to the generosity of the John and Joseph Dunn families, the parish was able to replace the old parish hall—cobbled from the old convent and school--in 1975 with the current brick facility. In 2011, St. Patrick Parish is made up of approximately 60 households, and shares Father Stephen Rudolphi with St. Polycarp Parish, Carmi, as part of the White and Hamilton County cluster.

St. Patrick Parish has produced one "native son" priest, Msgr. Wilfrid Hanagan, who was ordained in 1926. Women who have joined religious orders include Sister Mary Ida Donnelly, Sisters of Loretto; Sister Mary Pauline Mitchell, Sisters of St. Joseph; Sisters Mary Elexia Reagan, Mary Patricia McGuire, Mary Petronella Dolan, Mary Angela Dolan, Mary Ignatia Fyie, Mary Bonfilia Dunn and Avellina Dolan of the Servants of Mary; Sister Mary Gabriel Hanagan, Sisters of Mercy; Sister Gertrude Marie Mitchell, Sisters of St. Mary; Sister Carmalita Devoy, a Benedictine; and Sister Anna Marie McCloskey of the Adorers of the Blood of Christ.

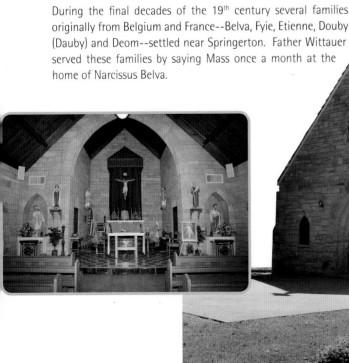

St. Joseph

EQUALITY, ILLINOIS

Founded 1873

Bishop Henry J. Althoff was born August 28, 1873 in Aviston.

■ The small Catholic community that was the origin of St. Joseph Parish was ministered to in the 1840s by Father Elisha Durbin and other missionary priests as they rode circuits throughout southern Illinois. In 1873, the parish began raising funds and obtained property. A frame building was built in 1881 at a cost of $800. A two-storey, nine-room rectory was constructed in 1893 and served the parish until 2010. Father Thomas Day was assigned as the first resident pastor. In 1900 the parish purchased five acres of land on a hill outside of town for a cemetery.

The present brick church was built in 1908 and was dedicated to St. Joseph on December 18, 1908. St. Joseph Parish celebrated the centennial of this historic church, which has watched the floodwaters of the nearby Saline River rise and recede over the years, many times lapping at the front steps. Most notably in 1937 when the river invaded the church, hall, and rectory to a depth of nine feet. During this trying time, Mass was held in the home of parishioner, Joseph Wathen, and the congregation rallied to make repairs. The church, itself, has been renovated several times in its century of existence. In 2000 beautiful etched glass windows were installed that present the Gospel story of the life of Christ.

Through the years, St. Joseph has proven to be a well-chosen parish patron. As the patron saint of workers, and in his role within the Holy Family, he is a good model for a parish made up of working class people with strong family values.

In addition to the guidance of their patron saint, St. Joseph parishioners feel blessed with the leadership of many priests, religious and laity. The School Sisters of Notre Dame and, more recently, the Adorers of the Blood of Christ have served in Equality. Thirty resident pastors have ministered in this parish, or, clusters that included this parish. At various times, St. Joseph has been partnered with parishes in Stonefort, New Burnside, Vienna, Ridgway and Metropolis. Currently St. Joseph Parish, Equality shares Father Steven Beatty with Immaculate Conception Parish in Shawneetown, St. Joseph Parish in Ridgway, and St. Patrick Parish in Pond Settlement. Each of these partnerships has brought new perspectives and has enriched spirituality.

In an area of the diocese that has a predominantly non-Catholic population, St. Joseph parishioners strive to set an example of Catholic Christianity while working in a spirit of cooperation with neighbors of other denominations in bringing about the Kingdom of God upon the earth.

St. Edward

FAIRFIELD, ILLINOIS

Founded 1878

Blessed Pope Pius IX died on February 7, 1878.

■ St. Edward Church in Fairfield can trace its history back to the early 1800's when a group of about twenty Catholic families began to gather. Their desire to build up their lives through the Eucharist and other sacraments led them to search for a priest to serve as their pastor. Circuit-riding priests on horseback visited and celebrated Mass in various Catholic homes around Wayne County.

In 1878, St. Edward Church was established as a mission of St. Stephen Church, Flora, with Father L. Riesen as pastor. L.J. Rider, Alexis Rider, and Edward Bonham donated the farmland for a new church, which was constructed of handmade brick and oak timbers, which were cut locally. The church in Fairfield was dedicated on September 18, 1881 and Father Riesen celebrated the first Eucharist in the new church. The new church was named after St. Edward the Confessor, eleventh century King of England.

On December 12, 1946, Bishop Henry Althoff appointed Father John Walsh as the first resident pastor. The ecclesiastical documents were read constituting St. Edward Catholic Church as a parish and attaching St. Sebastian Church in St. Sebastian as a mission.

Besides Mass and the celebration of other sacraments, St. Edward Parish has great devotion to the Rosary, which usually precedes the Mass. Prayer for vocations to the priesthood and religious life is ongoing, since parishioners are very aware that priests are needed in every stage of their Christian lives. In addition, the congregation has Eucharistic Adoration, usually during Lent.

From the first twenty families in the nineteenth century, the present congregation has grown to more than 100 families. An active parish life is maintained through a strong Pastoral Council, lectors, ushers, Ministers of Communion, Parish School of Religion program for children, the Rite of Christian Initiation for Adults, Ministers of Care, Men's Club, Altar Sodality, and a vibrant youth group.

Three men of St. Edward Parish have been called to priestly ordination: Father Henry Ray Engelhart in 1963; Father Ray Schultz in 1991, and Father Mark Reyling in 1998. Father Michael Moonu is the current parish administrator at Fairfield.

The spirit of cooperation and community, that has characterized the Catholic Church in Fairfield for over 100 years, echoes in the St. Edward Parish mission statement, which reads: "We, united as a family of God's people, strive to live out the Gospel of our Lord Jesus Christ through a community spirit of love and service to one another. We endeavor to touch the lives of all with God's living presence and love."

61

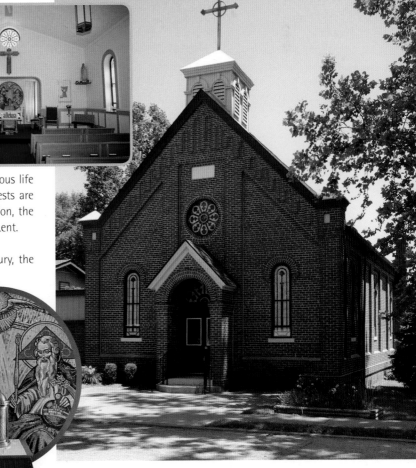

St. Stephen

FLORA, ILLINOIS

Founded 1854

Pius IX solemnly defined the Immaculate Conception in 1854.

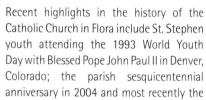

■ St. Stephen Church, Flora, is one of two parishes in Clay County, along with Holy Cross Church of Wendelin. The 150 families of St. Stephen Parish strive to fulfill their mission statement, which captures the spirit of the 157-year-old faith community: "United in the love of God and under the guidance of the Holy Spirit, to proclaim the Word of God by a life of witness in our community and beyond; to give God the glory through assisting the weak and the less privileged , putting things back together, binding, healing, affirming, serving, restoring and educating the People of God; to serve together in reconciling with one another and with God, sharing our gifts and ourselves for the sake of the Gospel."

The parish began in 1854, when Father Joseph F. Fischer celebrated the first Mass in Flora, at the home of Louis Valbert, who later donated two acres for a Catholic cemetery. For the next 12 years, Masses were celebrated in the Hagerty and Rider homes. By 1866, a small church was built on East Maple Street. St. Stephen Church was moved to a site on Ninth and Main, deeded to the parish by Sylvester and Ann Rider.

A parochial school was built in 1888 with 31 to 64 students taught initially by lay teachers and later by Adorers of the Blood of Christ. This school served as a temporary church after St. Stephen Church was destroyed by fire on Christmas Day 1892. On All Saints Day, November 1, 1955, Bishop Albert R. Zuroweste visited Flora to dedicate a new multi-purpose building which housed the parish school, church, convent, and auditorium. In 1965 the school was closed and religious instruction began on Saturdays.

Recent highlights in the history of the Catholic Church in Flora include St. Stephen youth attending the 1993 World Youth Day with Blessed Pope John Paul II in Denver, Colorado; the parish sesquicentennial anniversary in 2004 and most recently the remodeling of the church in 2008.

This faith community gathers for daily Mass and Rosary, monthly Eucharistic Adoration, and adult Scripture studies. St. Stephen's parishioners assist with the local Meals on Wheels and take part in the local food pantry. Parish organizations work on behalf of the parish and those in need. St. Ann's Altar Society hosts many activities including a pro-life baby shower. The Knights of Columbus Council collaborate with the local Shriners on various fundraisers for those in need. Both organizations make various donations to local and national pro-life and youth organizations.

The current administrator of St. Stephen Parish, Father Martin Edward Ohajunwa, has been instrumental in starting an Ave Maria Garden, which includes a new Virgin Mary statue and a walk made of bricks inscribed with family names and dedications.

St. Stephen Parish has given the Church one priest and four women religious. Father James Thompson, who was one of the priests who ministered to President John F. Kennedy when he was assassinated, was ordained in 1934 and is buried in St. Stephen Cemetery. Louise Willien entered the convent in 1895 and became Sister Aloysius SSND: Beatrice Day entered in 1897 and became Sister M. Nazaria, CSJ: Hattie Thompson entered in 1895 and became Sister M. Patricia, SSND; and Nellie Conroy entered in 1922 and became Sister Mary Agnes Lucille, CSD.

St. Mary

HARRISBURG, ILLINOIS

Founded 1907

"The Messenger"' made its debut as the quarterly publication of the Diocese of Belleville.

■ Harrisburg was settled as a coal mining town by English, German, French, Polish, and Slavonic families. The first Mass in the area was celebrated in a private home in 1902. St. Mary Church, Harrisburg, was established on December 8, 1907, the solemnity of the Immaculate Conception of the Blessed Virgin Mary with a permanent building formally dedicated on September 30, 1908. The present church, built in 1960, is located just west of Harrisburg and serves approximately two hundred families.

Today, the parishioners of St. Mary are more diversified than they were at the beginning but still are bound together in faith and love bearing witness to God's love for humanity as Christ commanded, "Go make disciples of all the nations." (Matt. 28:19)

In the light of this mandate, Harrisburg parishioners share time, talent, and treasure within and beyond the parish community. Members of St. Mary Church actively participate in the local Choisser Kitchen which feeds the hungry. The parish partners with the Community Christian Compassion Center, an interfaith effort to provide food, financial assistance, shelter to the poor and handicapped in our community.

More than twenty priests, including Father Vito Lopardo, Father Bert Iffert, Father Jack Stallings, Father Donald Abell, and, most recently, Father Ignatius Okonkwo, *a fidei donum*

of "gift of faith" priest from Archdiocese of Onitsha, Nigeria, have worked to make St. Mary Parish the Christian community imbued with strong faith, hope and love in God and one another that it is today.

Although St. Mary has not had a Catholic school to pass on the faith, many committed men and women of our parish have worked hard to hand on our faith to our young people. Marie Bridwell, Magdelin Klein, Eleanor Molinarolo, and George Dennis were few of the parish's outstanding catechists. Today, their legacy and tradition have continued at our Parish Center with dedicated teachers and song leaders, who work dilligently to hand on our faith to our young ones.

The late Father James Donovan and Sister Eloise Jarvis were two St. Mary parishioners who embraced priestly and religious vocations.

St. Elizabeth Ann Seton

KINMUNDY, ILLINOIS

Founded 1870

St. Anthony Mary Claret died on October 24, 1870.

◼ Located in the small town of Kinmundy, Illinois, St. Elizabeth Ann Seton Parish is a close-knit community of faith that was founded in 1870. Originally founded under the patronage of the virgin-martyr, St. Philomena, by Father Francis Moening, OFM, the church was renamed following the 1975 canonization of St. Elizabeth Ann Seton, the first American-born saint.

While 27 priests have been assigned to Kinmundy in over 140 years, a parish life coordinator was named for St. Elizabeth Ann Seton in 2001 to oversee the religious life and activities of the parish. Visiting priests, many of whom were retired, helped meet the sacramental needs of the parishioners. This period was marked by a significant increase in lay participation at every level of parish life. In 2010, the parish was blessed when Bishop Edward K. Braxton appointed Father Robert Zwilling as pastor of both the parish in Kinmundy and St. Theresa of Avila in nearby Salem.

Two parishioners of St. Elizabeth made generous donations that allowed the church to continue to grow. In 1951, Mr. Fred Kleiss donated the land where the current church was constructed. In 1968, Mrs. Mildred Kleiss donated land adjoining the church for a new parish hall. While St. Elizabeth Ann Seton parishioners live in various communities, some quite a distance away, they have been united in their hard work and sacrifices on behalf of their Catholic church in Kinmundy.

St. Elizabeth Ann Seton Parish reaches beyond the city limits of Kinmundy to help serve the less fortunate. A relationship has been established with Our Lady of the Sioux Mission Parish, Oglala, South Dakota. One Sunday each month, a monetary collection is taken up to help support this mission. Several times throughout the year, specific items are collected for Our Lady of the Sioux. For example, school supplies are collected in August to help the students at Our Lady of the Sioux. In the Fall, St. Elizabeth Ann Seton parishioners donate winter clothing items like hats, gloves, mittens, and scarves to help in the harsh South Dakota winter.

St. Elizabeth Ann Seton Parish also participates in the local adopt-a-family program at Christmas, with parishioners sponsoring an area child in need. The parish also contributes food, monetary donations and volunteers to the local food pantry.

Despite its small size, St. Elizabeth Ann Seton Parish has fostered two vocations to the religious life. In 1903, Catherine Kramer joined the Ursulines as Sister Mary Gertrude. On December 21, 1963, Father Wayne Like was ordained a priest of the Missionary Oblates of Mary Immaculate.

St. Elizabeth's mission statement is "to be a community that believes and proclaims the powerful and loving presence of Jesus Christ and extends His love to others. We are called and sent to pass down the Catholic Faith we have inherited through our worship, word, and work."

St. Lawrence

LAWRENCEVILLE, ILLINOIS

Founded 1899

Blessed Angela Truszkowska, foundress of the Felician Sisters, died October 10, 1899.

■ According to a history written by Father Patrick Slattery in 1923, a mission congregation existed at Lawrenceville as far back as 1899. At this time Father James Downey and later Father Joseph Taggart of St. Francisville came to Lawrenceville to offer Mass in the upstairs of the C. D. Carter Store, General Merchandise. The congregation started to build its first church late in 1909 and Mass was first celebrated in the unfinished church on Sunday, December 5, 1909.

By 1951, the parish had grown to 90 families and that growth indicated the need for a school for the parish. On Sunday November 6, 1955 ground breaking ceremonies took place for the school, which opened on September 5, 1956 with 74 students and the Adorers of the Blood of Christ as faculty. St. Lawrence Parish continued to grow as ground was broken for a new church on Sunday, August 28, 1960. Located on the southeast corner of Eleventh and Collins, the church is of modern Gothic construction and seats 380. Today, St. Lawrence Church has a faith community of 125 households and is currently administered by Father Bernardine Nganzi.

St. Lawrence strives to follow the command of Christ to "love our neighbor." The St. Vincent De Paul Society was formed in 1983 at St. Lawrence and continues to meet weekly to provide assistance to the poor. They have also enlisted church members to visit the sick in the parish, shut-ins, and those in long-term care facilities. St. Lawrence financially supports the St. Vincent De Paul Society, other charities and outreach programs in Lawrence County. For

those imprisoned in the local state correctional facility, a bi-monthly Bible study is conducted by a parishioner.

The Altar Society has been in existence since 1932 and remains active providing support to the parish in ways which include providing meals after funerals for parishioners. This seems fitting due to the fact that the parish's patron saint, St. Lawrence, is the patron for cooks. The Altar Society also represents St. Lawrence by providing a canteen for the American Red during local blood drives.

Although St. Lawrence School closed in 1985, the building continues to be used by such organizations as St. Vincent De Paul, Rite of Christian Initiation for Adults, Boy Scouts, Cub Scouts and Girl Scouts, 4-H, Knights of Columbus Council 7579, as well as parish committee meetings, parish council meetings and other church functions. The school building is also home to an active Parish School of Religion and Youth Group with parental volunteers overseen by the Coordinator of Religious Education. Church membership grows each year as new members are formed through the RCIA.

A Spiritual Life and Worship Committee cares for the spiritual needs of our parishioners by meeting to discuss the church year and providing parishioners with spiritual tools to nurture their faith. The committee also co-hosts a parish mission every two years along with the Parish and Community Life Committee.

St. Clement

McLeansboro, Illinois

Founded 1881

Angelo Roncalli, Blessed Pope John XXIII, was born November 25, 1881.

■ An anchor, a sign of hope and the symbol of the fourth pope, St. Clement, is molded in bronze on the front doors of St. Clement Church, a sign of faith and hope in Hamilton County for over 130 years.

The legendary circuit-riding priest, Father Elisha "Daddy" Durbin celebrated the first Mass in what is now McLeansboro in 1846 in the log home of Irish immigrants James and Mahalia McGilley. The celebrant had journeyed on horseback from his mission base at St. Vincent's Kentucky in Union County, Kentucky.

During his 60 years as a missionary, "Daddy" Durbin rode over 200,000 miles on horseback, often subsisting on cornbread, salt pork, and water. Father would stop at a Catholic home and the news would spread. As the faithful gathered, "Daddy" Durbin would first hear confessions and then celebrate Mass before leaving for the next cluster of Catholic homes.

In 1864, the area's first resident pastor, Father Edward Herman, was assigned to a community of German Catholics which would eventually be known as Piopolis, some seven miles north of McLeansboro.

McLeansboro experienced considerable growth. The pastor of the German settlement, Father John Niehaus and Sister Clementine Zerr, leader of the Adorers of the Blood of Christ who had settled there, began to teach religion to the youth of McLeansboro in 1872. When the idea of a new Catholic congregation for McLeansboro was broached, Sister Clementine suggested her own patron, St. Clement, because she had received a first class relic in Rome on the occasion of her final vows.

In 1880, St. Clement was made a mission of St. Mary Parish, Mt. Vernon. The pastors came by way of the new rail service of the L & N Railway on Saturday to celebrate Mass, returning to Mt. Vernon on Sunday morning.

The first recorded baptism in St. Clement's records was January 7, 1881, administered to Mary Scarbroug Pentecost. Eventually, Mary would marry James McGilley, Jr., son of the community's earliest pioneers. Bishop Peter T. Baltes of Alton dedicated the first St. Clement Church on October 2, 1881. The Lawrence Paul family loaded an organ in a wagon and brought it to the new church for use during the Mass.

The privilege of Mass every weekend throughout the year has been enjoyed since 1931, while sharing a pastor with St. John Nepomucene Parish, Dahlgren. In July 1931, a new paved road connected McLeansboro and Dahlgren and overcame a great travel difficulty.

The present church was constructed largely with local labor and the expertise of the Rapp Family, a company of four brothers under the leadership of their father and the dedication Mass was on June 24, 1964.

A parish annex, built under the leadership of the current pastor, Msgr. Joseph Lawler, is used for the Parish School of Religion classes, Rite of Christian Initiation classes, parish cluster activities, youth meetings, parish social gatherings and the annual Wurstmart.

The first man to be ordained a priest from the parish was Father George Mauck. Sister Anastasia Rubenacker, ASC, is another parishioner presently living her vocation to religious life.

About 150 households presently attend St. Clement Church, striving to be faithful to the legacy of faith handed down from the parish's pioneers and to live the parish mission statement: "We are a group of baptized Roman Catholics that celebrate our faith and are nourished by God's grace in the seven Sacraments attempting to bring the message of Christ to ourselves and our diverse community of neighbors."

St. Mary

MOUNT CARMEL, ILLINOIS

Founded 1836

Venerable Henriette Delille organized the religious community for women of color which became the Sisters of the Holy Family in New Orleans in 1836.

■ The first recorded gathering and celebrating of Catholics in the city of Mt. Carmel dates to 1836. A small group of German Catholics met in a home where a visiting priest celebrated the Eucharist, baptized their children and witnessed a marriage. As more families joined them, the Catholic community built a church overlooking the Wabash River in 1854. This church building was dedicated to St. Mary of Mt. Carmel.

spirited Catholics, married couples, enthused students, caring outreach groups, and dedicated workers. It has also offered more than sixteen women to serve as Sisters, one of whom - Mother Veronica Baumgart - helped establish the Adorers of the Blood of Christ Center at Ruma, and eight men to accept the priesthood. The mission continues today with Father Bill Rowe as pastor.

In 1881, the parish constructed a school, staffed by the Adorers of the Blood of Christ, to encourage the children to grow in the faith. By the turn of the century, the growing population required a new church building, a rectory, a parish cemetery, and a larger school all realized within the space of several years. In this way the mission of St. Mary of Mt. Carmel was fashioned: to share the Eucharist and Word, to pray for each other, to pass the faith on to others, to care for the hurt.

The twentieth century saw the need to expand the mission: to be an alive and hospitable community. The hall above the school building was used for the youth to gather - the beginnings of the former Catholic Youth Organization. It was these teens that took second and third place trophies in a Diocesan Holy Week Quiz sponsored in East St. Louis. A building for the Knights of Columbus was built and was shared with the Altar Society, the Cub and Boy Scouts. The school program was expanded once more with a new building in 1953, guided not only by the Adorers of the Blood of Christ and the Poor Handmaid of Jesus Christ, but also lay teachers from the parish.

The vision of Vatican II produced changes not only in the church building, but also gave birth to a Parish Council and School Board. Lectors, cantors, extraordinary ministers of the Eucharist, two choirs, Cursillo, the Rite of Christian Initiation of Adults, adult Bible study, and home discussion groups all emerged in the Vatican II spirit. A final touch of hospitality and celebration was added with the construction of a new church hall in 2004.

As the church of St. Mary has lived out its mission, it has blessed the community and greater church with countless

St. Mary

MT. VERNON, ILLINOIS

Founded 1880

U.S. population exceeded 50 million in 1880.

■ St. Mary Parish in Mount Vernon stand at a crossroad—and always has beenm. Settlers moved into the area in the early 1800s, because the Goshen Trail and Trace Trail crossed nearby. But it was 1866 before enough Catholics had settled in the area to bring Father Blasius Winterhalter to Mount Vernon for the first recorded Catholic Mass, which was offered in the home of Judge and Mrs. Thomas S. Casey. Although Judge Casey was not Catholic, his wife, the former Matilda Moran of Springfield, Illinois) was Catholic. So from its earliest days the Catholic community in and around Mount Vernon and Jefferson County worked to establish themselves as a respected religious minority working and witnessing to their closest neighbors--and even family members.

In the early decades of the parish, this mission meant establishing a strong Catholic community and a place of worship. To do the first, servant priests like Father Henry Hagen focused on building up Catholic organizations and sodalities that emphasized Catholic identity, devotion, and works of charity. Others, especially Fathers Louis Hinssen, Francis "Father Teck" Tecklenburg, Joseph Voll, and Edward Dahmus worked to build, furnish, and pay for a church that would serve the coming generations of Catholics.

The next stage of development at St. Mary Parish focused on the founding and development of a Catholic school. Planning for the school began in 1939, but the doors only opened in 1955, under the pastoral leadership of Msgr. James P. Burke. Catholic

parishioners sacrificed to build and grow a strong Catholic school in Mount Vernon, later demonstrating a similar desire to develop a quality Parish School of Religion and opportunities for youth ministry. Msgr. Melvin Vandeloo hired the reportedly first paid youth minister in the diocese in 1999. As in so many parishes in our diocese, passing on the faith to the next generation remains a passion for the Mt. Vernon Catholic community.

Today Mt. Vernon sits at another transportation crossroad—the intersection of Interstates 57 and 64. This confluence has contributed to economic growth and demographic stability in Mt. Vernon. It has also meant a Catholic presence in Mt. Vernon that is larger than our numbers, which is only approximately 10% of the total population. Yet, Catholic Social Services maintains a regional office in Mt. Vernon. St. Mary/Good Samaritan Hospital is now a regional medical center "continuing the healing ministry of Jesus Christ." Many diocesan meetings, programs, and catechetical events are scheduled in Mt. Vernon, providing a strong core of well-formed volunteers who are active in our parish and the diocesan church.

The mission of maintaining grace-filled Catholic worship, passing the faith on to our children, and witnessing to the Gospel of Jesus Christ by works of charity and faith, still guides the life of St. Mary Parish 146 years after that first Mass. To accomplish this mission, the parish has adopted goals, under the direction of Father John Iffert, pastor, that include building a new church, maintaining strong faith formation for children, becoming a center of excellence in adult faith formation, and re-evangelizing the Catholic community in Jefferson County.

St. Joseph

OLNEY, ILLINOIS

Founded 1857

The landmark Dred Scott decision was handed down in St. Louis in 1857.

■ Founded in 1857 by Father T. J. Loughren, St. Joseph Parish, Olney, has remained true to the example of its patron saint, Joseph the Carpenter, by being a community of builders. Masses were celebrated in the Raling home until the first church was built in 1861. The church was moved on rollers in 1892 to a new location. On January 1, 1906, the parish opened its Catholic school, which over 100 years later continues as the primary parish mission. Young children are the heart of St. Joseph Parish as well as a gauge of its future. Catholic identity, academic achievements, and sports successes are only a small measure of the school's effectiveness.

To build the people's faith on their life journey, the parish has been involved in adult faith formation as well since Vatican Council II. First, the parish served as a hub for the surrounding parishes for adult education programs. From Confraternity of Christian Doctrine gatherings at their inception to today's RENEW groups to monthly lectures by outside speakers, St. Joseph Parish offers programs to enrich parishioners' faith. Another significant element in building the faith is the Rite of Christian Initiation for Adults, which began in 1980 as a pilot program for the Belleville Diocese. Since then the parish has welcomed over 400 Catholic adults.

The parish has endeavored over the years to build good relations with other churches. With an ecumenical spirit, pastors and associate pastors have been very active members in the Ministerial Association to cordially work with other Christian denominations in joint projects and worship services.

St. Joseph is proud of its three priests and five religious sisters who answered God's call. Also, several parishioners have contributed significantly to church and community.

Dr. George T. Weber established in 1898 the Olney Sanitarium, which soon housed a training school for nurses. It was later named the Weber Clinic. Dr. George T. Weber was also instrumental in establishing St. Joseph School. Gus and Mary Sliva left an indelible mark on the community's appreciation for music with their outstanding work at East Richland High School, where the high school auditorium is named after them. They also served for years as church organist and choir director.

An unusual incident occurred in the early 1930's during the Great Depression, when the church was in serious need of repairs. Olney parishioner Mabel Litzelman purchased an Irish Sweepstakes ticket in 1935 and won the grand prize, $142,500. She exclaimed, "My God did this for me," and immediately stated that there were two things she wished to do: help build a new church and get a Packard. Both wishes came true.

The parish mission statement in part says "we minister to ourselves and others through prayer, support, and service." While continuing to encourage religious vocations through daily prayer and the chalice program in school, Meals for Moms, Healing Blankets, and working with Good Samaritan Hospital, Olney, along with many other seasonal outreach projects by school and church, are some of the efforts to serve those in need. The parish's faith life reflects Christ's call to love one another and the parish mission "to pass it on to future generations."

St. John the Baptist

PIOPOLIS, ILLINOIS

Founded 1841

President William Henry Harrison died on April 4, 1841, just one month after his inauguration.

On April 19, 1841 a special Mass was celebrated in the town of Ersingen in the state of Baden, Germany. Twenty-five individuals were leaving to start new lives in the United States. August 21 of that same year found the travelers in Hamilton County, Illinois. Two years later, additional German settlers, including Tobias Brummer and Nicholas Engel arrived in the community. Engel built a log cabin where the Holy Sacrifice of the Mass would be celebrated later that year. Father Elisha Durbin rode on horseback from St. Vincent in Union County, Kentucky to serve the German settlers. He started a Baptismal book for the growing community and wrote an inscription on the front page, "Mount St. John, Hamilton County, Illinois."

A 40 acre tract of land was purchased in 1844 by Cajetan Aydt from Thomas Whittaker and deeded to the Catholic Bishop of Chicago, Bishop William Quarters. Disaster struck the community in 1857 when a wind storm destroyed the frame church that the settlers had constructed. With the help of migrants from Clinton County, a new Church was completed in time for Bishop Henry Damian Juncker of Alton, to celebrate Confirmation in 1860.

Father Edward Harriman was the first resident pastor at Piopolis. Mr. Marcellus Zachman was hired as a lay teacher for the newly established St. John the Baptist School in 1865. In 1870 a two-storey school and a convent were completed for nine Adorers of the Blood of Christ, refugees of the Kulturkampf, who traveled from Gurtweil Germany, arriving by wagon after coming to Shawneetown by boat. In 1876, Bishop Juncker suggested the Sisters move their Piopolis Motherhouse to Ruma. It was a sad day, when the Sisters packed up their belongings and agricultural tools and departed with their cows on the L & N Railroad at Delafield.

The village of Piopolis, named after Pope Pius IX, who was celebrating 50 years in the priesthood, was laid out on 13 acres of church property in 1877.

In 1879, 16 orphan girls were sent to Piopolis to be taken care of by the Sisters remaining in Piopolis for two years. That same year, plans were drawn up to build a new church, and one half million bricks were baked in a local kiln for the project.

The Adorers of the Blood of Christ left Piopolis in 1964 after 94 years, and the following year their convent was converted to a rectory. A Parish Council was established at Piopolis in 1972. The twelfth and current pastor Father Joseph Lawler was installed July 10, 1983. In his 28 years as pastor at Piopolis, he was named "monsignor" in 2000 and celebrated his golden jubilee of ordination. With Msgr. Lawler's retirement in July 2011, Father Slawomir Ptak, a *fidei donum* priest of the Diocese of Tarnow, Poland, became administrator of St. John the Baptist Parish.

Thirty-four women from Piopolis have entered religious life, primarily the Adorers of the Blood of Christ. Five men have been ordained to the priesthood, including, Father William Fidelis Karcher, OFM, Father August Reyling, OFM, Father Albert Karcher, Father Eugene Kreher, and Father Mark Reyling.

St. Patrick

POND SETTLEMENT, ILLINOIS

Founded 1852

The controversial novel, "Uncle Tom's Cabin," was published on March 20, 1852.

■ St. Patrick Parish, Pond Settlement, has its origins in the arrival of Irish Catholic families, who settled in the area surrounding the Ohio River bottoms near Shawneetown. There were no Catholic churches established so the families relied on circuit-rider priests. Father Elisha Durbin from St. Vincent of Waverly, Kentucky was the first priest who came to the area then known as Doherty and later known as Pond Settlement. Father Durbin traveled thousands of miles on horseback ministering in this region from 1822 through 1859. He celebrated the first Mass in May 1824 at the home of John Lawler one of the first settlers of the area.

Masses were offered in the log homes of the various families until Fall 1853 when the first Catholic church of Gallatin County was constructed in Pond Settlement. This structure was 35' x 25' and was made from logs. The first Mass was celebrated on August 18, 1853 by Father Patrick McCabe. The first log cabin church was then replaced in 1880 during the administration of Father James Rensmann. This structure was then replaced in 1929 under the administration of Father Louis Ell with a small Tudor Gothic church, which was built of brick and dedicated by Bishop Henry Althoff on December 11, 1929.

St. Patrick parishioners remain very active in the life of the Church. As part of a county-wide cluster, including St. Joseph, Ridgway; St. Mary, Shawneetown; and St. Joseph, Equality, Pond Settlement Catholics assist as lectors, servers, greeters in each of the churches. St. Patrick parishioners are very active in the Parish School of Religion, classes, Parish Council and Youth Ministry. They participate in the meals for new mothers, food pantry collections, Altar Society, and Knights of Columbus.

The People of God of Pond Settlement recognize that the faith continues to build on the foundation that was set by those first pioneers who chose not to give up; but persevered. Being established by Irish Catholics who chose St. Patrick as their patron saint, this community annually celebrates his March 17 feast day with a Mass and potluck meal afterwards. St. Patrick's Parish goal is to continue growing the heritage of being a friendly and hospitable Catholic Community that draws friends, neighbors and families to a closer relationship with Jesus Christ.

This small parish community has been blessed with many religious vocations. The priests from our parish include Father Joseph Frey, Msgr. Joseph Lawler, and Father Donald Abell. Women religious, who call Pond Settlement home, include: Sister Mary Alma Lawler, Sister Mary Gabriel Lawler, Sister M. Lorita Lawler, Sister Mary Rachel Lawler, Sister Celeste Lawler, Sister Agnes Loretta Maloney, Sister Liberia Maloney, Sister Amadeus Lawler Raftis, Sister Marie Bowling and Sister Kathleen McGuire. A Memorial Niche for Sister Kathleen McGuire displays information and memorabilia of this Adorer of the Blood of Christ from her birth on December 28, 1937 to her being martyred on October 23, 1992, in Liberia, West Africa, along with four other missionary Adorers.

St. Joseph

RIDGWAY, ILLINOIS

Founded 1870

Bishop Peter J. Baltes became the second Bishop of Alton in 1870.

■ The first Catholic settlers arrived in the Ridgway area in 1843. Records indicate that Father Elisha Durbin celebrated the earliest Masses for these pioneers. He would come on horseback from St. Vincent, Kentucky, to administer to the faithful. Father Anton Demming of Shawneetown began visiting the rail town in 1870.

More Catholics made their homes in the town and in 1875 a church was built with Father James Rensmann as the first resident pastor. Official parish records date from 1879. Father Rensmann shared his vision of building a Gothic style church in Ridgway with his parishioners and the dream began to take shape in August 1892 when Bishop John Janssen laid the cornerstone. Dedicated in 1894, the crowning touch of

St. Joseph Church came in 1908 when an altar of Italian marble was installed. St. Joseph Parish sponsored a Catholic school from 1884 until 1991.

Thirteen resident pastor have served St. Joseph Parish and Father Steven Beatty, the current administrator, is the fourteenth priest to reside in Ridgway and minister to its Catholic families. A parish council was organized in Ridgway in 1966. In the 21st century, 204 families make up St. Joseph Parish. Organizations include youth ministry, the altar society, and the Knights of Columbus, who are celebrating the centennial of their council in 2011.

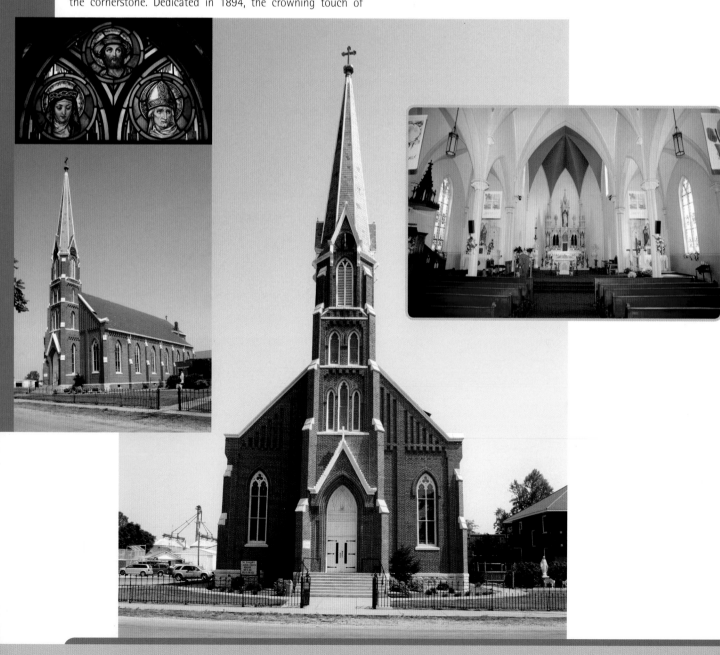

St. Francis Xavier

ST. FRANCISVILLE, ILLINOIS

Founded 1818

Illinois became the 21st state on December 3, 1818.

■ The Catholic Church at Saint Francisville, Illinois was originally established in 1818 on the bluffs of the Wabash River. The second log church was built in 1836 on the same bluffs. Then, in 1887, a wooden frame church was built near the site of the present church in the town at a cost of $3000. The present day church was built in 1916 of Brazilian pressed brick and Bedford stone and reflects the architecture of the Italian Renaissance era. The stained glass windows were imported from Europe, and are perhaps the most unique treasure in the East Deanery.

Jesuit missionaries dedicated this early church to the patronage of the great missionary of the Society of Jesus, St. Francis Xavier, who once said, "It is not the actual physical exertion that counts toward a man's progress, nor the nature of the task, but the spirit of faith with which it is undertaken."

Early settlers in this area were predominantly French and the French influence has been carried forth in the parish's annual "French Crepe Shrove Tuesday" fundraiser, sponsored by the parish's Altar Sodality with all the parishioners working side by side. St. Francis Xavier Parish also hosts an annual Advent Dinner to which parishioners from nearby cluster parishes are also invited. Parishioners maintain the practice of reciting the Rosary before Sunday Mass and conducting the Stations of the Cross after Mass during Lent.

Concern for the poor is addressed by the St. Francis Xavier Parish "Helping Hands" fund, which primarily reaches out to parishioners in need. The parish also offers financial assistance with tuition for parishioners attending nearby Catholic schools. The call to involve others is also founded by our annual "Advent Dinner" in which the other parishioners from our clustered parishes are welcomed.

This parish has always been served by priests from other surrounding parishes. Even today, we share one priest, Father Bernardine Nganzi, with two other parishes in Lawrence County. This has resulted in the formation of a Tri-Parish Pastoral Council which includes three representatives from each parish. The Tri-Parish Pastoral Council oversees five other committees established to care and guide all aspects of our pastoral way of life. Each parish is able to still maintain its own identity, culture, and values.

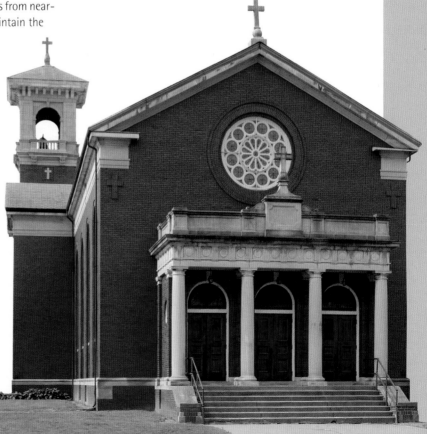

St. Sebastian

ST. SEBASTIAN, ILLINOIS

Founded 1870

Ulysses S. Grant was in his first term as President.

■ In 1870, a group of devout Catholics began to form a community in Wabash County and Mass was celebrated in their homes by visiting priests. The need for a church became obvious as the community grew. In May, 1870, Sebastian Ankenbrand donated one acre of land for the construction of a church which was dedicated to his patron saint, St Sebastian the third century Roman soldier-martyr. Father J. Meckel is credited with establishing the parish and Father William Walter was assigned as the first resident priest in 1909.

A school was then built in 1893 for the education of children and young adults. Over the years, the Adorers of the Blood of Christ of Ruma, Benedictine Sisters of Jonesboro, Arkansas and Sisters of St. Francis of Peoria served at St. Sebastian School, which was lost in a devastating fire in 1925. Sadly, the school was lost to a devastating fire outbreak in 1925. Education of children in the faith remains a great value to the parish and the Parish School of Religion is offered on a regular basis for preschool through high school youths and Vacation Bible School is organized annually.

A parish hall was constructed in 1980 to serve for all parish social activities and meetings with eight classrooms later added.

The parishioners of St. Sebastian drafted a Parish Mission Statement in 2010 and it reads: "We, of St Sebastian Catholic Church unite as one big family of God's people in the worship of God and faith sharing. We strive to live out the Gospel of our Lord Jesus Christ in response to the call of our baptism. Empowered by the Eucharist, through the presence of the Holy Spirit, we endeavor to: build and sustain a community of faith and love; offer our time and talents in the service of God, our parish community and religious education of our children; provide a welcoming environment to all who visit to worship with us and those who might like to join our parish; preserve the history of our parish while evolving to meet today's needs."

Members of St. Sebastian parish strive to participate in the Eucharistic celebration with devotion. Eucharistic Adoration is part of the parish's Lenten devotions. Praying the Rosary precedes the Sunday Mass. Parish fellowship is fostered by coffee and donuts following Mass on Sunday; the celebration of St. Sebastian's feastday; fall festivals and ice cream socials.

Parish outreach includes regular outreach to the Hope Pregnancy Center, Operation Share, and Wabash County Ministerial Alliance. St. Sebastian parishioners belong to the Knight of Columbus and Daughters of Isabella and St. Sebastian youth are regular participants in the diocesan youth conference. Father Michael Moonu is the administrator of St. Sebastian Parish.

St. Sebastian Parish has been blessed with six vocations to the priesthood and religious life and continues to pray for more vocations in addition to Father Anthony Keepes, Father Jerry Wirth, Father Patrick Peter, Sister Florian Berberich and Sisters Phillipine and Germaine Wahler.

St. Theresa of Avila

SALEM, ILLINOIS

Founded 1868

Ven. Michael McGivney, Knights of Columbus founder, entered seminary in 1868.

■ In 1868, St. Theresa of Avila Parish in Salem began with 8 families gathering in a newly constructed wood-frame building on South Washington Street in Salem. Until then, area Catholics attended Mass in nearby Odin. Mass at Salem was celebrated by assistant pastors from neighboring parishes with 46 families attending by 1933.

When oil was discovered in the area in 1938, parish membership skyrocketed to 67 families. Belleville Bishop Henry Althoff appointed Father A.B. Schomaker to Salem in the Fall of 1939 with the task to "organize a parish and erect a church." The church was built within one year and June 27, 1940, Father Schomaker was appointed pastor of St. Theresa of Avila. Further growth in population prompted the construction of a parish school, staffed by the Adorers of the Blood of Christ in 1954.

Within fifteen years the school closed, but by 1975, parents were concerned about declining religious values and education of their children and they petitioned their pastor and the Belleville Diocese to reopen the school. In addition, a large printing firm had relocated to Salem, and many of its 1,800 employees were Catholic. In 1976, the school reopened with three Felician Sisters from Chicago and three lay teachers staffing the school. Sister Margaret Schmidt, SSND, and her staff continue to nurture the school through declining economic times. School enrollment is currently 53 and parish families number 246.

While the parish was under the direction of a parish life coordinator for ten years, in July 2010, Father Robert Zwilling was appointed resident pastor.

Four vocations have come from the parish; one religious Sister and three priests. Most recently, Father Patrick (Michael) Cooney and Father Godfrey (Thomas) Mullen were ordained for the Benedictine Archabbey, St. Meinrad, Indiana. Sister Maureen Theresè Cooney, OSB, is a native of Salem. The parish has embraced the work of the diocese on behalf of vocations with daily and Sunday prayers and a weekly Holy Hour for Priests.

Eucharistic Adoration has continued over the years as a source of strength for individuals as well as for the heart of the parish. The reading and study of Sacred Scripture has long been encouraged with several sessions of classes being offered each year.

St. Theresa parishioners reach out to others in various ways including volunteer service in both the community and parish food pantry, ministry to the grieving, and visits to homebound Catholics as well as those in area nursing homes.

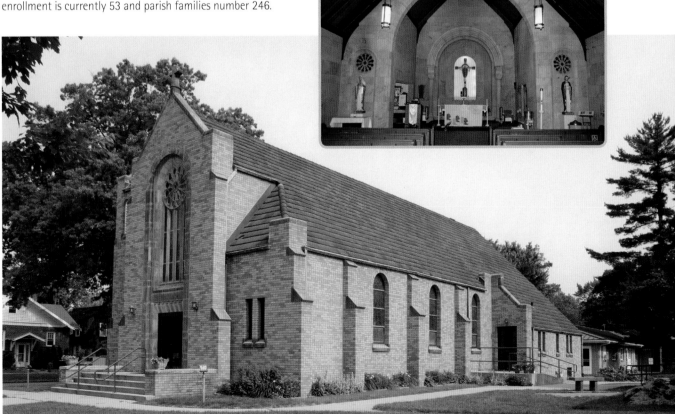

Immaculate Conception

SHAWNEETOWN, ILLINOIS

Founded 1842

St. Dominic Savio was born in Italy, April 2, 1842.

■ Immaculate Conception (St. Mary) Parish can trace its heritage to the early pioneers settling along the banks of the Ohio River at Shawneetown, "the Gateway to the West," as early as 1814. Since no Catholic church existed in this raw frontier boomtown, several priests from nearby Kentucky became circuit rider missionaries to serve area Catholic families. Perhaps the most famous of these traveling priests, Father Elisha "Daddy" Durbin rode thousands of miles on horseback ministering to his far-flung flock including Shawneetown, where he celebrated Mass in family homes and public buildings including the public school, the depot building and the home of Major Aaron Stout. One of Daddy Durbin's saddlebags was discovered and today his monstrance, chalice, paten and altar stone are treasured at St. Mary Church.

In 1860, Father John Brennan had a frame church, which was dedicated by Alton's Bishop Henry Juncker, who also confirmed 46 Catholics that same day. The early diocesan historian, Father Frederic Beuckman distinguished himself for his relief work and leadership following the devastating Palm Sunday Flood which devastated Shawneetown in 1898. Off and on throughout the ensuing years, the parish would deal with floods. Over fifty years ago, residents voted to form two towns which had come to develop, one on the Ohio River flood plain -- the Village of Shawneetown -- commonly called Old Shawnee or Old Town and the other on higher ground, the town of Shawneetown.

The present Immaculate Conception Church and rectory were completed in 1962 on approximately 5 acres, high on a hill in a residential neighborhood. The church features an area known as the Durbin Room, which houses the carved wooden altar from the former Benedictine monastery at Wetaug, Illinois. St. Mary Church honors its patron, the Mother of Jesus, with shrines to Our Lady Queen of Hearts and Our Lady of Fatima Shrine. In recent years, the St. Mary Parish School of Religion has held special Mother's Day celebrations complete with the crowning of a statue of Mary located in the canopy at the entrance to the church. There is also an annual Mass in Spanish for Hispanic parishioners.

During his 26 years as pastor, the late Father John Stallings introduced the parish council to St. Mary Parish, which became one of the first communities to participate in this form of church governance. Religious education has always been an important component of Immaculate Conception Parish and lay volunteers conduct religion classes throughout the school year. The parish participates in Pre-Cana programs and the Rite of Christian Initiation for Adults. At the time of the 125th anniversary of the Belleville Diocese, St. Mary Parish has hosted a bi-monthly Scripture study class for Catholics of Gallatin County. St. Mary parishioners work to address the issue of poverty in Gallatin County with the local food pantry and other community-based initiatives. Over the years, this parish has learned to survive and to help themselves as well as their neighbors. Currently Father Steven L. Beatty serves Shawneetown from Ridgway.

St. Joseph

STRINGTOWN, ILLINOIS

Founded 1841

St. John Neumann made his vows as a Redemptorist at Baltimore in 1841.

The former parish school had been staffed from 1908 to 1967 by the Adorers of the Blood of Christ and later by lay faculty. It is currently used for the parish religious education program. A new parish hall was built in 2010 and promotes fellowship in the community.

St. Joseph's Mission Statement reads in part, "We believe our call is to be a Community deep in our religious faith and rich in our heritage. One of our growing concerns is to keep our parish together for future generations by working, playing, learning, and praying together for the common good of the parish. We also believe that we must continue to grow in faith through our celebration of the Liturgy and our education in the teachings of the church as renewed in the Second Vatican Council. We must be willing to serve one another in the parish community and in the community at large. Particularly, we are called to hear the cry of the poor, those who are hurting materially, emotionally, and spiritually."

■ St. Joseph Catholic Church at Stringtown was organized in 1841. The first Mass was offered November 5, 1841 at Casimier Kloepher's residence by Father M. Mullins, who organized the parish. The first church, a log building, was finished on February 15, 1842, and was dedicated in honor of St. Joseph on March 19, 1848. The people of Stringtown worshipped in this church for 59 years.

Bishop John Janssen of Belleville decided that a new church should be built in a better location for the parishioners. In 1899, construction began on the new church, a frame building in Gothic style with brick foundation, and it was dedicated in 1901. The new church was located a mile from the original church. Actually, the first building constructed on the present parish grounds was a small horse barn for the priest to stable his horse and buggy. It was built in the autumn of 1897. The following winter rough lumber was cut from the Embarras Bottom for the rectory which was constructed in the fall of 1898. In October, 1902, two bells, 500 pounds and 700 pounds respectively, were blessed and lifted into position in the steeple.

Since 1841, forty-seven priests have served St. Joseph Parish with Father Mark Stec as the current pastor. The first native son priests of Stringtown, Father Matthew Elie and Robert Zwilling, were ordained on June 4, 2005. St. Joseph's Parish has had many women enter religious life. The most recent is Sister Janice Schneider, a member Hospital Sisters of St. Francis, Springfield, Illinois, since 1989. She has been a member of the leadership of her community.

Holy Cross

WENDELIN, ILLINOIS

Founded 1871

The Great Chicago Fire broke out on October 8, 1871.

Father Henry Ader was appointed the first resident pastor of Holy Cross in 1883. From 1887 until 1971, Holy Cross Parish operated a school, which was staffed by women religious of various orders until 1967. In 1930, under the guidance of Father Edmund Niess, the old Holy Cross Church was torn down and the current Holy Cross Church was constructed and dedicated on April 7, 1931 by Bishop Henry Althoff.

Today the Holy Cross Parish includes 248 families, who make use of the physical plant made up of church, cemetery, rectory, and parish hall. The current pastor of Holy Cross is Father Mark Stec.

The rural parish of Holy Cross in Wendelin is very proud of its Catholic heritage. In over 140 years, ten men and thirteen women have heard God's calling and taken up the mission of Holy Cross to praise the Father, to encounter the Son, and to live in the Spirit through a calling to a vocation. The parish has sometimes been referred to as the "vocation parish" because of the extraordinary number of vocations that have come from this rural community. Among the diocesan priests who hail from Wendelin are Father Wilbert Iffert, Msgr. Marvin Volk, Msgr. James Buerster, and Father Stephen Rudolphi.

■ In the late 1830s, German settlers began to arrive in the vicinity where Clay, Jasper, and Richland Counties come together. This area would come to be known as St. Wendel and later as Wendelin. The first Catholic church was built in 1860, two-and-one-half miles southeast of Wendelin. Originally named St. Ignatius, this church was later renamed to honor St. John the Baptist. With the continued increase in population, in 1870 construction began in Wendelin on a new church, which was dedicated to the Holy Cross in 1871.

Holy Family

CAHOKIA, ILLINOIS

Founded 1699

Williamsburg was founded as the capital of the Virginia Colony in 1699.

■ "Ever Ancient, Ever New" is the motto of historic Holy Family Parish, Cahokia, a faith community that can trace its origins back to the seventeenth century. In 1698, Fathers Francois de Montigny, Antoine Davion, and Jean Francois Buisson de St. Cosme set out from the Seminary of Foreign Missions in Quebec. They traveled down the Great

Lakes, the Illinois River, and then the Mississippi River until they arrived on the western bank of the Mississippi River across from Cahokia on December 7, 1698. On the morning of December 8, 1698, the feast of the Immaculate Conception, they crossed the river and were warmly received by the Tamaroa Indians who inhabited the area. The missionaries celebrated the first Mass in Cahokia on that day.

They then continued traveling south on the Mississippi River to what is now Arkansas. Having failed to find a better site to establish a mission than Cahokia, they returned in January of 1699 to make a permanent mission there. They named the mission *Sainte Famille*, French for Holy Family. Father St. Cosme became the first pastor of Holy Family. A log church, a log rectory, and a missionary cross were erected. The church was dedicated on May 14, 1699, the date regarded as the founding of Holy Family Church.

Father St. Cosme served as pastor of Holy Family for one year. In 1700 he left Cahokia and was martyred later that year in the lower Mississippi Valley. He was succeeded by Father Jean Bergier, who died in 1710 and is the first priest buried in the row of priests' graves behind the current Log Church.

French settlers, especially fur traders and farmers, gradually replaced the Indians in the Cahokia area. In 1763, as part of the treaty ending the French and Indian War, the French turned over their holdings in North America, including the area of Cahokia, to the British. British rule continued until 1778. Father Pierre Gibault, the "patriot priest," and the people of Cahokia opposed British rule and supported the American Revolution. On July 6, 1778 General George Rogers Clark entered Cahokia and captured it for the Americans without any bloodshed. Many men from Cahokia joined the Revolutionary Army. Fifty-five of

these men are buried on Holy Family's grounds. A large cross marks the area and a plaque lists their names, but their individual grave markers are no longer there.

In 1783 the original log church was destroyed by fire and all parish records were lost. However, several items, including the chalice and paten used in the parish's first Mass in 1698, a Latin missal printed in 1668 in Antwerp, Belgium, a monstrance made in France in 1717, five candlesticks which were a gift from King Louis XIV of France, and a bell given as a gift to Holy Family from King Louis XV and suspended from a tree in the churchyard, were saved. The present Log Church was built in 1799. It is still used for Latin Mass on Sundays, for weddings, and for other special events.

In the 1800's Cahokia continued to grow. In 1836 the Sisters of Saint Joseph of Carondelet came from France and established their first school in America at Holy Family with 39 students. However, due to the frequent floods the Sisters of Saint Joseph gave up their work at Holy Family and the school was closed in 1856. Holy Family was then without a school for 33 years until 1889 when the Sister Adorers of the Blood of Christ from Ruma came to staff the school.

Holy Family Parish and its school flourished in the years after World War II and the Korean War. Due to the rapid population growth of Cahokia, the former St. Catherine Laboure Parish and School were founded to serve the eastern half of Cahokia. In 1972, the present Holy Family Church was constructed to accommodate the fast growing parish. However, by the 1980's Cahokia's fortunes reversed and Catholic families began to move out of Cahokia. Both Holy Family and St. Catherine Laboure Parishes, which only a few years earlier had experienced such rapid growth, were now experiencing an equally rapid decline in both numbers and income. The parishes of St. Catherine Laboure and Immaculate Conception in nearby Centreville were suppressed in 2006 and joined to Holy Family Parish. Because of the continued decline in enrollment and income, Holy Family School was forced to close in 2010 with most of its Catholic students and some of its non-Catholic students transferring to St. James School in Millstadt and Immaculate Conception School in Columbia.

"Ever Ancient, Ever New" continues as Holy Family Parish's motto. Years of boom and prosperity have been replaced with decline and poverty. As an Indian village became a French, then a British, and then an American settlement, so now Cahokia has become increasingly African American and Hispanic. Yet while its numbers and income decline, Holy Family's faith remains strong. Three religious vocations have come from Holy Family during these changing times: Father Albert Jerome, Sister Janet McCann, ASC, and Sister Susan Catherine Wade of the School Sisters of St. Francis of Christ the King. Holy Family's evangelization within the Cahokia area is strong as it reaches out through an active St. Vincent de Paul Society and with other churches to serve the needs of the poor. Holy Family is "Ever Ancient, Ever New" as it treasures its past but also meets new challenges.

St. Stephen

CASEYVILLE, ILLINOIS

Founded 1893

The Adorers of the Blood of Christ purchased land
for the former St. Teresa Academy in East St. Louis in 1893.

■ Area Catholics recognized the need for a church that would be more accessible than St. Philip Church in East St. Louis. They petitioned Bishop John Jansen to establish such a parish, which was established as a mission of St. Philip in 1893. Area priests would take a local train from East St. Louis or travel by horse to celebrate the Sacraments in the simple church that was constructed for the new St. Stephen Parish. Records show that baptisms and weddings were regularly celebrated at the church by visiting priests.

At times though, the viability of the parish's life was threatened. Over the course of its history the church building was not used and parishioners had to travel elsewhere, but they did not give up on their local church. In 1948, Bishop Albert Zuroweste sent Father John Grote as the first resident pastor in Caseyville. He was specifically charged with building a Catholic school, which was dedicated in 1960 to assist parents in the formation of their children in the faith. St. Stephen School was consolidated with Our Lady of the Assumption School in nearby Fairview Heights to create the former St. Elizabeth Ann Seton School.

Father Grote led the parishioners in a capital campaign to build the present church on the south end of town. St. Stephen Church was dedicated in 1963.

Over the years, pastors have collaborated with Directors of Religious Education and pastoral Associates to realize the mission of St. Stephen Parish. Under the leadership of the most recent pastor, Father Joe Rascher, St. Stephen has been a pilot parish for the diocesan initiative for comprehensive youth ministry and has begun efforts to address the growing needs of the "new immigrants" who are drawn to the parish from Mexico and other Latin American countries.

Among the vocations nurtured by St. Stephen Parish are two permanent deacons, the late Deacon Julius Gasawski and Deacon William DeWolf, who has since moved from the parish.

St. Stephen Parish strive to live its motto, "Our people make the difference!" For 115 years, the presence of the people of St. Stephen Parish has been making a difference in Caseyville, the Diocese of Belleville and in the lives of many. "

Sacred Heart of Jesus

DUPO, ILLINOIS

Founded 1914

World War I broke out on August 3, 1914.

In the late nineteenth century, the area south of Prairie du Pont Creek south of Cahokia began to develop into a railroad town. Originally called Prairie du Pont, meaning the "prairie beyond the bridge -- or beyond the creek," eventually the community became known by the shorter name of Dupo. As a town grew to the east of the railroad yard, there was a strong push for the Dupo area to have its own Catholic church.

At first, St. Joseph Church was established in nearby East Carondelet, Illinois, as a mission of Holy Family Church in Cahokia, but this fledgling parish was short-lived due to the frequent flooding of the Mississippi River. Among Bishop Henry Althoff's first acts in 1914, the year of his consecration as the second bishop of the Diocese of Belleville, was the relocation of St. Joseph Church to Dupo. The relocated community was placed under the patronage of the Sacred Heart of Jesus Parish. Father John Wiemar was the first pastor of Sacred Heart of Jesus Parish.

The first church for Sacred Heart of Jesus Parish was built in 1915 and a school was also opened for the parish children in 1923. Before it closed in 1971, Sacred Heart School gave the Church one vocation: Georgia Braun entered the Adorers of the Blood of Christ Convent at Ruma and took the religious name of Sister Mary Bernard. She is the one religious vocation from Sacred Heart of Jesus Parish.

Sacred Heart of Jesus Parish built its current church in 1989. Through nearly a century, Sacred Heart Parish has continued to thrive. The laity of the parish stepped forward to run a Parish School of Religion for the grade school children who did not attend the neighboring Catholic grade school. Others worked with the youth of the parish, while still others provided adult education opportunities. An active Women's Club has greatly served the parish in various ways.

The Catholic Church in Dupo had been served by 13 resident pastors until 1999. In 1999, Sacred Heart of Jesus Parish returned to its roots and was again ministered to by the priest residing at Holy Family Church in Cahokia. This has led to Sacred Heart of Jesus and Holy Family Parishes having a combined Parish School of Religion, Rite of Christian Initiation of Adults, and Ministry of Care. The celebration of the Easter Triduum is alternated each year between Sacred Heart of Jesus and Holy Family Parishes.

Sacred Heart of Jesus Parish now has Masses on Sunday, Tuesday, and Thursday. The Rosary and the Prayer for Vocations are prayed before each Mass. Sacred Heart of Jesus Parish also has a very active St. Vincent de Paul Society which reaches out to serve the poor, regardless of faith background, in the Dupo and East Carondelet area. Through prayer and outreach, the parish continues to fulfill its mission statement, which reads in part: "United in Christ we try to support one another through the blessings and challenges of life, always seeking to discern God's presence and guidance in our daily lives, the call to ongoing conversion, and the practice of charity."

Immaculate Conception

EAST ST. LOUIS, ILLINOIS

Founded 1895

St. Luigi Orione, founder of the Sons of Divine Providence,
was ordained April 13, 1895.

■ In 2005, the East St. Louis Lithuanian-American community published a bilingual history entitled, *One Hundred Ten Years of Faith in East St. Louis.* The work provides a pictorial tribute to the congregation's present church on Baugh Avenue, which features traditional Lithuanian styles of architecture including a distinctive steeple with Lithuanian tulip motifs. Designed by architect Jonas Mulokas, the small church has 55 stained glass windows, sixteen of which depict Mary, the Mother of Jesus in her various titles. A replica of a Lithuanian shrine to Our Lady of Siluva can be found on the church grounds.

The commemorative text includes a comprehensive history of Immaculate Conception Lithuanian Catholic Church by parishioner Zygmunt Grybinas. Most early Lithuanian immigrants to East St. Louis were young men, who hoped to bring "their brides and sweethearts" to the city once they were settled. These men promoted the establishment of a Lithuanian language parish.

Bishop John Janssen approved their proposal, provided 25 families made up the original congregation. The number of founding families was renegotiated and in 1895 Father Juozapas Servetka became the parish's first pastor. Father Anthony Deksnys led the drive to build the present church, which replaced a structure that burned down in 1943. At this time, Father Deksnys and the people of Immaculate Conception also helped resettle more than 200 Lithuanian refugees from Soviet persecution. In 1969, he became bishop-at-large ministering to the spiritual needs of Lithuanian exiles living in Europe. Bishop Deksnys died in 1999.

Various priests of the Belleville Diocese enable the parish to continue to celebrate Sunday liturgies, which include a monthly "Sweet Sunday" of refreshments and various cultural celebrations hosted by the East St. Louis Chapter of the Lithuanian-American Community.

St. Augustine of Hippo

EAST ST. LOUIS, ILLINOIS

Founded 2006

St. Theodore Guerin, a woman religious from Indiana, was canonized on October 15, 2006.

■ On March 5, 2006, four Catholic churches in East St. Louis were merged under the new Patron, Saint Augustine of Hippo, The four churches were: St. Philip, established in 1841; St. Patrick, established in 1862; St. Joseph, established in 1902; and St. John Francis Regis, established in 1909. The new church continues the long and proud legacy of Catholic presence and ministry in a city which at one time boasted of thirteen Catholic churches. The population in this struggling community, with the departure of most major businesses in the 1960's and 1970's, has dropped from almost 90,000 to a little over 27,000.

The mission statement of St. Augustine of Hippo states that "We are a community of Catholics from the East St. Louis metropolitan area who choose to celebrate our faith together at St. Augustine of Hippo Church. In response to God's call to grow in our faith through Word and Sacrament, we give witness that we are all brothers and sisters in the Lord crossing traditional race, ethnic and economic divisions. We share together in worship, in fellowship, in hospitality, in service to and involvement in the life of the surrounding community."

In five years, the parish has lived out this mission statement by providing worship services that are authentically Catholic incorporating the rich traditions and spirit of the African-American community. This community is a warm and open community that reaches out to the visitor and the stranger to make them feel welcome. St. Augustine Parish is committed to the promotion of Catholic education by actively supporting

Sister Thea Bowman School and providing financial assistance to parents who choose to send their children to a Catholic school.

Concern for the poor and those in need is shown through direct giving of "time, talent and treasure" to Catholic Urban Programs. Parishioners make financial contributions, give volunteer hours, and serve on the CUP Board of Directors as well as various committees of the outreach agency. St. Augustine is also involved in the activities of Health Visions East through participation in efforts to promote healthy living and special services to the elderly and handicapped in the community. Ecumenical and Interfaith efforts include participation in United Congregations of Metro East and Metro East Interfaith Partnership. The parish is also blessed with both an active Senior Citizen group, that meets monthly, and a Youth Group that includes outreach to the youth of the community particularly through our Community Youth Gospel Choir.

Franciscan Friars serve St. Augustine of Hippo Parish with Father Carroll Mizicko, OFM, pastor.

Fr. Augustine
Tolton
1854-1897
First African-American Priest

Holy Rosary

FAIRMONT CITY, ILLINOIS

Founded 1922

Pope Benedict XV died January 22, 1922.

■ "Viva Cristo Rey!" "Long live Christ the King!" These were the last words uttered by the young Jesuit priest, Blessed Miguel Pro, as he stood, arms outstretched, in front of the firing squad in Mexico City in 1927. At that time the churches in Catholic Mexico were closed, and, if you were a priest, you could be shot. Father Joseph Pico, a Spaniard, who was ordained to the priesthood in Vera Cruz, Mexico, in 1912, was forced to flee for his life.

At that same moment in time an industrial area on the north side of East St. Louis was growing rapidly. Workers and their large families came from all over to work in Fairmont City, which consisted of a chemical plant, a zinc manufacturing plant and a railroad yard. The population was almost ninety percent Catholic composed of seventeen national groups, including large numbers of Polish, Lithuanian, Croatian, Mexican and Spanish residents. Bishop Henry Althoff requested that Father Pico, who had landed in the Archdiocese of St. Louis at St. Patrick Church, be assigned to the Diocese of Belleville for the purpose of establishing a parish in Fairmont City.

Land was donated and a six-room wood-frame building was built. On the Feast of St. Joseph, March 19, 1922, Father Pico celebrated the first Mass in the living room of the rectory with twenty-six parishioners in attendance. The Catholic faith was planted well in 1922 by this refugee priest and these families who had come from far away to begin a new life amid the many insecurities that immigrants so often face. Amidst the uncertainties of day-to-day living , there was one sure and true footing, the security that their Catholic faith gave them. Parish life and the Sacraments meant everything. It was the one language that everyone understood.

The mix of cultures caused a few problems in the early years, but the uniqueness of the parish inspired a strong loyalty. Holy Rosary has stood at the heart of the life of this town for ninety years and its vocations include Father Andy Knopik, Jr.. Despite the steep decline of many of the surrounding communities, Fairmont City has maintained a high level of cohesion and stability. Many of the original families are still here, including children and grandchildren. In the past twenty or thirty years there has been a sizable influx of new families from Mexico, bringing with them a new injection of devotion and religious faith into the parish. Although the school closed two years ago, Holy Rosary continues to pass on the faith to the young people through an extensive Parish School of Religion program. Father David Wilke serves as pastor of Holy Rosary Parish.

Fairmont City has experienced many vicissitudes during its history. The zinc plant is gone, and many of the small family-owned stores also, but the foundations of the faith continue to hold strong at Holy Rosary. **"Viva Cristo Rey"**

Holy Trinity

FAIRVIEW HEIGHTS, ILLINOIS

Founded 2003

Pope John Paul II promulgated his encyclical
"On the Eucharist in Its Relationship to the Church," on April 17, 2003.

■ In many communities of the Belleville Diocese, declining resources and demographic shifts impacted once well-established Catholic parishes such as those in Fairview Heights. In times of significant growth, St. Albert the Great Parish was established in Fairview Heights in 1951 and fourteen years later, a portion of this community formed Our Lady of the Assumption Parish. Each parish sponsored a parochial school, which supported ongoing faith formation within an academic environment. With increasing operational costs, Our Lady of the Assumption School and St. Stephen School, in nearby Caseyville, were consolidated to form St. Elizabeth Ann Seton Catholic School.

In the 1990's the issues of demographic shifts, decreasing resources and clergy availability for pastoral assignments were once again considered. These challenges initiated regional planning sessions. Location and shared history led to the two parish communities of Fairview Heights along with the neighboring Caseyville parish entering into dialogue.

After a lengthy discussion, and with an offer to purchase the St. Albert the Great property, a proposal was made to merge the two Fairview Heights parishes. The process concluded with the merger of the two Fairview Heights parishes forming Holy Trinity Catholic Church. Fairview Heights' Catholic schools consolidated to form Holy Trinity Catholic School, while remaining in partnership with St. Stephen Parish.

Father Ray Schultz, who had been appointed administrator at Our Lady of the Assumption was named pastor and continues to serve in this capacity, and Father Jim Long, who had been pastor at St. Albert the Great, was appointed Senior Associate until his retirement.

Holy Trinity Catholic Church was established of the Solemn Feast of the Body and Blood of Christ in June 2003. As the merger began, special attention was given to the joining of the two communities of faith. The pastoral leadership and councils of both parishes began a process which involved plans to unite the communities, to select a new building site, and to determine building needs.

Through the celebrations of Eucharist, the two communities began to come together, especially through the sign and symbol of special liturgies. A final liturgy was celebrated at the former Our Lady of the Assumption Church during which its Paschal Candle, a vessel containing Holy Water from their font, Parish Records and liturgical vessels were prominently displayed. Then a liturgy of welcome was celebrated at the former St. Albert the Great Church during which the Paschal Candle of each parish was extinguished after a new Paschal Candle was blessed and lit; Holy Water was commingled; Parish Records were joined and vessels from each parish were used to celebrate Eucharist. The centrality of Eucharist would serve to continue the process of merger.

The gymnasium at Pontiac School, Fairview Heights, served as a temporary site for worship until construction was completed at the present site of the new parish. The dedication of Holy Trinity School by retired Bishop-in-Residence Stanley G. Schlarman took place in August 2007. The dedication of the new worship space was held December 2, 2007 by Bishop Edward K. Braxton.

In order to retain a sense of shared history, some furnishings from each former site were either incorporated into the new structures or placed in storage until future use. These include crosses from each former site, art and stained glass windows and church bells, which are now in storage until a bell tower can be built. The new worship space is furnished in part through the efforts of parishioners who continue to share their gifts and talents.

St. Bernard

ALBERS, ILLINOIS

Founded 1908

The Servants of Mary moved their motherhouse from Enfield, Illinois to Cherokee, Iowa.

■ St. Bernard Parish was established in July, 1908 with 44 families. Presently about 300 households make up the parish, which was named for the patron saint of the founding pastor, Father Bernard Peters. August 20 is the parish feast day, celebrating St. Bernard of Clairveaux. The desire of the Albers parishioners has been to follow his example of sharing God's Word through word and deed. His life of simplicity and prayer as a Cistercian has instilled in us a prayerful spirit.

Over the years, members of St. Bernard Parish have deepened their faith and trust in God through frequent celebration of Eucharist and other Sacraments; the Rosary and bi-weekly faith-sharing sessions; RENEW 2000; parish prayer chain, intention book and youth prayer box; weekly Eucharistic adoration; and prayer breakfasts, in addition to a prayer blanket ministry.

Additional ministries in the parish serve God and neighbor, with the on-going desire to also build up our faith family as the Body of Christ. With talented adult and youth choirs and musicians, a daily faith formation program, and

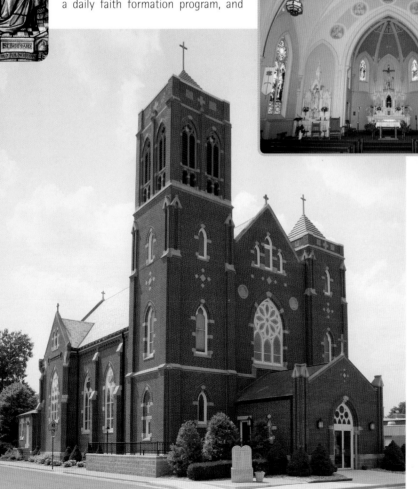

parish youth group, the parish strives to respond to Christ's call to discipleship. Outreach ministries have included the annual Thanksgiving Food Drive to support local St. Vincent DePaul societies; Giving Tree sharing at Christmas; spiritual and emotional support to the sick, homebound and bereaved of the parish; and on-going support for our Guatemalan Sister Parish, San Agustin. Community building activities through the Ladies Sodality, Men's Club, Knights of Columbus and American Legion are numerous.

Recently, a new organ was dedicated to our former organist, Frances Tonnies, who served the parish in music ministry for over 50 years. She began a Men's Choir in 1962 that continues to sing with some of its original members.

Vocations to the priesthood, diaconate and religious life have been supported throughout the parish history. Two native sons have been ordained to the priesthood, and one deacon who is presently ministering at St. Bernard. Eight young women entered various religious congregations and professed a life of service in the Church. Five of them followed in the footsteps of their grade school teachers, the Adorers of the Blood of Christ, who began their mission in Albers in 1912. Presently, at each weekday Mass a Vocation Prayer is prayed to encourage young people to listen to God's call to serve in ordained ministry, religious life, or in a lay capacity. God continues to invite.

Stewardship is a significant component of St. Bernard Parish, developing attitudes and actions that reflect how all of life is "gift", and "giving back" is "key" to a life well-lived.

St. Francis of Assisi

AVISTON, ILLINOIS

Founded 1865

U. S. Civil War ended at Appomattox, Virginia, April 9, 1865.

■ St. Francis of Assisi Parish has been tending the spiritual needs of Catholics in the vicinity of Aviston since October 4, 1865. The new Clinton County church was dedicated on the feast of its patron, the Poor Little Man of Assisi. German settlers came to the area in the late 1830s and 1840s and had attended Mass in either Breese or Hanover, now called Germantown.

In 1854, the Ohio and Mississippi Railroad was built one mile south of Aviston As more Catholics moved into the new town along the railroad, a movement started to build a church. The project took two years due to lack of funds and labor. Many women joined in the hauling of materials and other necessary work since many men were serving with the military in the Civil War. Father Henry Boeker was the first pastor of St. Francis and the first church picnic in 1866 was held to pay for a new organ.

Education was of the utmost importance even in the early years of St. Francis and an early public school was located on the grounds of St. Francis. The second public school was built also on parish property and it was used later as a convent for the School Sisters of Notre Dame.

Father Frederick Lohman was pastor of St. Francis from 1876 until 1917 and during this time, the present St. Francis Church was built. The former Sacred Heart Hospital and Home for Aged was built in 1881 with care given by the Poor Handmaids of Jesus Christ. The hospital was needed with bouts of both small pox and cholera.

Through all of the years of St. Francis there have been common threads. For example, St. Francis parishioners once supported both a parish elementary school and a high school. Although both schools have closed and most Aviston Catholic students attend public schools, a majority of the youth take part in the Parish School of Religion. This is a five-day a week, early morning program. The students attend class three days per week, and Mass with Father Dan Friedman, the current pastor, two days each week.

Another common thread has been the dedication given to the care of the elderly that began with the Sacred Heart Home and continues today as the parish reaches out to the elderly residents of Countryside Manor, the long-term care facility in Aviston.

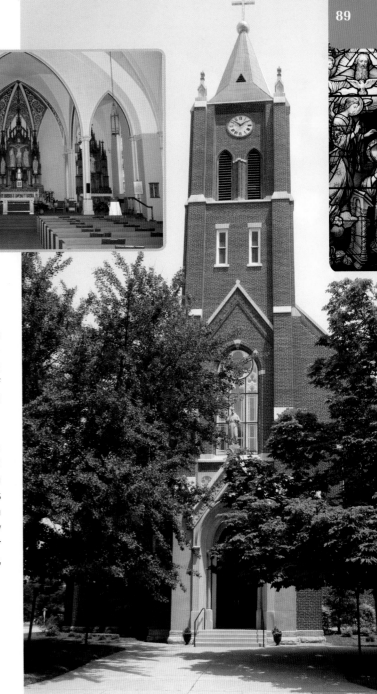

St. Cecilia

BARTELSO, ILLINOIS

Founded 1885

St. Damian, apostle to the lepers of Hawaii, contracted leprosy in 1885.

■ St. Cecilia Church was built on ground donated by Father Bartholomew Bartels, the parish's second pastor for whom the village was named. The cornerstone was laid on June 10, 1884 and the first Mass was celebrated on January 22, 1885.

The German Catholic settlers of this area made great sacrifices not only to build a church in a wheat field but also to pass on the faith to future generations. Their spirit and commitment remain the foundation of the Bartelso community today.

From the first pastor of St. Cecilia Parish, Father Joseph Spaeth to the ninth and current pastor, Father Henry Fischer, priests and women religious have shared gifts of faith and wisdom through their talents of creativity, music, teaching, oratory and humor. Nine young men from Bartelso have been ordained to the priesthood and forty-two women entered religious life.

The church stands at the focal point of our community where parish and village activities are often entwined since the community evolved with and around the church.

Parish organizations bring people together for fun, fundraising, and service. The Mother of Perpetual Help Sodality provides scholarships to Mater Dei Catholic High School students, in addition to cleaning the church and providing funeral lunches. Catholic Youth Ministry offers spiritual, cultural, social service and athletic activities for high school age students. Knights of Columbus Council 4745 organizes religious, educational and charitable projects.

After over 125 years, St. Cecilia Church remains both a beautiful landmark of faith in Clinton County as well as a Christian community, struggling to live the command of Jesus, "love one another."

St. Felecitas

BEAVER PRAIRIE, ILLINOIS

Founded 1883

The Diocese of Helena, Montana, was established in 1883.

■ "It was a grand undertaking, September 19, 1883, when St. Felicitas Parish of Beaver Prairie was officially born in Wheatfield Township, Clinton County, Illinois." Father Nicholas Dietrich wrote in the first parish history, which dates to 1933. "Beaver Prairie is that treeless tract of virgin land running north and south, bounded on the west by the Shoal Creek and on the east by the Beaver Creek in Clinton County. About 25 mostly German families had settled in the northern part of this Prairie. south of Bond County and the distance to the nearest Catholic church (Carlyle, Breese, and St. Rose) being rather far, especially considering the bad roads and the crossing of one or the other creeks, where the waters often came high over the road, it was considered advisable to establish a mission church in that part of Beaver Prairie."

From its beginning of 25 families, the parish continued to grow. In spite of the fact that, or maybe because of the fact that the pastor lived in Marydale, the members of St. Felicitas Parish have taken special responsibility for their parish. For example, when a tornado did much damage to the church in 1967, it was decided to dismantle what remained, store the church furnishings in some of the farmers' barns, and set up the parish hall as a temporary church. Under the watchful eye of Father Francis X. Heiligenstein and Father Jerome Feldmann, the next months were spent on plans to build a new church. The dedication of this new church was held on November 30, 1969. Father Feldmann was the pastor at that time and remained so until shortly before his death in 1998.

Following the death of Father Feldmann, with no priest available to serve as pastor, Barb McQuade was appointed the parish's first Parish Life Coordinator, serving the parishioners for a term of three years. Sister Diane Marie Turner, SSND, serves in that capacity currently.

Over the years, some of the people have changed but the parish remains a community faithful Christians, willing to serve their God and each other through an active Pastoral Council and Finance Committee, a small but effective Parish School of Religion, a social group for the parish and the regular "work crew" that takes care of any maintenance around the physical plant. Parish musicians add much to liturgical celebrations with Father Larry Nickels, OFM, who serves as sacramental minister.

A highlight of the year at Beaver Prairie is the parish chicken dinner, which is known throughout Clinton County and beyond.

St. Anthony of Padua

BECKEMEYER, ILLINOIS

Founded 1905

Three Marianist Brothers arrived in Belleville to start Cathedral High School on September 1, 1905.

■ In December, 1905, St. Anthony of Padua Parish in Beckemeyer was dedicated by Bishop John Janssen, first Bishop of Belleville, with Father Joseph Hoellmann as founding pastor. St. Anthony's mission statement, "continuing to create a future together" allows the community to reflect on the past, recognize the present and contemplate the future.

Within this context, the parish remembers those ancestors, who built both the original parish church in 1905 and the present St. Anthony of Padua Church in 1938, as well as the eight pastors and three administrators who have served in Beckemeyer. The present pastor of St. Anthony is Father Chuck Tuttle and Deacon Bob Lippert serves as Parish Life Coordinator.

The former St. Anthony of Padua School was served by the Poor Handmaids of Jesus Christ until it closed in 1994. Catholic education is now a collaborative effort. Catholic elementary school is provided by All Saints Academy, Breese, and Catholic secondary education is available at Mater Dei High School, Breese. For students attending District 12 elementary, St. Anthony shares the Parish School of Religion with St. Augustine and St. Dominic in Breese.

This "mini-cluster" also shares in semi-annual Reconciliation Services, Confirmation, Baptism Preparation, as well as the education of youth. The parish also shares the faith through the Rite of Christian Initiation for Adults.

While the Eucharist remains the summit of worship at St. Anthony Church, the parish promotes certain de-

votions. The Rosary is prayed before each Mass. A statue of St. Anthony of Padua, accompanied by a booklet of prayers, is available for parishioners to have in their home for a week of prayer for the parish and personal intentions. During Lent, the parish also prays for missionary Sisters from the parish and takes up special collections to help support their ministries.

The Pastoral Council reaches out to others in need through monthly charity drives, which have benefited programs such as The House of Manna, Sister Thea Bowman School and Cosgrove's Kitchen. St. Anthony Parish joins with the local Methodist Church for Ecumenical Stations of the Cross on Good Friday and a Thanksgiving Service in November, when the two congregations share prayer and loaves of bread.

Priests, who are natives of Beckemeyer, include Father James Dieters, pastor of St Clare Parish, O'Fallon; the late Father Jerome Feldmann and the late Father Joseph Dearworth, SVD. Among the 14 women religious from Beckemeyer are those who followed in the footsteps of the parish's pioneer Poor Handmaids. Sister Germaine Hustedde, PHJC, served as former Mother General of her order and most recently a missionary in Kenya. Sister Edith Schneider, PHJC, is a missionary in Mexico. Sister Virginia Kampwerth, PHJC, is a member of the order's Leadership Team. Sister Carole Langhauser, PHJC and Sister Pat Peters, PHJC also call Beckemeyer home.

St. Anthony Parish continues to encourage this tradition of church vocations from the parish by praying the Vocation Prayer at each Mass and discussing church vocations with adults and youth alike.

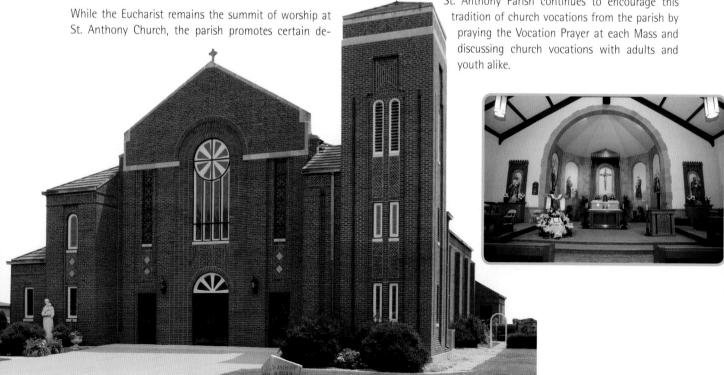

St. Augustine of Hippo

BREESE, ILLINOIS

Founded 1912

Albino Luciani, Pope John Paul I, was born October 17, 1912.

to celebrate God in life and to recognize Him in one another. St. Ambrose, Bishop of Milan and mentor of St. Augustine, stated, "Faith is to believe what you do not see; the reward of this faith is to see what you do believe."

Christ, the Eucharist, and Scripture are kept at the center of the parish's faith life, while encouraging and enabling the laity to be involved. Each Sunday, an extraordinary minister of the Eucharist is commissioned to take Holy Communion to those who could not be present at Mass. They pray with the homebound, share the Scriptures, and offer them the Body of Christ.

Through faith sharing, stewardship, and the work of the Ladies' and Men's Sodalities, St. Augustine Parish evangelizes by living and sharing the Word of God. After every Mass, the congregation prays in unison Bishop Edward Braxton's Prayer for Vocations. In nearly 100 years, St. Augustine of Hippo Parish has been blessed with three vocations to the priesthood, one to the permanent diaconate, and sixteen to the religious life in five different orders.

St. Augustine Parish has a very strong devotion to Our Lady of Perpetual Help. Each Wednesday, before Mass, a lay person leads her novena and the Rosary. Lenten services include the presentation of the Passion according to St. Matthew's Gospel by our eighth-grade students preparing for Confirmation and our ecumenical way of the cross.

■ On July 1, 1912, Father Vincent Hartung arrived in Breese as the first of eleven pastors of the newly established St. Augustine Parish. The first meeting of the congregation was held four days later, and St. Augustine of Hippo, Doctor of the Church, was chosen as the patron of the parish in memory of Father August Reineke, the first pastor of neighboring St. Dominic Parish, Breese. Prior to that date, St. Augustine formed part of that faith community.

Christ's command to love of neighbor is practiced through parish support of the House of Manna, pro-life events, Cosgrove's Kitchen and most recently, Sister Thea Bowman School in East St. Louis. Also, St. Augustine Parish sponsors a sister parish in Guatemala.

The present parish family, through the guidance of Father Charles Tuttle and Deacon Robert Lippert, tries to mirror a prayer of St. Augustine, "...Let love be rooted in you, and from that root, nothing but good can grow." The parish's mission/vision statement, "called to welcome, serve and celebrate," echoes this prayer as these words are put into action.

Through Baptism, members of the parish are called, and through stewardship, a welcome is extended to those who volunteer talent and time to serve as the People of God come together

Outstanding contributions from members of our parish date back to the pioneers, who came together to give of themselves to establish St. Augustine Parish. So many hands at work, coming together to champion Christ's cause, because all are called to welcome, serve and celebrate.

St. Dominic

BREESE, ILLINOIS

Founded 1858

Blessed Charles de Foucauld was born September 15, 1858, in Strasbourg, France.

■ Thanks to the spirit and dedication of early settlers, St Dominic Parish in Breese has been bound by Christ in a community of faith for more than 150 years. The parish's 875 households gather in a church that shows a history of sacrifice and dedication to God and to each other. The cornerstone of St Dominic Church was laid on August 2, 1857. The first bishop of the Alton Diocese, Bishop Henry Damian Juncker, blessed the new Roman style brick church on October 18, 1858.

Bishop Juncker was accompanied by the newly ordained Father August Reineke, who was then installed as the first pastor of St. Dominic Parish. In 1908, Father Reineke observed his golden jubilee both as a priest and pastor of St. Dominic Parish. The beloved parish priest had watched his parish grow from infancy to the size of 425 families. His parish development included a church, rectory, school, convent, cemetery, and hospital.

The steady flow of German immigrants from 1858 through 1864 made it apparent that the parish needed a larger church. In early 1867, Father Peter Baltes, pastor of St. Peter, Belleville, and future Bishop of Alton, laid the cornerstone of the new and present church. In December 1868, the Gothic-style stone church of St. Dominic was completed, with a steeple rising 175 feet high. Following a major renovation which restored the interior to its original architectural style, the church was rededicated on May 26, 2002.

Father Patrick Peter has been pastor of St. Dominic Church since 1995. He is only the eighth pastor who has served at St. Dominic over its 153-year history.

In imitation of their patron, St. Dominic de Guzman, members of the parish strive to identify how Jesus Christ is at work in their lives and how they can spread His Good News within parish, community, and the world. Father Peter and Deacon Linus Klostermann spread God's Word and enrich the lives of youths by regularly visiting their classrooms to teach and be present in their lives.

St. Dominic de Guzman taught that a missionary fire must always burn in the heart of the Church and that the faithful should all be resolute in prayer, courageous in living the faith, and devoted to Christ. St. Dominic Parish shares its love and faith with its sister parish in Guatemala. The resources brought to them have helped to build a church building and much more.

St. Dominic Parish believes and proclaims the powerful and loving presence of Jesus Christ and extends His love to others through worship, ministries and work. This faith community celebrates God's love; fosters growth in God's love through Christian formation; and extends God's love through service. Every five years the parish hosts a parish mission. St. Dominic Parish prays weekly devotions to St. Jude and offers monthly devotions to Padre Pio.

Many St. Dominic parishioners have answered Christ's call to a life of friendship with God or to specific vocations, including twelve priests, four religious Brothers, one deacon, and thirty-one religious Sisters. Numerous others serve in the parish's many ministries and programs aimed at developing our faith and furthering spiritual lives.

St. Mary of the Immaculate Conception

CARLYLE, ILLINOIS

Founded 1853

Diocese of Springfield in Illinois erected July 29, 1853 as the Diocese of Quincy.

■ The cornerstone of St. Mary Church, Carlyle, was laid in 1853, with Father Roderick Heimerling as the first pastor. The parish chose to honor the Blessed Mother and was named St. Mary of the Immaculate Conception, with news of the dogma of Mary's Immaculate Conception, and following the United States choice of Mary as national patroness under this title.

The St. Mary Mission Statement reads, "Our mission is to involve ourselves in lay ministries, living and spreading the gospel message of justice and peace." In order to fulfill this commitment, St. Mary Parish has joined with neighboring Catholic communities to help feed the hungry at Cosgrove's Kitchen in East St. Louis with donated casseroles; to support drives for school supplies and clothing for "Gear Up" and "Dress for Success" programs; and to purchase books for students at Sister Thea Bowman School, all in East St. Louis. Parishioners volunteer at Carlyle's food pantry, Matthew 23 and extend temporary emergency assistance to those in need through Carlyle's Ministerial Alliance. St. Mary Parish "adopted" a sister parish, St. Catarina Mita in Guatemala 15 years ago.

The Good News is proclaimed through parish programs such as the Rite of Christian Initiation of Adults and small Bible study/prayer groups for parishioners. Religious education classes are offered to grade school students; and the Youth Ministry Council reaches out to teens in the parish. Students from St. Mary's Faith Formation classes cantor and occasionally plan and participate in the Liturgy for weekend Mass. Parish missions are also a regular part of life in the Carlyle Catholic community. The parish maintains a website and publishes a quarterly newsletter, *Voice of St. Mary's.*

Mother of Perpetual Help devotions are held on Tuesdays and Sacred Heart devotions on First Fridays. St. Mary Parish has given the Church 16 priests and 54 women religious.

Following the early example set by the Poor Handmaids of Jesus Christ Sisters at St. Mary's in nursing the sick in their homes and keeping night watches with the dying, Father George Mauck, pastor, and

Extraordinary Ministers of the Eucharist bring Holy Communion to shut-ins and the sick. Parishioners also volunteer at the Carlyle Healthcare Center, a nursing home which has evolved from the former St. Mary Hospital and Home for the Aged established in 1910.

St. Mary's supports Catholic education through All Saints Academy and Mater Dei High School in Breese and St. Ann Grade School in Nashville. Catholic students from St. Mary Parish attend all three of these schools, which receive financial support from St. Mary Parish.

St. Mary Church serves as a place of worship to the many weekend campers at Carlyle Lake, offering them food for thought as they enjoy God's great outdoors.

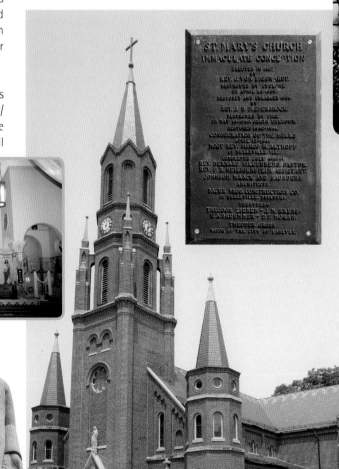

Assumption of the Blessed Virgin Mary

CENTRALIA, ILLINOIS

Founded 1857

The Archdiocese of Omaha was first established on January 6, 1857.

■ Saint Mary of the Assumption Church has served the spiritual needs of Catholics in Centralia and the vicinity since 1857. Among the visiting priests that ministered to the pioneer Catholics of the area was Father Rudolph Heimerling who later became the first resident priest in Centralia.

Over the years, Centralia Catholics have grown in their devotion to their parish patroness, the Blessed Mother. Among the strongest ongoing religious practices of the parish is the weekly Our Lady of Perpetual Help Devotions.

The essential mission statement of St. Mary Parish today is "to be a community of faith, empowered by the Holy Spirit, to spread the Gospel of Jesus Christ. The parish strives to keep Christ, the Eucharist and Scripture at the center of the faith community through Adult Bible study, small faith communities, baptismal preparation, Rite of Christian Initiation of Adults. A new generation of Catholics is encountering Christ at St. Mary Elementary School and through the Parish School of Religion for other elementary student. St. Mary Parish offers an active Youth Ministry program. All day Eucharistic Adoration is also held once a month.

Social outreach activities are coordinated by the St. Mary Social Justice Committee and include supporting a sister parish, St. Patrick Parish, Cairo, Illinois, working at the area recycling center, holding food drives and adopting families for Christmas gifts.

In order to further the parish efforts at evangelization, the parish began a Parish Outreach Observance on Pentecost, 2011.

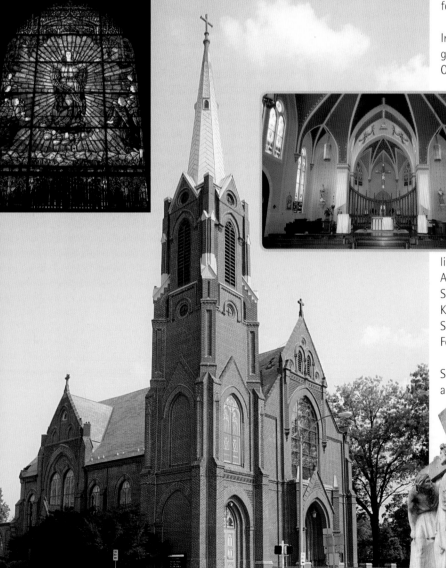

In the 154-year history of St. Mary Parish, six men have responded to God's call to the priesthood and religious life: Father Robert R. Boyle, SJ, Father Thomas R. Parrott, CM, Father Joseph C. Hays (1951), Brother Camilus Pollock, CPPS, Father James Nall, and Father David Darin. Women from the parish called to religious life include: Sister Berthulda Garnier, PHJC, Sister Amelia Garnier, PHJC, Sister Dolores Atkinson, PHJC, Sister Antonella Tillman, PHJC, Sister Godoleva Klein, PHJC, Sister Mary Paul Foley, OSU, Sister Stephen Brueggemann, PHJC, Sister Antonette Feldhake, OP, and Sister Raineldis Addison, CSS.

St. Mary parishioners have served with distinction in a variety of venues. For example, Miss Mercedes Campbell served as parish secretary for 70 years. Perhaps the most prominent person from St. Mary Parish at the national level is James Brady, who served as White House Press Secretary for President Ronald Reagan.

St. Damian

DAMIANSVILLE, ILLINOIS

Founded 1861

St. Eugene de Mazenod, founder of the Missionary Oblates of
Mary Immaculate, died on May 21, 1861.

■ With loyalty to the faith of their homeland, German immigrants worked to establish a Catholic church in the village once known as Dempter, where they had settled. The church's cornerstone was laid on September 27, 1860, and Father Augustine Berger celebrated the first Mass on February 10, 1861. On September 27, 1863, Feast of Sts. Cosmas and Damian, Alton's Bishop Henry Damian Juncker visited Dempter to dedicate and bless this church. He placed the parish under the care and protection of his own patron saint, St. Damian. The name of the village was changed from Dempter to Damiansville.

St. Damian was a man of science, who used his knowledge of medicine and his talents to help people heal physically, performing these services without payment. Inspired by his generosity, many were led to conversion to Christianity. For 150 years the example and spirit of their patron, St. Damian, has continued to inspire generations of parishioners at Damiansville to give generously of their time, talents and resources in service to God, Church, and neighbor. A 1911 Parish Golden Jubilee souvenir book cited St. Damian parishioners' spirit of Catholicism, their trust in the Church, and their unselfishness.

The physical presence of St. Damian Church is an outward symbol of the faith and the spirit of cooperation of the parishioners. Through the years, the community's inner spiritual life has been sustained and nurtured under the guidance of pastors and by women religious, all carrying out their ministry and fulfilling their vocations. Msgr. Donald Eichenseer has served as pastor during the parish's 150th year. The Mass and reception of the Sacraments have always been a regular part of the faith life of the parish. Homilies relate Scripture readings to daily Christian living. Other devotions and services include the Rosary, Eucharistic Adoration, Penance Services, and the Way of the Cross.

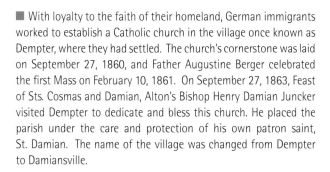

Parishioners are encouraged to more fully participate in liturgies by becoming good stewards as Eucharistic ministers, lectors, choir members, organists, servers, and sacristans. Nurturing the faith life of the young parishioners is further enhanced by a faith formation program in grades kindergarten through eighth and formation of a high school youth group.

In the past, St. Damian Parish has had four native sons serve the Belleville Diocese as priests and 21 daughters have become women religious. Vocation anniversaries and jubilees are noted and celebrated and remind parishioners that the willingness of men and women to dedicate their lives to serving God's people has enabled St. Damian Parish to sustain a viable faith community.

Like their patron, St. Damian, whose generous good works aided those in need of healing, the parishioners of St. Damian also are willing to share their resources with those in need of a helping hand. They readily participate in food drives, Christmas gift drives, and a monthly needy fund collection. Parishioners visit nursing home residents and shut-ins.

In its jubilee year, this parish built by German immigrants now opens its church and parish facilities to a new generation of immigrants, members of the area Hispanic community, who gather at St. Damian Church for Sunday Mass in Spanish and other celebrations of the Hispanic community.

St. Boniface

GERMANTOWN, ILLINOIS

Founded 1833

Andrew Jackson served as President of the United States.

■ Amid the unrest and hard times of their homeland, a group of low German settlers from Westphalia and Hanover came to a prairie of "...tall grasses, trees and snakes". In this swampy land which reminded them so much of their home land, they established a settlement in 1833. St. Boniface Church, the mother church of Clinton County, had its humble origins as a frame, one-room building next to Shoal Creek. Bishop Rosatti assigned Father Casper Ostlangenberg as the parish priest with two weeks in Germantown and two weeks in St. Libory.

When Father J.H. Fortmann took the place of the visiting priest in 1839 as the first pastor at St. Boniface, he undertook the job of planning a new stone church with a dirt floor and no benches. It also served as the priest's quarters. The church as it stands today was erected in 1854 and at first was called St. Henry's but that was later changed to St. Boniface. As the town grew so did the church. The bell tower was added in 1866 by Father Bartholomew Bartels. The bell tower contains four bells, each having significance and a name. The largest two are St. Cecilia and St. Joseph and the two smaller bells are named for St. Maria and St. Henricus.

After the cholera epidemic in 1849 the parish built a new cemetery on a parcel of ground south of town. Here the parishioners erected an ornate wooden entrance. Above it were the words "Today Me, Tomorrow You." In 1894 Stations of the Cross arrived from Germany and were installed in the cemetery along with a Crucifixion group. St. Henry's Men's Sodality upgraded the entrance in 1995.

St. Boniface has been the patron saint of the church since 1867. He was a teacher and a missionary. In bringing Christianity to the German people he gave us the tradition of the Christmas tree as a symbol of Christ's light and guidance. Today the Germantown parish carries on the legacy of St. Boniface by lighting the way as a 'spiritual compass' offering many opportunities for service of God and neighbor.

Time and Talent ministries involve the entire parish with the youngest preschoolers taking part in a special Sunday morning liturgy. The Faith Formation Program is set up for grade school children in kindergarten through eighth grade. The Youth Ministry draws teenagers from 8th grade through high school and involves them in volunteering their time as well as organizing a toy collection, caroling for Guatemala, and pro-life activities. Younger students help support the St. Vincent de Paul Food Pantry, which serves all of Clinton County. The children of the parish also have fun participating in organized sports and Vacation Bible School.

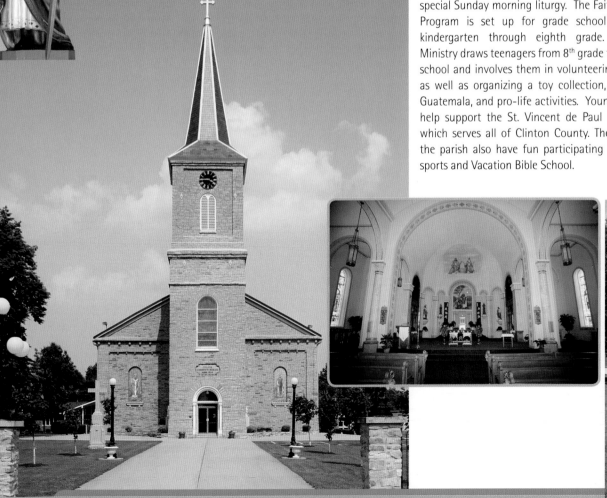

St. Teresa of Avila

MARYDALE, ILLINOIS

Founded 1920

Karol Wojtyla, the future Blessed John Paul II, was born May 18, 1920 in Wadowice, Poland.

St. Teresa of Avila Parish, Marydale, was founded in 1920, in rural Clinton County, six miles north of Carlyle. The Marydale parish was originally dedicated to St. Edward located in Keyesport, Illinois. St. Edward Parish closed after ten years and sold to the newly established St. Teresa of Avila. The church building was moved to five acres donated by John Schaefer in Marydale. The building was moved over logs and was pulled by a steam engine. Hagen Brothers Construction of Breese reportedly completed the project in three days.

In a letter dated October 14, 1919, Bishop Henry Althoff of Belleville instructed Father Edmund Niess, "In our latest communication to you in regard to the new congregation at Irishtown, we granted you permission and authority to procure the deed securing the ground for a new church and also to remove the church at Keyesport to the new site... we declare... that the new congregation at Irishtown shall be organized and is hereby established... We would suggest that the patron of the new church at Irishtown be St. Teresa, whose feast occurs tomorrow."

The first Mass was celebrated on April 7, 1920 and with the formal rededication on June 20, 1920, Marydale was born. St. Teresa Parish has had thirteen resident pastors, the last pastor being the late Father Jerome Feldmann who served St. Teresa Parish from 1969 to 1998. As a parish without a resident pastor, the People of God at Marydale are challenged in special ways to witness the Gospel message of Jesus. St. Teresa of Avila Parish strives to be a caring, charitable and loving community, dedicated to teaching all our members of God's love, reaching out to all those in need, spiritually and materially, living the true Gospel message.

A bit of wisdom is credited to St. Teresa of Avila, who once observed, "Yours are the feet with which Christ walks to do good. Yours are the hands with which Christ blesses the world." St. Teresa Parish strives to realize this wisdom. Parishioners' hands and feet work at canned food collections, making casseroles for Cosgrove's Kitchen in East St. Louis, collecting books for Sister Thea Bowman School, East St. Louis, and coordinating an annual school supply drive, rummage sales and donations to the local ministry alliance.

IN MEMORY OF
OUR BELOVED PASTOR
FATHER
JEROME
FELDMANN
SEPTEMBER 29, 1924
TO
JANUARY 1, 1998
"I HAVE LOVED
EVERYONE
YOU HAVE SENT ME
TO THE END."

St. George

NEW BADEN, ILLINOIS

Founded 1894

St. Maximilian Kolbe was born January 7, 1894.

■ The earliest settlers in the town of New Baden emigrated to southern Illinois from Germany. On November 11, 1894, Father Gerard Toennies celebrated the first Mass in New Baden. Over 115 years later, St. George Parish includes 475 households, made up of 1,200 souls, with Father Gene Neff as pastor.

Having survived devastating tornadoes in 1896 and 1982, the town and parish have flourished through agriculture, mining, and easy access to employment at nearby Scott Air Force Base and St. Louis, Missouri.

Hospitality, charity, joy, forgiveness, service, compassion, and acceptance are the values that guide the parish. St. George Parish strives to realize a vision of a Catholic community which is "...in communion with the one, holy, catholic, and apostolic church..." and which is becoming "...a Eucharistic community of faith, knowing, loving, and serving God." The parish mission is to build "... a community of faith, guided by Christ's example of charity, lived in a spirit of joy, hospitality, compassion, charity, and service."

St. George Parish is active in a cluster of neighboring parishes, which includes St. Joseph, Lebanon; St. Mary, Trenton; St. Bernard, Albers and St. Damian, Damiansville. The Catholic communities collaborate primarily in the Rite of Christian Initiation of Adults, youth and Hispanic ministry. The parishes at New Baden, Albers and Damiansville share office staff.

St. George Parish School of Religion and its ministry with junior and senior high school students are concrete ways in which the parish passes on the faith. Adult faith formation is promoted by small group Lenten discussions, which include a simple meal and consideration of different topics. Over the years, St. George Parish has nurtured many vocations to the priesthood and religious life. In private prayer and during Mass, the parish continues to pray for vocations to the priesthood, permanent diaconate, religious life and lay ministry.

Faith in action is evident as St. George parishioners take part in various outreach programs, including the ecumenical food pantry; parish meat voucher program, special seasonal outreach at Christmas, Lent, and the Back-to-School season. The New Baden parish has also adopted a sister parish in Guatemala. Ecumenical relationships with New Baden sister churches are strong. Annual Thanksgiving and Lenten services are times to pray together. For a quarter of a century the pastor of Zion United Church of Christ has served as organist for the Saturday evening Mass at St. George Catholic Church.

Parish organizations include ladies sodality, Marian prayer group, parish and finance councils with their respective committees; cemetery committee and many volunteer opportunities, including taking Communion to the homebound and serving with the parish ministry of consolation. The parish celebration of the Eucharist is rich and meaningful. Scripture-based homilies, a beautiful music ministry, lay liturgical ministers and a magnificent edifice built in 1908 nurture the Catholic Christian Faith and strengthen St. George parishioners as they take that faith into the marketplace.

St. Barbara

OKAWVILLE, ILLINOIS

Founded 1867

Redemptorist missionary, Blessed Francis Xavier Seelos died in New Orleans on October 4, 1867.

■ The first Catholic settlers, mostly immigrants from Germany and Ireland, arrived in what was then called Bridgeport in 1860. At first, they attended Mass in St. Libory. The first Mass in Bridgeport was offered at the home of John Reitz in 1867 by Rev. H. Jantzen. (The village name was changed from Bridgeport to Okawville in 1871 when it was discovered that there was already another town named Bridgeport.)

The six or eight Catholic immigrant families in the area decided to organize a Catholic parish in Okawville. They built the first St. Barbara's Catholic Church in 1868, a brick structure with a seating capacity of 125 at a cost of $800. The cemetery was also purchased in 1868. It is assumed that the new church was placed under the patronage of St. Barbara since she is the patroness of miners and many of the Okawville pioneers worked in the area coal mines.

Okawville did not receive a resident pastor until 1904 when Father Ferdinand Mumbour was transferred to St. Barbara Parish from Mt. Vernon.

In the mid-1970s, parish groups for women, men and youth were organized under the guidance of Father Gerald C. Miriani. The parish board was also enlarged from seven to thirteen members to allow for elected board representatives. St. Barbara Parish, with 161 households, has grown to include a Parish School of Religion, an active Youth Ministry program, a Knights of Columbus council, and an Altar Sodality. The Rite of Christian Initiation is also offered. Father John Joyce and Father Steven Poole serve St. Barbara's.

For over a century and a half, pastors and parishioners have strived to live the ideals which are now stated in the St. Barbara Parish Mission Statement: "...work to make our parish family and parish a warm place to come together and share our faith with others; encourage participation for members of all ages; continue the strong personal commitment to spread the good news to worship and grow in the Lord; continue to educate our children in the faith of God and the Catholic Church; provide a means of allowing the Good News of God to spread to one another through the daily and weekly ministry of the Word of God..."

101

St. Rose of Lima

St. Rose, Illinois

Founded 1868

St. Josephine Bakhita was born in 1868 in the Sudan.

■ In the center of St. Rose Township in the town of St. Rose, the foundation and cornerstone for St. Rose Church was laid on August 30, 1868, the former feast of St. Rose of Lima, the first canonized saint of the New World. The earliest settlers came to the area from Germany and Switzerland and many of their descendants still live in the community. These pioneers had impressed Bishop Henry Juncker of the Alton Diocese with their determination and deep faith and he had given permission to build the church and form a new faith community.

With the church building and rectory completed, Father Theodore Kamann arrived in August 1870 to become the founding pastor. He served St. Rose as pastor for the next 49 years. During Father Kamann's pastorate the parish cemetery was established with the unique feature of uniform, identical headstones and the custom of sequential burials; people are buried in the order that they die.

The parish school was constructed in 1881 and was staffed by the Sister Adorers of the Blood of Christ, a community of women religious that has had a continuing presence in the parish to the present day. The parish expanded the school over the years to include a gym and cafeteria. This educational complex has been leased by the local public school district since 1924.

Promotion of vocations to the priesthood and religious life has always been an important part of parish life. Thirty-four women have professed vows in religious life over the years. Four men have been ordained to the priesthood, the most recent being Fr. John Ozella, who was ordained for the Diocese of Pueblo, Colorado, on May 25, 2007.

The parish's patron saint, St. Rose of Lima, was devoted to the care of the needy and the parish also has tried to imitate her generosity. St. Rose Parish has adopted a sister parish, **La Sagrada Familia** or Holy Family, in Guatemala. Contributions are made to Cosgrove's Kitchen and Holy Angels Shelter, both in East St. Louis, and various other local charitable groups.

Father Edward Schaefer is the pastor of St. Rose, following a succession of priests who have ministered in this rural community, including Msgr. John Quack, who served the community for 37 years. and retired Bishop Stanley Schlarman. In over 143 years, St. Rose of Lima Parish has witnessed to faith and determination, which continue to find new ways in which God can be reflected in these People of God.

St. Lawrence

SANDOVAL, ILLINOIS

Founded 1871

St. Alphonsus Ligouri was named a Doctor of the Church in 1871.

In 1871, Father Theo Wegmann celebrated the First Mass in Sandoval in a private home. The following year, Father Herman Hegemann arrived as the first pastor and the first St. Lawrence Church was constructed by 1875.

While the parish once sponsored a parish school that was staffed first by lay teachers and later by the Poor Handmaids of Jesus Christ, the Church in Sandoval currently passes on the faith through its Parish School of Religion. Bible study groups also delve into the Scripture and the weekly Liturgy of the Word.

St. Lawrence Church maintains a high profile in the community and provides opportunities for social interaction between different denominations. The parish collaborates with "Shalom," an organization that provides food, clothing, and basic supplies for Sandoval residents in need. St. Lawrence parishioners practice Christ's commandment on love of neighbor by donating food, clothing and time to this program.

Through outreach to the needy, Sandoval Catholics imitate their parish patron, St. Lawrence, the third century Roman deacon and martyr who counted the poor and sick and beggars as "treasures" of the Church.

St. Lawrence Parish has an active Knights of Columbus Council and St. Monica's Altar Sodality, which cares for the church and serves luncheons after funerals in the parish.

At every Sunday liturgy, before the dismissal, the St. Lawrence Parish Mission Statement is read: "We, the Catholic Church of St. Lawrence in Sandoval, Illinois, unite as a Eucharistic people to spread the Good News of Jesus Christ through prayer and worship, faith development and faith sharing, hospitality and serving those in need."

Father Justin Olisaemeka serves as administrator of St. Lawrence Parish.

St. Mary

TRENTON, ILLINOIS

Founded 1864

The first African-American Catholic church in the United States was dedicated in Baltimore in 1864.

■ The sanctuary of the St. Mary Church, Trenton, features a triptych, which depicts the disciples on the road to Emmaus, recounted in the Gospel of St. Luke. Like Cleopas and his companion, St. Mary parishioners hope to recognize God's presence along the journey of faith. This parish's journey of faith began in 1858 when a small group of Catholic families settled in Trenton, Illinois. A church was built in 1864 and then a school and parish hall. As the parish grew, the parishioners started organizing themselves in various societies and sodalities. Today, St. Mary Parish has a Ladies Sodality with a sizeable membership, along with the Knights of Columbus, the Holy Name Society and Catholic Fraternal Life, among other dedicated committees that keep the parish flourishing.

The present church was built in 1953. After the Second Vatican Council, a Pastoral Council, a Finance Council and various committees were established. Small faith sharing groups were formed through RENEW and parish retreats have been organized with significant input by the parishioners. When St. Mary Parish celebrated its 150th anniversary in 2008, there were approximately 1700 parishioners from 600 families. The parish continues to live out the mission statement by being united by faith, mindful of stewardship, and being one heart and mind toward a common purpose: to serve the community and pass on the Faith.

In honor of the parish's patroness, there is an outdoor scene of statues of Our Lady of Fatima. Morning strollers stop by and meditate on the bench before it. As a devotion to Mary, the Parish School of Religion prays the Rosary there every year at the close of school. In the months of May and October, the Rosary is said before the Masses.

Perhaps the most remarkable aspect of St. Mary's is the number of vocations that have come from this community; a total of forty-one: twenty-seven women religious and fourteen men!

The three largest organizations of our church are Christ-centered. Along with providing numerous items for the liturgy, the Ladies Sodality has an annual women's ecumenical service and Luncheon with the focus being on Scripture. Over seventy-five women of various faiths gathered recently together to pray and hear about Scriptures. The Holy Name Society gives grants to Mater Dei High School for tuition assistance so students can further their faith formation. The Knights of Columbus support vocations and the Newman Centers for college students to go for Christ-centered activities, meetings and Masses. All three organizations donate to youth, especially the Confirmation Retreat, which focuses on following Christ as a disciple.

St. Mary's is also affiliated with the Trenton Council of Churches, and together have Ecumenical Services, and an outreach to the poor. The "Green Bean Pantry" serves the needs of many in the community.

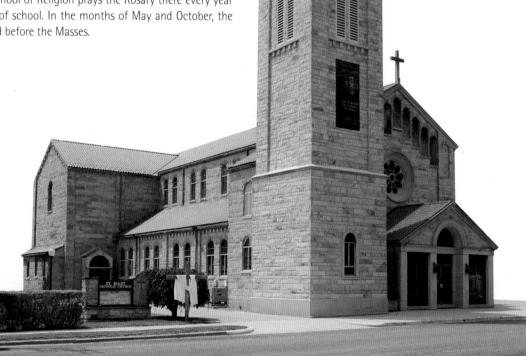

St. Mary

ANNA, ILLINOIS

Founded 1857

St. Dominic Savio, patron of boys, died March 9, 1857.

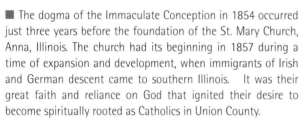

■ The dogma of the Immaculate Conception in 1854 occurred just three years before the foundation of the St. Mary Church, Anna, Illinois. The church had its beginning in 1857 during a time of expansion and development, when immigrants of Irish and German descent came to southern Illinois.   It was their great faith and reliance on God that ignited their desire to become spiritually rooted as Catholics in Union County.

The Immaculate Conception dogma proclaimed Mary as the "New Eve," conceived without original sin, and Jesus Christ as the "New Adam." This dogma has become vital to the mission of St. Mary Church, which strives to be a great spiritual light for the entire region. The two main stained glass windows in the rear of the church at Anna symbolically display Eve as the mother of fallen humanity and Mary the Mother of God as the mother of redeemed humanity. The message written in Latin on these two windows is **Quod Heva Tristis Abstuli, Tu Reddis Almo Germine** (What man had lost in reckless Eve, thy sacred womb in man restores).

 As one of the first churches in southern Illinois to be placed in Mary's patronage under this title, St. Mary Parish became a splendid "amen" to the Immaculate Conception over the years. By this title the church was given a special charisma and identity for the mission of the church.

As early as 1854 missionaries celebrated Mass and the sacraments in the homes and farms of the faithful people. It is believed that the first Mass was in the home of Michael Brady. Father Theodore Elshoff was appointed the first resident pastor in 1861.

On June 13, 1893 fire destroyed the entire church complex and with determination, the people did rebuild. For a period of 54 years St. Mary Church became a mission of St. Joseph Church, Cobden, with the spiritual needs of the people being cared for by the Benedictine monks, who brought with them a great love for liturgy, prayer, and religious education.

In 1948, St. Mary's Church once again had a resident pastor, Father Fred Renschen, who was instrumental in building the present church, which was completed in 1957 to accommodate the growing population of Catholics in the area. St. Mary's membership has grown from its humble beginning of approximately 30 families in 1957 to the 250 households who currently make up the St. Mary faith community with Father Federico Higuera as pastor.

St. Elizabeth of Hungary

AVA, ILLINOIS

Founded 1890

Mt. Carmel Cemetery, Belleville, was purchased on November 13, 1890.

■ In the late 1800's, fertile farming land and nearby coal mines created a thriving community in Ava, preparing it for the establishment of a Catholic mission attached to St. Andrew Parish in Murphysboro.

Father Kasper Schauerty offered the First Mass in Ava on May 19, 1890. Parishioners later built a frame church with white wooden siding that still stands today; though, it is presently covered with imitation brick siding. Bishop John Janssen dedicated this church to St. Elizabeth of Hungary in the fall of 1892.

Assistant pastors at St. Andrew Parish served St. Elizabeth of Hungary Parish until November 5, 1925, when Father Robert DeGasperi was appointed resident pastor. The parish rectory was built in 1899, but was rented out until Father DeGasperi moved in. His assignment included the missions of Willisville and Raddle, which removed the mission churches permanently from the jurisdiction of St. Andrew Parish. These three parishes became the first and oldest "cluster" in the diocese.

The varied life of St. Elizabeth of Hungary, who was wife, mother, widow, religious, rich and then poor, reflects the varied lives of the Ava Catholic congregation. The parishioners are a community of diverse people: Irish, German, Bohemian, Yankee, rich, poor, city dweller, and farmer; all striving to worship their God, through Christ, as Catholics.

The Eucharist is the center of parish life, celebrated daily and especially on Saturdays at 6 p.m. This accomplishes the first goal of the present pastor, Father Leo Hayes: to deliver a Scripture-based homily each week centered in a participated, joyful celebration of the sacred, sacramental, sacrificial supper of the Mass. Father Hayes, who has served this cluster of parishes for over 40 years, has as a special, ministry the bringing of Christ in the Eucharist to the sick.

Christ's command for love of neighbor takes a unique form at the Ava parish. Father Hayes explains that everyone who asks for a handout is given a hand-up. They are given a job and they are paid money, which they can then use to fulfill their needs.

St. Elizabeth Parish has nurtured three permanent vocations to the religious life: Sister Mary Anton Slechticky, S.L., her brother, Brother Dominic Slechticky, D.S.F., and Sister Irene Blette, S.S.M..

St. Joseph

BENTON, ILLINOIS

Founded 1872

St. John Bosco founded his order of women religious in 1872.

■ Documentation exists that Alton's Bishop Peter Joseph Baltes officially instituted St. Joseph Parish, Benton, on May 20, 1872. Official parish records do not exist before 1910, when Father Charles Klocke, then of Harrisburg, was named pastor. This document is signed by John Deno and Dominic Spani, trustees.

The history of the parish in the first half of this century seems to have been a time of struggle for survival. Among the more noteworthy events were two fires, in 1920 and 1922, that destroyed the modest church buildings that had been built in Benton. Most of the church support in those times came from the coal miners, who, for the most part, had come to this area from Poland, Lithuania, and Italy. The mines were not working regularly, and it was a difficult time for the parish.

With the help of financial support from throughout the Diocese of Belleville, another church was in place by the end of 1922. This served the parish until the present Church was completed in 1952. People who were around at the time it was built give great credit to Father John Venegoni as the driving force behind building the church and the adjoining rectory. Father Joseph Trapp currently serves as pastor of St. Joseph Parish.

Throughout its history, St. Joseph Parish has been blessed with perseverance, particularly in the catechetical ministry with the assistance of various women religious from the Polish

Franciscans, Adorers of the Blood of Christ, and Sisters of the Divine Providence as well as lay teachers and catechists.

Perseverance is reflected in the parish mission statement: "'You are Peter and upon this Rock, I will build my Church.' (Matthew 16:18) Like a Rock, we are a parish built on a solid foundation of Faith, Hope, and Charity. The defining traditions of our Faith are to celebrate the Eucharist, to receive the Sacraments, to proclaim God's Word, and, upon death, to celebrate a life. We strive to remain faithful servants to our Lord Jesus Christ by our actions and our word. Our hope is to achieve eternal life. We go in peace to love and serve the Lord."

St. Patrick

CAIRO, ILLINOIS

Founded 1838

Forced removal of the Cherokee people on the «Trail of Tears» began in 1838.

■ Vincentian Father C. M. Collins of Cape Girardeau, visited the pioneer Catholics of Cairo and led the construction in 1838 of the original church which is believed to have been the first church of any denomination built in the river city. The small frame building set on posts and the bell was hung in a tree in front of the structure. Baptismal records for the parish opened in 1840. Various priests served the community with Father Francis Zabel -- along with the Holy Cross Sisters -- distinguishing himself for his service during the yellow fever epidemic of 1878. The present stone church in Romanesque style was built in 1894.

In 1879, the congregation was divided into two parishes -- St. Patrick and St. Joseph -- to better serve Catholic of German and Irish heritage and in 1928 Irish priests from the Society for the African Missions established St. Columba Mission for African-American Catholics in Cairo. The three congregations returned to one when St. Joseph closed in 1961 and St. Columba closed in 1968 amid the racial turmoil of those times. Father John Agbasiere serves as administrator of the parish. Poor Handmaids of Jesus Christ, Sisters Jeanette Schutte and Mary Carolyn Welhoelter, continue to work with Cairo's Daystar Community Program, where Sherry Miller serves as interim administrator.

Among the vocations that the Cairo Catholic community has given to the Church is the late Father Tom Stout.

ST. PATRICK CATHOLIC CHURCH
ESTABLISHED 1838
(PRESENT BUILDING CONSTRUCTED 1894)
THIS PROPERTY PLACED ON THE
NATIONAL REGISTER OF HISTORIC PLACES

St. Francis Xavier

CARBONDALE, ILLINOIS

Founded 1900

The former St. Clement Hospital in Red Bud was dedicated on August 5, 1900.

Saint Francis Xavier Church was officially established in 1900 by Father Bernard Hilgenberg. The community was placed under the patronage of St. Francis Xavier, S.J., one of the seven founders of the Society of Jesus, who evangelized in India, Japan and other Far East countries and is patron of the world missions. He has proven to be a most appropriate patron for this community. Since the parish of St. Francis Xavier is located in the hometown of Southern Illinois University, students and faculty from a great variety of countries and ethnicities are quite evident at the weekend liturgies as well as in the parish life of the community in general. A parish pilgrimage to the birthplace of Saint Francis Xavier in Spain took place in the fall of 2009.

The opening sentence of the pastoral council's preamble makes clear that "our parish is centered in the Eucharist. The ambo and the altar are the focal points of our life together, and enable us to be a community of love. The Word and the Body and Blood of Christ nourish and strengthen us as we become Christ's presence in the world today."

For a number of decades, the parish has been host to a Sunday Spanish Mass. Since the year 2000, an annual combined liturgy and fiesta has been held on the Feast of Our Lady of Guadalupe. The Hispanic children have also been incorporated into the religious education programs of the parish, pre-school through grade twelve.

The parish's care reaches beyond its own boundaries. St. Francis Xavier is actively involved in the monthly Carbondale Interfaith

Council meetings and its quarterly Interfaith Dialogues. Ecumenism is a special interest of the pastor of the Carbondale Catholic community, Father Bob Flannery, who is co-chair of the Illinois Conference of Churches and chair-elect of the National Planning Committee for the National Workshop on Christian Unity. The parish offers monthly support to St. Andrew Catholic School in nearby Murphysboro. The Newman Catholic Center and the Good Samaritan Ministries, a community outreach of the Carbondale Interfaith Council, first began and continue to be sustained by parishioners from Saint Francis Xavier. The parish also opens its doors to several twelve-step and other community-based programs which are held weekly.

Since the year 2000, the parish has been involved with the RENEW program and small Christian communities. St. Francis Parish regularly hosts parish missions, including several which were collaborative events with cluster members St. Andrew Parish, and the Newman Catholic Student Center in Carbondale.

For the past eleven years, St. Francis has had a Holy Hour of Eucharistic Adoration following the 12:15 p.m. Monday liturgy. For the last three years, a quarterly 24-hour Eucharistic Adoration has been organized by the local Knights of Columbus Council. General intercessions for an increase in church-related vocations are offered regularly in the parish.

The present lieutenant governor of the State of Illinois, Sheila Simon, is a parishioner of St. Francis Xavier.

Holy Spirit

CARTERVILLE, ILLINOIS

Founded 1974

Bishop Albert R. Zuroweste established the diocesan Ministry
to the Sick and Aged with Father Gene Neff in 1974.

■ A Catholic parish, under the patronage of the Immaculate Conception was established in Carterville in 1879, as a mission of St. Andrew Parish, Murphysboro. Father Bernard Hilgenberg, the "apostle to the coal fields," was the pastor of the parish in the late nineteenth century. During anti-Catholic and anti-German activities in the area in 1917, Immaculate Conception Church burned down under suspicious circumstances. Carterville Catholics attended Our Lady of Mount Carmel Church, Herrin, until the Church of the Holy Spirit was established in 1974.

The power and strength of the faith community are captured by the design of three stained glass windows that grace the Church of the Holy Spirit: the Pentecost Window, the Dove Window, and the Cross Window.

Located near the votive candles, and the artistic rendition of Pentecost, this Pentecost Window calls to mind the flames of fire that came down upon the 120 persons gathered in the upper room on the day of Pentecost, fifty days after Easter. The swirl-like inserts show the power of the Spirit in the wind that blew through the room where the disciples were gathered and the flame is reminiscent of the call of the parishioners to be on fire with the Holy Spirit.

The Dove Window, near the ambry where the sacred oils are kept, depicts the Holy Spirit as a dove. Again, the swirls indicate motion. The Spirit constantly moves in the lives of parishioners.

The Spirit, as dove, descended on Jesus during his baptism and through the sacramental life of the Church, Carterville Catholics are anointed with the Spirit as priests, prophet and royalty.

In the Cross window, the resurrected Christ, lifted high on the many-colored cross, indicates that the many, are one in Christ participating in the Paschal mystery of the life, death and resurrection of Jesus. As individuals and as a faith community, the members of the Church of the Holy Spirit live the Paschal mystery.

The Carterville Catholic community has reached out to others at both the global and local levels. The parish supports twelve Sri Lankan students in their quest for education. The parish Women's Group is active in battling cancer by supporting the Relay for Life. Carterville Catholic youth carol for Guatemala, collect food for Souper Sunday and participate in yearly mission trips. The parish feeds the hungry on the fourth Sunday of each month at a homeless shelter. The Knights of Columbus support Special Olympics. Through Eco-aware, Holy Spirit recycles materials and cultivates a parish garden.

These are ways in which Holy Spirit Parish fulfills its mission statement, which reads in part, "We strive to continue the mission and ministry of Christ's Church, which is a sacramental sign of His presence and activity in the world, by proclaiming the Word of God; celebrating the Liturgy; serving the people; building community."

St. Andrew

CHRISTOPHER, ILLINOIS

Founded 1908

Bishop John Janssen celebrated the Golden Jubilee of his priestly ordination.

■ The city of Christopher has this boast: "The one and only." This is because it is believed that there is no other town or city in the United States with the same name. Christopher, Illinois, began as a very small settlement before the coal industry in the area was developed. The population jumped from 2600 in 1910 to 5700 by 1920.

A Catholic community had been organized in 1908. Father Charles Klocke, pastor of St. Joseph Parish, Benton, was visiting and ministering to the Catholics of Christopher. A parish was soon formed with Msgr. Bernard J. Hilgenberg serving as the first pastor. Because Msgr. Hilgenberg served several parishes in the area, he was assisted by other younger priests. Originally, the Christopher parish was named for St. Joseph the spouse of Mary, the same patron as the parish in Benton just a few miles down the road. In 1915, the parish was officially placed under the patronage of St. Andrew the Apostle.

Catholics in Christopher did not have an easy time of it in the 1910's and 1920's. There was a great deal of anti-Catholic, anti-foreign born sentiment that expressed itself in many ways. The Ku Klux Klan made targets of Catholics in the area most of whom were first generation Americans from Italy, Poland and Lithuania. Another hard reality was that most of the people in the area depended upon coal mining for their living and there were often violent union strikes and mine shut-downs.

A church building had been erected during these difficult years and the parish opened a school in 1922 under the supervision of the Franciscan Sisters of Our Lady of Perpetual Help. This order of religious women would serve at St. Andrew's for decades. The parish supported the school generously. One of the fundraising traditions were "ravioli dinners" which many of the older parishioners today remember with fondness.

After the closing of the school in the late 1970's, a renewed commitment to religious formation of young people began with Parish School of Religion program that continues to this day. Msgr. Angelo Lombardo led a drive to build a new church and rectory in 1964. Father John O' Keefe would later spearhead the building of a new multi-use parish center after the closing of the school. Pastors of recent decades have included Father Walter Barr and Father Steven Poole. Beginning with the pastorate of Fr. Poole, pastoral and financial councils were formed as well as the beginning of various committees. The Rite of Christian Initiation for Adults was introduced and St. Andrew joined with the other parishes in Franklin County to form a Franklin County Catholic Cluster which today is one of the most active clusters. St. Andrew Parish also made a new commitment to outreach to other area Christians through a revitalized Ministerial Alliance, hosting joint prayer services throughout the year and assisting the needy in the community.

Several young women from Christopher have responded to God's call, primarily through the Franciscan Sisters and the later Father Stephen Boros and the late Father John Venegoni were parishioners with vocations to the diocesan priesthood. Recently, St. Andrew Parish marked its 100th anniversary.

St. Joseph

COBDEN, ILLINOIS

Founded 1879

Pope Leo XIII, champion of workers, headed the Catholic Church in 1879.

■ The first Catholic settlers in Cobden, which was originally known as South Pass, were the families of Matthias Clemens, Joseph Bigler, Frank Manzer, Joseph Metz, Benjamin Basler and John Sweitzer. They migrated from Germany in 1853. The Flamm, Stadelbacher and Ihle families came from Germany a few years later. Traditionally they were all farmers, The first Masses were celebrated by a "traveling priest" from Kentucky in the home of Matthias Clemens, The priest would commute on horseback throughout the area.

St. Joseph Parish was formally organized and a church built in 1879. A few rooms were built onto the original church to accommodate the Benedictine Father who would visit Cobden and the surrounding area from the monastery in Wetaug, Illinois. In 1893 the church in Anna was destroyed by fire. Father Alto Herr transferred his residence to Cobden and purchased a small three room house adjacent to the church property. This lot is where the rectory currently stands. In 1893, two parcels of land were donated by Anna Petsch and Joseph Bigler for a cemetery.

In 1894, the first resident priest, Father Christopher Goelz arrived and traveled the area by horse and buggy or train. In 1905, a two-story combination school and convent was built and the Benedictine Sisters had their first graduating class in 1907. The graduates included Elizabeth Cerny Bigler, Louisa Bigler Earhadt, Regina Bigler Schrodt and Cecilia Schumacher Rendleman. The School Sisters of Notre Dame conducted the school from 1912-1962 when the school was closed. The last graduating class included Rita Hamilton Ahlberg, William Musgrave, Mary Musgrave Fox, Mike Spiller and Leonard Basler.

The original frame church was leveled in 1922 to make way for a larger brick church to accommodate the growing faith community. The new church was dedicated by Bishop Henry Althoff on May 31, 1962. In 1973 the old school building was demolished to make way for a Parish Hall. The first potluck dinner in the new hall was celebrated in June of 1974. In 1977, St. Joseph Parish celebrated its first one hundred years, continuing to follow in the footsteps of the Carpenter's son who was born in Bethlehem.

Father Uriel Salamanca is the administrator of St. Joseph Parish.

Sacred Heart of Jesus

DU QUOIN, ILLINOIS

Founded 1857

Kansas ratified an anti-slavery state constitution in 1857.

■ The first Catholics in the Du Quoin area probably included Chief Jean Baptiste Du Coigne and members of his Native American tribe, which lived in the vicinity in the late 1700's. The first Mass in this area was celebrated by Father Cusack of Vandalia in the home of Michael Bradley. A marble topped chest was used as an altar. From 1857 to 1866, Masses were celebrated every three or four months in the homes of Michael Bradley, Henry Horn, John Bradley, Dr. O'Rielly, Timothy Kelly, Mr. Day and Mr. Molter.

The Sacred Heart of Jesus Congregation was formed in 1863, just ten years after the incorporation of the City of Du Quoin itself. The first church stood on the north side of Perry Street between Hickory and Walnut Streets. Its estimated cost was $4,000. While it was being constructed, a storm blew down one wall on Christmas day, 1867, and the completion of the church was delayed. The damage was soon repaired, however, and the dedication was held on April 19, 1868. Parish membership continued to grow, so that in 1871 a decision was made to divide the parish and establish St. Bruno Parish in Pinckneyville and St. Mary Magdalen Parish in Todd's Mill.

A parish school was conducted in the rectory. In November 1872, Father Charles Klocke announced plans to build a new school to accommodate the increasing enrollment. In 1891, the School Sisters of Notre Dame began their century-long association with Sacred Heart School, which closed in May 2008. Father Klocke served as pastor of the Du Quoin parish for 43 years.

The present church on West Main Street was dedicated on November 4, 1890, after a farewell Pontifical High Mass was celebrated at the old church with the languages of the congregation, English, Italian, German and Polish, incorporated into the ceremonies. Three bells were hung in the belfry and dedicated in March, 1908 to Jesus, Mary and Joseph. For 29 years before the bells were electrified, Victor Ritter and members of his family rang the bells in the Angelus devotion, three times a day, every day of the year.

Sisters from the area include Sister Mary Charles Knetzger; Sister M. Cajetan Steins; Sister M. Andrea Schubert; Sister Illuminata Schleper; Sister Ignatiius Koener; Sister Francesca Fritzp; Sister Clara Stein; Sister Emilia Louisa Vettese; Sister Mary Agnes Childs and Sister Edith Schneider.

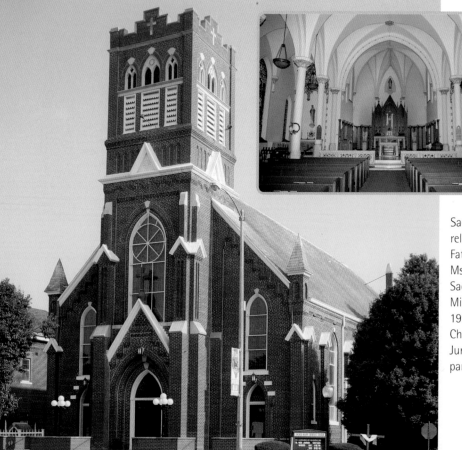

In 1908, Du Quoin Knights of Columbus Council 1298 was formed. Organizations of women have been an integral part of Sacred Heart Parish throughout most of its history. Among them were National Council of Catholic Women, Catholic Daughters of Americas, the Altar Society and the Sewing Circle, now known as the Quilters.

Sacred Heart Parish has been a rich source of religious vocations. Native son priests include Father John Bergmann, Father Clement Dirler, Msgr. Harry Jerome, who served as pastor of Sacred Heart from 2000 to 2009, Msgr. Thomas Miller and Father John Iffert, whose June 7, 1997 ordination took place in Sacred Heart Church, a first for the parish. Father Nicholas Junker currently serves as administrator of the parish.

St. Charles Borromeo
Cathedral of the Prairie
DUBOIS, ILLINOIS

Founded 1877

Rutherford B. Hayes began his term as U.S. President in 1877.

German settlers came to this area of Washington County in the middle of the nineteenth century and were followed several decades later by Polish immigrants who sought to take advantage of cheap land offered through agencies working to advance the railroads,. like the Illinois Central. Many of the Poles came to escape the brutal partitioning of their homeland by the superpowers of Germany, Prussia, and Russia.

These settlers came with a deep faith and they sought the assistance of neighboring clergy to nurture that faith. The parish was named after the patron saint of Father Charles Klocke, who traveled from Du Quoin to serve the spiritual needs of the early Catholic settlers in the area and who was instrumental in forming the parish. It was placed under the patronage of St. Charles Borromeo, the sixteenth century cardinal who was involved in the Council of Trent and who worked for the reform of the clergy.

The first St. Charles Borromeo Church was a frame structure built in 1877. Planks laid on empty kegs served as pews for the first Mass celebrated in the church on the Third Sunday of Advent, December 16, 1877. From these humble origins came today's St. Charles Borromeo Church, which is called the "Cathedral of the Prairie" by some. It was designed by Msgr. Joseph Ceranski, whose pastorate extended from 1898 to 1962!

One man from St. Charles Borromeo Parish was ordained to the diocesan priesthood, Father Stanley Ksycki. Another served the Church as a religious brother. Women from DuBois have entered the School Sisters of Notre Dame, the Adorers of the Blood of Christ, the Franciscan Sisters and the Our Lady of Victory Noll Missions. Father Oliver Nwachukwu has served as administrator of St. Charles since 2008. Born in Nigeria, Father Oliver was featured in an article in the St. Louis Post-Dispatch on *"fidei donum"* or "gift of faith" clergy from other lands assisting the United States Church during the current priest shortage.

St. Catherine of Alexandria

GRAND CHAIN, ILLINOIS

Founded 1891

Pope Leo XIII's landmark encyclical Rerum Novarum was published in 1892.

■ The first Mass offered in the Grand Chain area was celebrated by Father Engelbert Leist, OSB, at the home of Frederick Reichert. Father Leist celebrated Mass at local homes or at the public school until 1891. On April 1, 1896, Father Bernard Peters was appointed as pastor of the new parish in Grand Chain. In October 1896, the cornerstone of Saint Catherine of Alexandria Church was laid and Bishop John Janssen, Bishop of Belleville, dedicated the church on August 10, 1897.

Through the years, St. Catherine Parish promoted Catholic education, operating through a parish grade school from 1896 to 1908, when it closed for lack of funds, and again from 1921 to 1941, when student enrollment declined. From 1921 to 1925, St. Catherine Parish operated both a Catholic high school and grade school. Since the school's closing, volunteers have conducted religious education classes for the parish's youth. Adult formation is offered through Scripture study courses held twice each year along with the neighboring parishes of Saint Mary, Mound City, and Saint Patrick, Cairo.

Saint Catherine was blessed to have resident pastors from its founding until 1973. Since 1973, Saint Catherine has been clustered with Saint Mary Parish, Mound City and the former Our Lady of Fatima Parish, Ullin. Strong bonds of friendship and family have been formed between all the parishioners. After the closing of Our Lady of Fatima Parish in 2007, St Catherine and St. Mary Parishes have been clustered with Saint Patrick Parish, Cairo.

Parishioners of Saint Catherine and members of the local Protestant congregations work together to benefit the greater community of Grand Chain and Pulaski County. Members of Saint Catherine Parish participate in an annual county-wide ecumenical service. Saint Catherine regularly opens the doors of the parish hall to host luncheon gatherings following funerals, with individuals from every local church assisting to provide food and comfort to family and friends of the deceased.

Through the last 114 years, Saint Catherine Parish has experienced growth and loss. Yet the parishioners are united in faith, hope and love in God our Father and the Lord Jesus. The parish continues to see itself as a close faith family.

Our Lady of Fatima Parish, Ullin. ■

Our Lady of Mount Carmel

HERRIN, ILLINOIS

Founded 1900

St. Rita of Cascia, saint of the impossible, was canonized in 1900.

■ Our Lady of Mount Carmel Parish expresses a unique desire; the desire to be "the hands and feet of Christ on earth." For over 100 years, this Catholic parish has reached out to the people of Herrin, Illinois. This parish was organized in 1900 with immigrants from all over Europe. The first pastor, Father Bernard Hilgenberg, spoke eight languages and was able to communicate with the Italians, Lithuanians, Hungarians, Poles, Slavs, Germans and Irish. He successfully kept them all under one roof.

The parish's patron, Our Lady of Mt. Carmel, reflects the strong Italian influence of immigrants who came to Herrin from Cuggiono, Italy, where this particular feast of Mary was celebrated since the 1600's. Mount Carmel is also the mountain mentioned in the Bible where Elijah met the prophets of Baal. So, Our Lady of Mt. Carmel stands as a rock of Catholic presence in the middle of southern Illinois.

Our Lady of Mount Carmel School began in 1912 and continues to be an avenue for evangelization. The children's liturgies throughout the week attract parents and grandparents who are not Catholic but they begin to see the Catholic faith in a new light. As one parent said, "I find myself coming back again and again because I find it is hopeful!" The school makes it a priority to pass on to children and young people the traditions of feast days and saints' days.

Parish evangelization efforts and the Rite of Christian Initiation have brought many new Catholics into the sacramental life of the Church.

Through the Sunday Eucharist at Our Lady of Mount Carmel, people come to experience Christ in worship, prayer and celebration. A strong choir and music ministry complement the Sunday worship. Again, the parish mission statement urges parishioners to "celebrate the death and resurrection of Jesus Christ in Word and Sacrament" every Sunday, "in union with the Catholic Church throughout the world." This is the faith that lived and shared with the community at large.

Our Lady of Mount Carmel Parish has a vibrant relationship with several parishes in the Diocese of Kasana-Lowerro in Uganda. The Herrin parish has helped build chapels and churches in very remote areas as well as installing electricity in schools and digging wells in villages that had to travel miles for water. Catholics in Herrin have helped feed Ugandan orphans and have sent tools, educational materials, and religious articles to be distributed through the parish priests. One of the churches built by the people of Herrin has now been officially named "Our Lady of Mt. Carmel."

The Catholic Church in Herrin continues to have considerable influence in Williamson County and people from the entire region enjoy the hospitality of this faith community. Today the ethnicity of the parish and school is more global than in the last century. The faith community now encompasses African-American families and people with origins in Peru, Colombia, Haiti, Panama, Mexico, the Philippines, China and Uganda. They are all bound together by faith in Jesus Christ and the celebration of the Word and Sacrament every Sunday.

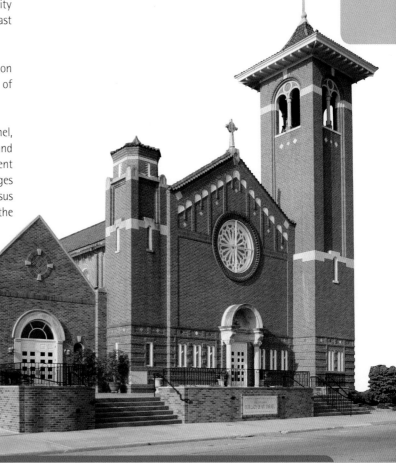

St. Paul

JOHNSTON CITY, ILLINOIS

Founded 1904

Blessed Pope John XXIII was ordained Father Angelo Roncalli on August 10, 1904.

From the latter part of the nineteenth century people from different parts of the world came to Johnston City, Illinois, to work in the coal mines. Catholic immigrants from Italy, Lithuania, Poland and some from different parts of the United States came and dreamed of having their own Catholic Church. Through the efforts of Father Bernard Hilgenberg, with financial backing from those companies that thrived in town, these immigrant miners built a simple frame church, which was blest and dedicated by Bishop John Janssen of Belleville on Labor Day in 1904. The church was placed fittingly under the patronage of the great missionary of the New Testament, St. Paul the Apostle.

In the early years of the parish, it was challenging to be Catholic and to openly profess faith in this area of southern Illinois. Catholics were not allowed to teach in the public schools of Johnston City and they were targeted by the active Ku Klux Klan. Despite these difficulties, the parish grew and in 1921, St. Paul Grade School was opened and was staffed first by Franciscan Sisters and later Trinitarian Sisters.

In 1945, at the request of Bishop Henry Althoff, the Trinitarian Fathers from Baltimore were assigned to St. Paul. During the pastorate of Fr. Albert Burrato, O.SS.T. a new church was built with Bishop Albert R. Zuroweste dedicating the sacred space on October 14, 1958. The Church was debt free!

The Parish School of Religion began in 1981 when St. Paul School closed. The Trinitarians left in 1990

and after diocesan clergy resumed ministry in the parish, Msgr. Paulin Dobkowski laid the groundwork for a much needed parish center, where the Parish School of Religion, Rite of Christian Initiation for Adults, Faith Community groups, and other activities could be headquartered. Sister Catherine Wellinghoff, ASC, has served Johnston City as Parish Life Coordinator since Msgr. Dobkowski retired in 1998.

Top priority is given to participation in the Sunday Eucharist as well as Masses on holydays. Parishioners take active part in worship as ministers of hospitality, servers, choir members, lectors, and Extraordinary Ministers of the Eucharist. During Lent, the parish follows the tradition of praying the Stations of the Cross with Adoration of the Blessed Sacrament. Members of the First United Methodist Church and St. Paul Church gather in prayer and fellowship during Christian Unity Week.

As part of their community outreach, St. Paul Parish prepares and serves a monthly dinner at the Lighthouse Shelter for the homeless in Marion and supports the Night's Shield which houses children. Pregnancy Matters, Adorers of the Blood of Christ missions in Bolivia, and the Johnston City Ministerial Alliances benefit from regular gifts from St. Paul Church, which also partners with the Williamson County recycling program.

During the Universal Church's Year of St. Paul, 2008-2009, the Johnston City parish celebrated its patron saint with special hymns, prayers and other activities, ever mindful of the prayer in Paul's Letter to the Church in Ephesus, "Glory be to God, whose power working in us, can do infinitely more than we can ask or imagine." (Ephesians 3:20)

St. Joseph

MARION, ILLINOIS

Founded 1927

Rose Philippine Duschense of St. Charles, Missouri, was beatified on May 12, 1940.

■ St. Joseph Catholic Church in Marion was established as a mission in 1927 with just 30 families. A church was built and dedicated on December 11, 1927, and the First Communion lass of 1928 numbered just 30 children. On October 21, 1940, Bishop Henry Althoff gave parish status to the Catholic community in Marion and Father Paul Holthaus was appointed the first resident pastor.

St. Joseph Parish was placed under the care of the Trinitarian Fathers in 1960 by Bishop Albert R. Zuroweste. In 1967. the Marion parish's only church vocation, Father Stephen Humphrey, was ordained by Bishop Zuroweste. In early 1990, the Trinitarians left southern Illinois and Father Richard Mohr was named pastor, serving in this capacity until his retirement in 2009 when Msgr. Thomas Flach was appointed pastor by Bishop Edward K. Braxton.

Through the years, various School Sisters of Notre Dame assisted thse pastors as Directors of Religious Education, with Mr. Bill Harper most recently serving in this capacity.

From its roots as a small mission to its over 70 years as a parish, the Catholic community in Marion has met its responsibilities to its own parishioners and to its brothers and sisters around the world. In its parish mission statement, the people of St. Joseph aver, "In our sincere efforts to imitate the words and example of the Lord Jesus, we recognize our own human and personal limitations, but nevertheless strive to live out the Lord's message, as proclaimed in the Bible."

They continue, "We reaffirm and joyously proclaim our One, Holy, Catholic, and Apostolic heritage of faith in union with Edward, the Bishop of Belleville, and Benedict, our Holy Father in Rome. As a People of Faith, we are summoned to sustain and encourage each other, regardless of age, social, economic, racial, or educational background. We are called, through word and deed, to be the living presence of the Lord on earth... With the continuing help of the Lord, may we, as a faith-filled community, give back to the Lord, a rightful portion of the time, talent, and treasure that He has given us."

St. Rose of Lima

METROPOLIS, ILLINOIS

Founded 1892

A Benedictine monastery was opened in the Diocese at Wetaug, in 1892.

■ The roots of Catholic life in Massac County and St. Rose of Lima Parish date back to the year 1702 with the arrival of Jesuit missionary, Father Jean Mermet who brought the Good News of Jesus Christ to the Mascouten, Chickasaw, Shawnee, and Cherokee Nations of this area. He celebrated Masses and administered sacraments for the soldiers at Fort de L'Ascension (later Fort Massac) and the early settlers, as well as for the Native American converts.

Masses were celebrated in the homes of Catholics of the area until the first church was built in 1894 for $1,400.00 and donated materials and labor. St. Rose of Lima Church was a mission until 1946 when Father Herbert Kopff was named the first resident pastor. The original frame building was used until May 1968 when the current church was built and then dedicated in 1969.

St. Rose of Lima School was opened in 1949 and staffed by the Adorers of the Blood of Christ. The school operated for twenty years until it closed in 1970. That building now houses the Parish School of Religion and also serves as parish center.

The people of St. Rose of Lima Catholic Church are continuing to strive to live their mission statement: "St. Rose of Lima Parish is a community of Roman Catholics in union with the Diocese of Belleville on a pilgrimage to God in response to the call of Christ. We come to recognize the Lord Jesus by a re-awakening of faith through the opening of Scriptures and the celebration of Eucharist. We strive to develop an atmosphere of acceptance, through prayer, and reconciliation. We encourage promoting the quality of parish life by inviting people to be participants in church ministries and activities. We respect the dignity and value of every person and reach out to human need. In a spirit of good will we respond with openness to all brothers and sisters of every faith."

One way in which the Metropolis parish lives this pledge to "reach out to human need" is their Ugandan Sister Parish. In 2009, the Parish Council decided to "adopt" the home parish of St. Rose of Lima Parish's administrator, Father Michael Christopher Mujule's rural community of the Bwikara area in Kibaale District, Hoima Diocese, western Uganda, East Africa. Support from the southern Illinois parish helps build village chapels, promote education, support and care for those left homeless by the death of a spouse or parent due to AIDS.

St. Joseph

MOUND CITY, ILLINOIS

Founded 1857

Ambrogio Ratti, the future Pope Pius XI, was born in 1857.

■ Popularly known as St. Mary's, the Church of the Immaculate Conception, Mound City, has a rich history, woven throughout with threads of love and dedication, joys and sorrows.

The formation of St. Mary Parish dates to 1857, when Father Thomas Walsh of Cairo began visiting Catholics who lived in Mound City. Mass was celebrated in private homes and later in the schoolhouse. The people wanted a resident pastor, but Bishop Henry Damian Juncker of the Alton Diocese withheld the appointment until a church was built. The first St. Mary's Catholic Church was completed in 1863 and served the congregation for thirty years. The cornerstone of the current St. Mary Catholic Church was laid on October 21, 1892, by Bishop John Jansen, the first Bishop of Belleville.

Between 1868 and 1870, the property for St. Mary Cemetery was acquired with Mrs. Florida Casey playing a prominent role in collecting the $200 to purchase the twenty acre plot.

St. Mary Parish is strengthened by the celebration of the Mass, adoration of the Blessed Sacrament, and praying the Rosary. Mound City parish organizations include St. Mary's Sodality, which dates back to 1869, and the Cairo Knights of Columbus Council 1027, which has a strong backing of members from St. Mary Parish. Both organizations promote spiritual and material interests. For example, since the 1940s, the Sodality has hosted a St. Patrick's Day Breakfast for the community. The members of these groups exhibit a spirit of cooperation, love, service, dedication, and prayer.

Several from the parish have entered religious life. Father Walter Mulroney was ordained in the Josephite Order in 1920. In the early 1950s, a Mound City young convert, Sherman Wall, joined the Missionary Oblates of Mary Immaculate and was ordained in 1957. The parish hosted a marvelous celebration for the occasion of his First Mass. Three women from Mound City have entered religious life: Sister Sebastina of the Holy Cross Sisters, Sister Placide of the Sisters of Loretto; and Sister Rosanna of the School Sisters of Notre Dame.

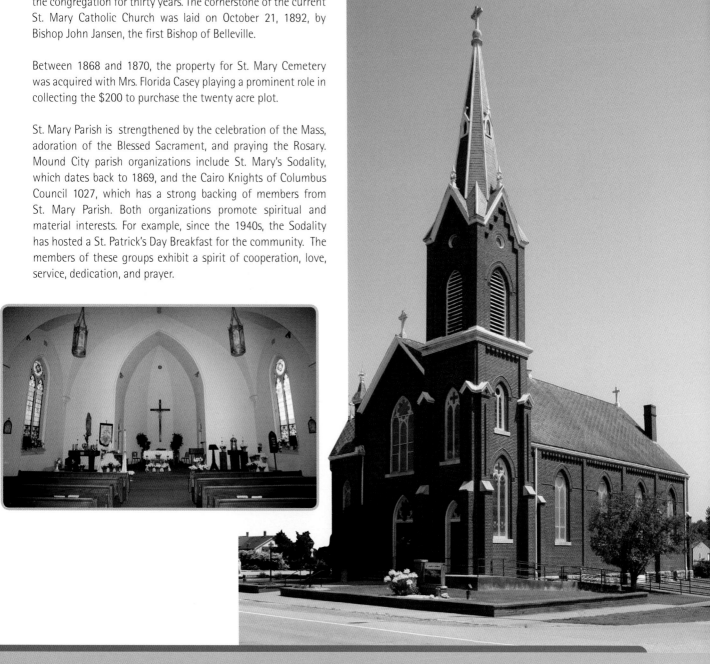

St. Andrew

MURPHYSBORO, ILLINOIS

Founded 1868

Andrew Johnson served as U. S. President.

■ The first Mass at St. Andrew Parish, Murphysboro, was celebrated in the Lucier home on May 21, 1868 by Bishop Henry Damian Juncker, the first Bishop of the Diocese of Alton. On that day, the Bishop baptized thirteen infants and children. Father F. Fockele was assigned by the Bishop to Murphysboro and a parcel of land was purchased to build a church in 1869. Father Fockele also helped to build a rectory and established the Altar Society, which remains an integral, active part of our community.

St. Andrew Catholic School was opened on the second floor of the parish rectory in 1872 and continues today, offering quality Catholic education for children ages pre-kindergarten through eighth grade. Students of St. Andrew School participate in weekday liturgies throughout the academic year.

"The mission of the Catholic Community of St. Andrew is to strengthen, to build and to ensure our faith community's growth, by proclaiming God's word and being led by the Spirit. As members of the Body of Christ, we can bring about this transformation. As we strive to be witnesses of our faith through awareness of our community's needs, may we be led by the light of Christ." This mission statement is realized in various ways.

St. Andrew Parish conducts exposition of the Blessed Sacrament at the chapel of nearby Saint Joseph Memorial Hospital on the first Friday of the month. Some small Christian communities that began as RENEW groups in 2000 still meet along with Scripture study groups.

St. Andrew Parish, under the guidance of Father Gary Gummersheimer, pastor, engages in evangelization by welcoming people to worship, by opening the doors to dialogue, and by providing study aids on the faith. Opportunities for outreach to others are also opportunities to evangelize. Direct assistance is given through the parish's Caring Fund and the local community Food Pantry. A parish 'Giving Tree' at Christmas fulfills the gift requests from children. The parish, school and Knights of Columbus collaborate on diaper drives several times a year to benefit Pregnancy Matters. The Murphysboro Catholic parish is a diverse community from farmers to college educators and each one makes a contribution in a significant way.

St. Andrew Parish has been blessed in our history to have provided three priests, three deacons and sixteen religious Sisters from our faith community. Father Jim Chambers, OMI, was ordained here at Saint Andrew.

St. Ann

NASHVILLE, ILLINOIS

Founded 1874

The Archdiocese of San Antonio, Texas,
was established August 28, 1874.

■ Begun as a mission and was served by priests from Belleville and neighboring parishes, the first Mass of St. Ann Parish was celebrated in 1874 in the home of Philip Wolf by Father Bernard Rossmueller of Lively Grove. In 1893, the Old Turner Hall building on North Mill Street was purchased at a cost of $900 and was remodeled as the first St. Ann Church. The congregation built successive sanctuaries until 1941 when ground was broken for the present St. Ann Church, which was dedicated on Sunday, July 26, 1942, the Feast of St. Ann the Mother of Mary.

Father Fred Halbig was named the first resident pastor of St. Ann Parish in 1942 and St. Ann School opened in 1949.

"There is a heritage bequeathed to us by our fore-bearers which becomes more sacred as the years pass to eternity," states the preface to the parish centennial history book, continuing, "This heritage has been responsible for great tasks, begun with a none too glorious future, has carried hopes and enthusiasms to higher and loftier heights while the work was in progress,

and has testified to work well done. One of the results of this heritage we see about us — staunch and eye-pleasing buildings to house God and God's children; another is unseen — it is within us... This heritage is our Catholic Faith."

With an eye to this history of over 130 years, the St. Ann Parish mission statement reads, "As a pilgrim people, we, the parish family of St. Ann, hope to build on the foundation of faith given us. By providing for the spiritual, educational, and social needs of all ages in our parish family, we hope to draw others into our family of faith — together setting the course for future generations of Catholics."

Two men of St. Ann Parish heard the call to the priesthood: Father Peter Augustine (Harry) Pierjok, OSB and the late Father Edmond Perjak of the Belleville Diocese. Another native of St. Ann Parish, Sister M. Marlene Geppert, OSF, joined the Franciscan Sisters of Our Lady of Perpetual Help.

St. Bruno

PINCKNEYVILLE, ILLINOIS

Founded 1872

The former parishes of Holy Name of Jesus, Grayville, and St. George, Grand Tower, also opened in 1872.

■ Named after the founder of the Carthusian order, St. Bruno Catholic Church was founded in Pinckneyville 1872. Although St. Bruno led a contemplative life, he continues to inspire the Pinckneyville parish to live the Gospel in the world, by sharing time, talents and other blessings.

St. Bruno Parish began as a mission of Sacred Heart Parish, DuQuoin, with Father Charles Klocke as administrator. An influx of immigrants from Baden and Bavaria led to Father L. Reisen being named the first resident pastor of the parish. Since then, this faith community has continued to grow and share the love of Christ with others.

Founded in 1887, St. Bruno School is a particular source of pride to the parish community. Students are provided with both the solid academic skills needed to reach life goals as well as spiritual formation. The school's mission statement sets the goal "...to develop and pass on the parish's faith and religious values ..."

A number of religious and priestly vocations have come from St. Bruno School. Most recently, these have included: Father Benjamin J. Stern, Father Trevor Murry, twin brothers the late Fathers David and Dean Braun. Father Joseph Fontana was ordained for the Society of the Divine Word.

The parish contributes to the wellness of the community through various charitable works including Giving Back Sundays, Advent and Lenten ecumenical services, Back to School and Jesse Tree drives as well as the St. Vincent de Paul Society outreach.

The Rite of Christian Initiation program calls new members to the church. St. Bruno Youth Ministry offers young parishioners opportunities to grow in Christ through mission trips, Advent projects, and Scripture studies.

Knights of Columbus Council 2921 and the Catholic Daughters of the Americas Court 1385 are also significant parts of St. Bruno Parish, which has as its pastor Father Brian Barker.

Our Lady of Perpetual Help

POSEN, ILLINOIS

Founded 1901

Bishop John Janssen dedicated the former St. John's Orphanage
just outside of Belleville on October 17, 1901.

■ The area known as Posen was settled in 1875 and 1876 by immigrants who came primarily from the Province of Poznan in Poland, which at that time was under the domain of Germany. The original settlers attended some of the neighboring parishes in the area whose parishioners were also of Polish heritage. Martin Gryna donated 100 acres of land so that a parish could be established for the community as the condition of the roads, the weather, and the terrain often made it difficult for people to travel to neighboring churches. He requested the area to be named Posen after Poznan, his native town in Poland.

On October 21, 1901, the Most Rev. John Janssen, first Bishop of Belleville, established Our Lady of Perpetual Help Parish at Posen. Father Andrew Janiszewski was named the parish's first pastor and during the next three years he built the first church, rectory, and combination school and convent. The school, staffed by the Polish Sisters of St. Joseph, and the convent were destroyed by fire in July 1909. A new school and convent were not built until 1911 when the Franciscan Sisters of Our Lady of Perpetual Help came from St. Louis to staff the school. They served in Posen until 1959 when the school was closed because of declining enrollment. A new church and rectory were built in 1967.

Over the years the parish has had many different priests who served as pastor, most of whom were either native Polish or of Polish heritage. These pastors resided in the Posen community and were only responsible for caring for the members of Our Lady of Perpetual Help Parish. In 1994, the parish was made part of a team ministry and in 1995, Our Lady of Perpetual Help Parish and its neighboring parish to the south, St. Mary Magdalen Parish, Todd's Mill, began to share a pastor, who currently is Father Bernard Goedde.

Today the parish has approximately 100 households, who are mainly engaged in farming and agriculture. At one time, many families had herds of milk cows, but today there are only a few left due to the many changes in the rules and regulations that govern the dairy industry. The people of Our Lady of Perpetual Help Parish are very proud of their Polish heritage. They exhibit a strong and lively faith, and participation in church and church activities is still an important component of their life. They serve and love through their strong dedication to family and friends and their commitment to be good stewards of the land that is entrusted to their care and from which they earn their livelihood.

St. Ann

RADDLE, ILLINOIS

Founded 1875

The former St. Ann Church, Patoka, also opened in 1875.

■ In 1875, the pioneers of St. Ann Parish, Raddle, felt the need for a church of their own. Frank Radl donated property for a site and a church measuring 18 by 32 feet was built in 1888. This community was known as the Mississippi Bottoms parish.

Frank Radl emigrated from Bohemia to American, the "land of promises." He brought his wife, Clara, and two of her brothers, Matthew and Vincent Korando. Later, an Irish family of brothers, Pat and Jim Shields, arrived to farm the land. Eventually, they were joined by the prolific Gale family. A post office and general store were located in what was then called Raddleville.

The present St. Ann Church was dedicated on October 12, 1912. It was characterized by those in attendance as "coming as near the ideal mission church as scarcely any other in the diocese." The patron, St. Ann, was presumably chosen because she is the patroness of a girl finding a good husband. With only three Catholic families in the parish, there were limited opportunities for finding a Catholic partner as then required by church law.

Following the completion of the church, Father Fred Witte came twice a month from St. Andrew Parish in Murphysboro to celebrate Mass. Father Robert DeGasperi was appointed resident pastor at St. Elizabeth Church in Ava on November 5, 1925. He was also assigned the missions of Raddle and Willisville. This assignment permanently removed these churches from the jurisdiction of St. Andrew in Murphysboro. The activities of St. Ann from then on would merge with those of St. Elizabeth's in Ava and St. Joseph's in Willisville, which share long-time pastor, Father Leo Hayes.

St. Ann parishioners keep Christ at the center of parish life by gathering each Sunday morning at 8:30 a.m. to hear God speaking to them through the Scriptures and celebrating Christ's presence among them in the Eucharist. A special ministry of the parish is to provide hospitality and lunch after funerals in the parish.

In 1981, St. Ann Parish began an event that characterizes its hospitality and concern for others. A young man lost his leg in a motorcycle accident and the parish wanted to assist. They organized a fundraiser which has continued ever since. On the first Saturday of October, St. Ann hosts its annual Duck Booya and Country Chicken Supper on the first Saturday in October. The Booya soup is an ancient Bohemian recipe concocted around the ducks, which are shot so plentifully in the Bottoms. (St. Ann parishioners omit one ingredient, duck's blood, from the traditional recipe.)

St. Ann Parish is remarkable for its dedicated trustees. Over the years, they have lovingly cared for and maintained the physical plant, always helping in harmony with the pastor, Father Leo Hayes.

St. Michael the Archangel

RADOM, ILLINOIS

Founded 1873

The future St. Therese of Lisieux was born on January 2, 1873 in Alcon, France.

■ St. Michael the Archangel Parish was founded when immigrants arrived on St. Michael's Day 1873 at Radom, a Polish settlement founded by Brig. Gen. John B. Turchin and Nicholas Michalski on tracts of land purchased form the Illinois-Central Railroad. Early immigrants to Radom included such family names as Mikolaj, Madojowie, Kowalski, Kozielek, Pieszchalski, Kurzynski, Nowak, Grajek, Zgonina, Labuda, Franc, Kwiatkowski, Wita, Pero, Minda, and Glaskowski. The first church was completed in one year with a rectory, convent, school, and even a high school soon following. Franciscan Priests served St. Michael Parish in the early years, with Franciscan and then School Sisters of Notre Dame teaching in the school.

Today Father Jean-Marie Mondji serves as administrator of the parish, where in addition to the usual Mass schedule, Eucharistic adoration is held every Wednesday before the 6:30 p.m. Mass. Keith Senior serves as principal of the parish school, which has the following Mission Statement: "St. Michael School is dedicated to pursue the mission of Jesus Christ by fostering spiritual growth nurtured through respect and service to others. Emphasis is placed on academic excellence with a positive self concept gained through cooperation, commitment, discipline and integrity.

One interesting fact of history is that in 1933 during the Depression, there was a threat of a run on Ashley State Bank, St. Michael Church agreed to leave 30% of the parish account in the bank as a loan so the bank could reopen. This is just one instance of St. Michael Parish and parishioners seeking to be a vital part of their community.

The present St. Michael Church was completed and dedicated on September 29, 1924. The structure is 60 feet wide at the front and 156 feet, 6 inches long, in the Roman/Byzantine style. There were 32 tons of steel used in the roof's framework, but thanks to that, there are no inner supporting columns. The highest point inside the church measures 33 feet from the floor. The exterior walls raise 23 feet above the foundation, and the bell tower raising 90 feet into the air. At the time of its completion it was the largest church in Southern Illinois with a seating capacity of about 700.

St. Aloysius, Sacred Heart

ROYALTON~ZEIGLER, ILLINOIS

Founded 1919

**Bishop Henry Althoff bought Priester's Park in Belleville
as the site of the future St. Henry Preparatory Seminary in 1919.**

■ In July 2009, St. Aloysius-Sacred Heart Parish reached a milestone, celebrating 90 years of faith and ministry. The recently combined parish continues to move forward in faith and love.

The individual parishes of St. Aloysius at Royalton and Sacred Heart at Zeigler were founded in 1919. After World War I, Bishop Henry Althoff asked Father Charles Siefert, an Army chaplain, to organize a church or churches to serve the coal mining towns of Franklin County. Parishes at Ziegler and Royalton were begun within six months of each other and were always served by the same pastor.

Although the building projects took place during difficult times for the European immigrant families who made up these faith communities, Father Siefert's lively spirit of faith and generosity inspired his parishioners to take pride in their parishes and to help them grow. The parish pastor also did much of the church construction work himself. He spent boundless energy on the youth in both communities, regardless of their religious backgrounds. Also, he was well known in civic organizations.

A great spiritual foundation was built during those first 35 years; the parish sacramental record books were meticulously kept and contain hundreds of names. Special elongated group pictures of First Communion and Confirmation classes, with many visiting clergy, remain in the parish archives. Those beginning years created lasting memories that are still shared today.

Subsequent pastors continued to build on the strong foundation of faith of the early years of the two parishes. The number of parishioners increased, and new structures were built: a church in Zeigler, a parish hall and rectory in Royalton. And always the spiritual and social needs of the people were met with many religious celebrations and parish dinners that kept the people together in faith and community.

The year 1999 was very significant. The parishes were merged to become St. Aloysius-Sacred Heart Parish, with Masses celebrated during alternate months at one or the other church. Parishioners assumed more duties in administering the merged parish, such as counting and recording the Sunday collections, assigning lectors and Eucharistic minister, and visiting the sick. In the struggle to assume a "one parish" mentality, a Long-Range Planning Committee and later a Pastoral Council were formed. Together the parishioners have faced the religious challenge of living the Gospel by witnessing Christ to others, while taking care of the temporal needs of the parish.

The faith of these parishioners was challenged once again in 2007, when it became financially necessary to sell the Sacred Heart Church building in Zeigler. Tears, memories, fears, and new hopes were shared after much prayer and many meetings. In the end, this very difficult decision has called St. Aloysius-Sacred Heart Parish to increase trust in God's providence and care. Father Trevor Murry serves as pastor.

ST. ALOYSIUS

1919

St. Barbara

SCHELLER, ILLINOIS

Founded 1898

St. Joseph Hospital, Breese, and the former St. Andrew Hospital, Murphysboro, both opened in 1898.

■ St. Barbara Parish began in 1898 when the community was a mission of St. Michael, Radom, and served by Father Remijasz Berndt, OFM. When a church was built in that year, Barbara Gajewski and Barbara Scheller purchased a large statue of the virgin-martyr St. Barbara for the altar, and the church was placed under her patronage.

The original members of the parish were German and Polish immigrants, who continued many of their customs and religious practices in the parish. For example, during his 28-year pastorate at St. Barbara Parish, the late Father Joseph Wieczorek, FDP, liked to have at least one hymn from his native Poland sung at each Mass. The parish continued this practice until younger members of the parish no longer spoke Polish nor learned the traditional hymns. Another Old World custom of St. Barbara is that the altar has always been decorated with beautiful fresh flowers. For over fifty years, Charles Millowshewski has grown the flowers free for the church. even in years of severe drought. He explained to fellow parishioners that God would always provide flowers for him to bring to church.

St. Barbara Parish has always worked to pass on the faith tradition from one generation to another. The parish progressed from religious education in the home in the early years of the parish to a parish school staffed first by lay faculty and then by Franciscan Sisters. After the St. Barbara School closed in 1967, women religious came from Radom to teach religion and now lay volunteers assume responsibility for sacramental preparation and weekly religious education from primary grades through youth in high school. Neighboring parishes cooperate in the effort. St. Barbara Parish hosted Bishop Edward K. Braxton, who celebrated Confirmation at the church on June 8, 2009.

In addition to the usual parish liturgies and devotions, St. Barbara Parish has an annual farm blessing in the Spring, and May devotions in honor of the Blessed Mother. Members of the St. Barbara Altar Society lead the recitation of the Rosary before each Mass, a service that they have performed for over fifty years.

Volunteers bring the Eucharist to the homebound each Sunday. Since 1990, parishioners have participated in the St. Barbara Parish Council. Young families have joined St. Barbara Parish in recent years and for the first time in parish history, the Scheller Catholic community numbered 100 households in 2010.

St. Mary

SESSER, ILLINOIS

Founded 1909

The first Mass was celebrated at the former St. John Francis Regis Parish, East St. Louis on June 30, 1909.

■ One of the pioneering priests of the Belleville Diocese, Msgr. Bernard Hilgenberg, was the founding pastor of St. Mary Catholic Church in Sesser. Msgr. Hilgenberg's "base of operation" was in Carbondale, but, over time he organized some ten other parishes to serve the needs of Catholics, who were involved in the coal mining industry.

Around 1908, Msgr. Hilgenberg was celebrating the Mass and other Sacraments in a vacant building in Sesser. On April 18, 1909, a new parish was formed in Sesser under the patronage of Our Lady of Mount Carmel. Quickly, the parish began to be referred to as St. Mary's. At its incorporation as a parish, there were officially seventeen registered households. The area was a true "melting pot" of nationalities and tongues with miners and families who had left their native lands for the opportunities that awaited them in southern Illinois. Msgr. Hilgenberg was referred to as the "tireless apostle to the coal fields" as he was multi-lingual and could communicate directly with many of the first generation Catholics.

St. Mary Church in Sesser was soon attached as a mission to St. Andrew Church in Christopher with one pastor serving both communities for over fifty years. The pastor of the Christopher parish also served the Sesser parish. for over 50 years. In 1965, under the leadership of Msgr. Angelo Lombardo, a rectory was built for a resident pastor. The first resident pastor at St. Mary Parish was Father Peter Hsu. Pastors who followed include Father Paul Holthaus and Fr. Fred Renschen, who persuaded the Diocese to purchase land nearer to the newly established Rend Lake for an outdoor worship space.

"The campers Mass" was a tradition in the Rend Lake area and was a part of the ministry of the resident pastors of St. Mary Parish.

One of the venerable aspects of life at St. Mary has been the Altar Sodality. It was organized in 1925 and helped the parish "stay afloat" in the years of the Great Depression and the closing of area coal mines. Today, the Altar Sodality still helps form the backbone of the parish. Although the parish never had a parochial school of its own, it has, over the years, sponsored children to attend area Catholic grade schools. Also, there has been since the St. Mary's earliest days a Parish School of Religion that has helped form young people in the faith.

In 1983, Bishop John N. Wurm laid the cornerstone of a new building for a new church. In 2002, Father Steven Poole was named pastor of Christopher and Sesser and was the first non-resident pastor since 1965. The two parishes began working together becoming a part of the larger Franklin County Catholic Cluster.

A milestone for St. Mary's came in 2009 when Bishop Edward K. Braxton joined Fr. Poole and former pastors in opening the centennial year of the parish.

St. Francis de Sales

STONEFORT, ILLINOIS

Founded 1879

Thomas Edison invented the incandescent light bulb in 1879.

■ St. Francis de Sales Church is nestled high on a hill at the edge of town overlooking the small village of Stonefort. Although the original wooden building was constructed around 1890 and later replaced by the present brick building in 1954, the history of St. Francis de Sales can be traced as far back as 1862. Father Louis Lambert, pastor of St. Patrick Parish, Cairo, would ride fifty-four miles to the Thomas McCabe residence in Reynoldsburg where families gathered from miles around including Stonefort to celebrate Mass.

St. Francis de Sales was the most fitting patron saint for the Stonefort parish. St. Francis defended the Catholic faith by his pastoral work and writing at the time of the Protestant Reformation. The Stonefort parish has often been challenged to defend its Catholic faith as well. One story in the parish history recounts how an elderly widow in particular was often sent hate mail challenging her Catholic faith. She would patiently reply with kind words and a Bible reference to justify and validate her Catholic beliefs. Today some prejudice and misconceptions still remain among some of St. Francis de Sales' neighbors, but the parishioners through example and faith still maintain a strong spirituality.

The St. Francis de Sales faith community keeps Christ, the Eucharist, and Scripture at its center through attending and participating in Mass. Religious devotions such as praying the Rosary before Mass each Sunday, attending first Saturday Masses, and attending special devotions during Lent and Advent all move the parish along its spiritual journey. Since the parish family is small, most everyone participates in Mass as lectors, ushers, music ministers, and servers.

Parish outreach involves expressions of love for neighbor by welcoming visitors, collecting food and money for the poor and those affected by natural disasters, funding special projects such as the local ministerial alliance, visiting the sick and shut-ins, and volunteering at the Veterans' Administration hospital. In the aftermath of Hurricane Katrina, St. Francis de Sales Parish "adopted" a family who lost everything and provided them with food, clothing, and furniture. The parish serves its own members by encouraging fellowship through cook-outs and special parties, providing Bible study, and teaching the faith to new generations of Catholics. Parishioners also volunteer to maintain the grounds of this little church, nestled high on a hill.

Immaculate Conception

TAMAROA, ILLINOIS

Founded 1904

Bishop John Janssen dedicated the former St. Vincent Hospital in Belleville on October 28, 1904.

■ Immaculate Conception Catholic Church in Tamaroa came about through the foresight of a small group of faithful Catholics along with Father Joseph Ceranski, the founding pastor. On December 8, 1904, the feast of the Immaculate Conception, Bishop John Janssen granted permission to them to form a new parish under the patronage of the Immaculate Conception of Mary, who continues to serve as an inspiration to the parish over a century later.

The first Mass was celebrated at Tamaroa by Father Ceranski on Christmas Day, 1905. The church was dedicated in 1906 as a mission of St. Barbara Church, Scheller. The original church was destroyed by fire in 1958 during a thunderstorm. By shear devotion, the parishioners of Immaculate Conception rebuilt the church on the current site. That same devotion of parishioners kept the parish functioning in these trying times without a resident pastor. Today, Father Oliver Nwachukwu serves as administrator of the Tamaroa parish.

In recent years, the parish has worked at remembering their forebearers. Three acres of ground located two miles west of town were acquired from Victor Rekosz, a parishioner, for a Catholic cemetery in July 2005. A Memorial Brick Garden was installed at the church in 2008, so that past, present, and future generations will recall those who have sacrificed to maintain the Church's presence in Tamaroa.

Over the years, a few parishioners from Tamaroa have responded to God's call to the priesthood and religious life. Father Trevor Murry has been the most recent of three priests that have answered God's call. A Franciscan Sister and Franciscan Brother also answered the call of God: the late Franciscan Sister Louise Schubert and the late Franciscan Brother Honoratus Michael Schubert called Tamaroa home.

Immaculate Conception Catholic Church in Tamaroa has one main objective: to grow in relationship with God, others, the community and the environment; to respond to God in love and obedience.

St. Mary Magdalen

TODD'S MILL, ILLINOIS

Founded 1868

The first Bishop of Alton, Bishop Henry Damian Juncker, died on October 2, 1868.

■ St. Mary Magdalen Church, Todd's Mill, is situated in the northern end of Perry County, in an area that was originally settled by Irish and German immigrants in the 1850's and 1860's. Among these early settlers was Joseph Todd, the owner and operator of a mill who had come here from Ireland, and after whose family business the area is named. He donated twenty acres of ground so that a church could be built, and on June 19, 1868, St. Mary Magdalen Parish was established by Bishop Henry Damian Juncker, the first Bishop of Alton. Although a church was immediately built on the site of the present parish cemetery, St. Mary Magdalen had no resident priest until the beginning of 1896 and was served primarily by the pastors of St. Anthony Church, Lively Grove, and then St. Bruno Church, Pinckneyville.

The first school was a room set aside in the rectory which was built in 1896, when Father Anton Stern was appointed the first resident pastor. He taught both religion and the three R's. A separate one-room school was built in 1901 and during that same year the church was destroyed by fire. A new church was built and blessed by Bishop John Janssen on May 27, 1903 and this structure served as the parish church until about 1970

when a new church was constructed. In Fall 1917, the Franciscan Sisters of Our Lady of Perpetual Help began staffing the two-room parish school. The school was closed in 1978 at the end of the school year. In 1960, a new rectory was built after fire destroyed the old rectory and took the life of Father Stephen Kraus, pastor at the time.

Over the years a variety of priests have served as resident pastors of St. Mary Magdalen, each with their own unique gifts and talents and each enriching parish life in their own ways. In 1994, St. Mary Magdalen Parish was made part of a team ministry that cared for parishes in the communities of Todd's Mill, Posen, DuBois, and Tamaroa. In 1995, the team ministry ended and a new pastor was appointed who would be responsible for both St. Mary Magdalen Parish and Our Lady of Perpetual Help Parish, Posen. This pastoral leadership arrangement continues today with Father Bernard Goedde.

At present there are approximately 100 households that make up St. Mary Magdalen Parish, many of German, Irish, or Polish ancestry. Since many of these people are related to each other, family and family functions are still very important. These people seek to grow in their own faith and devotion and to hand on that faith to their children as did their rugged ancestors in the faith who came to what is now known as the Todd's Mill area. Family, faith, and service of others are important priorities for them.

St. Paul the Apostle

VIENNA, ILLINOIS

Founded 1895

Grover Cleveland was in his second term as U.S. President in 1895.

■ Members of the Dennis Dwyer family from Ohio were the first Catholics in Vienna, arriving in 1858. For the next 26 years, participation in Mass and sacraments required a 20-mile trip to Reynoldsburg, which is now known as New Burnside, where a visiting priest would occasionally celebrate Mass in a private home. In February 1884, Father C.J. Eckert, pastor of Mound City, requested permission of the Bishop of Alton to provide an opportunity for the three Catholic families of Vienna to make their Easter duty. When Father John Duffy was appointed resident pastor of New Burnside in 1895, he was charged with the care of the eleven families of Vienna as a mission.

Vienna's first Catholic church was built on a donated lot in 1896 and given the name of St. Paul the Apostle. For two years until he was reassigned, Father Duffy resided in Vienna. In the spirit of their patron, the Apostle to the Gentiles, in succeeding years, St. Paul parishioners endured the hardships of rough hewn seats for pews, no screens, cold in winter and heat in summer, and Mass only twice a month.

Thomas McCabe, who came to Johnson County as an infant in 1854 wrote in his reminiscences, "My mother's faithful perseverance and labors in a very great measure provided the preservation of the faith among the early pioneers. In the absence of a priest, she taught the catechism and consoled and encouraged those early Catholic settlers." In 1932 three children from Vienna attended the religious vacation school at Elizabethtown. Beginning in the late 1940s the sisters at Mounds taught summer school religion classes at St Paul. Beginning in

the late 1970s , the Adorers of the Blood of Christ and School Sisters of Notre Dame sisters joined with St. Paul parishioners in providing religious education for Vienna Catholic youth.

Around the time of the Second Vatican Council, St. Paul Parish experienced significant growth. Development of Lake Egypt, construction of a prison and building I-24 interstate highway contributed to the expansion. It is interesting to note that the Rite of Christian Initiation for Adults brought greater growth than infant baptisms. A formal structure for parishioner participation in setting priorities with the pastor, currently Father Thomas Barrett, came into existence as the Parish Council. That council developed a parish mission statement, which reads, "St. Paul Church members will reflect God's saving love by living Catholic teachings and traditions. We as parishioners will support each other by active participation in the Sacramental and Liturgical celebrations. We will live out our Catholic Faith, and as Christians will serve our community."

St Paul parishioners live this spirit of service through various ministries. Vienna Hospitality House provides overnight lodging for families visiting prison inmates. Parishioners also assist with Faith Alive, a ministerial alliance sponsored store that offers clothing, assistance with utilities and food. St. Paul Parish also lends direct support to the local food pantry, which is operated at the First Baptist Church. St. Paul Parish also works to ensure celebration of the Sacraments and Eucharist at Shawnee and Vienna Correctional Centers.

St. John the Baptist

WEST FRANKFORT, ILLINOIS

Founded 1916

The former Central Catholic High School in Cairo opened its doors in 1916.

■ In response to the threat of attack during Tecumseh's War in the early 1800's, a man named Francis Jordan from Tennessee constructed a fort in this area with the help of his seven brothers. It became known as "Frank's Fort," and the community which arose around it in the following years came to be known as Frankfort. As the railroad entered the area just west of town, this new commercial center came to be known as West Frankfort. The name was maintained once both communities merged.

Once, West Frankfort had a population which rivaled that of Chicago, due to the thriving coal mines in the area. These mines attracted men, women, and children of many different ethnicities and faiths, including numerous Catholics, particularly those of Lithuanian, Polish, and Italian heritage. Before a church had been built in town, the first Catholics received their Lord in Word and Sacrament in the neighboring town of Johnston City, making the six-mile journey sometimes by wagon or by following the railroad tracks on foot. As the Catholic population grew, the pastors of neighboring parishes celebrated Holy Mass first in homes, then at the Old Opera House, the faithful often kneeling in the debris from the Saturday night shows.

In 1916, West Frankfort received its first pastor, Father Joseph Tragessor, and soon its first church, named St. John the Baptist. It was a humble structure whose yard was often the grazing pasture of cattle. Once the congregation outgrew it, plans were made for the current church, which was built in 1921. A parochial school

was also opened and its first graduation was held in 1922. In the early years, in addition to meeting in the convent, students used the church kneelers for chairs and the pews for desks until a building was completed. Their teachers were the Franciscan Sisters of Our Lady of Perpetual Help, a community which is based in St. Louis, Missouri, and who still have a presence in the parish today.

From its humble beginnings to the present, St. John the Baptist Catholic Parish has, in the spirit of its patron saint, continued to call the faithful to repentance and to prepare His way. The trail has been blazed by faithful priests, religious and lay teachers, and devoted parishioners who have opened many hearts to the love of God. As a place of solace, it has brought Christ's healing to the town of West Frankfort through times of tragedy, such as the Orient coal mine explosion of December 21, 1951, which took the lives of 119 men. As a place of belonging, it has through the years welcomed many converts to Catholicism, and continues to do so. As a place of learning, it carries on its long tradition of service to the community through the education of the mind and the cultivation of the soul. As a place of prayer, it is the meeting place where with St. John, young and old, wealthy and poor, healthy and ill, may "behold the Lamb of God." The pastor of St. John the Baptist Catholic Church is Father Trevor Murry.

St. Joseph

WILLISVILLE, ILLINOIS

Founded 1903

Pope Leo XIII, the champion of workers, died on July 20, 1903.

■ Bishop John Janssen sent a priest from Italy, Father Francis Sannello, to Willisville in January 1903 to organize a parish of those who had been attending Mass at Murphysboro and Pinckneyville. The present church, the second one built by the Willisville Catholic community, was dedicated in 1906. Parish activity thrived during the next several years. More than 90 were receiving a Catholic education at Willisville with the help of the Adorers of the Blood of Christ. Father Sannello purchased five acres outside of town for a cemetery.

Saint Joseph Parish was originally comprised of Sicilians who came to Willisville to work in the Dickie Willis coal mine. The town also had a thriving dairy business in operation. Unfortunately, hard times nearly wiped out the town and parish. Strikes at the coal mine and dairy. that could not be settled, were followed by the Great Depression until Willisville became a virtual ghost town. At one point, Mass was celebrated at St. Joseph Church only once a year, on Christmas, and the parish survived mainly due to the support of the Catholic Mission Society.

The dedication of a core group of parishioners produced the St. Joseph Spaghetti Supper in 1950. It made the difference in the parish's financial and social success. Currently, this event is held on the first Saturday in August and contributes to a thriving parish spirit.

Christ lives at the center of St. Joseph parish life in two main ways. First, parishioners gather each Sunday morning at 10:30 a.m. to attend to the Word of God through Scripture readings and to participate in a joyful celebration of the sacred, sacramental, sacrificial supper of the Mass. Second, several qualified volunteers teach the weekly Parish School of Religion to children from the cluster of parishes in Ava, Raddle and Willisville. Currently, there are about 24 children attending four levels of classes. The high school level recently prepared ten teenagers for the Sacrament of Confirmation. Religious education, both formally and through the Sunday Mass, brings Christ to life at St. Joseph Parish with Father Leo Hayes as pastor.

OUR·LADY·
OF·
PERPETUAL
†ĦELP†

Mary Help of Christians

CHESTER, ILLINOIS

Founded 1842

Australia native St. Mary MacKillop was born January 13, 1842.

■ The first Catholic immigrants settled in Chester in 1842. As a result of their repeated requests, Father Nicholas Perrin provided for their spiritual needs from Kaskaskia and began celebrating Mass monthly in private homes. The first church was built in 1850 and was dedicated to Mary Help of Christians. During the next decade, Chester continued to grow as pioneers made their way up the Mississippi River from New Orleans.

Mary Help of Christians Parish shared in the growth and the main section of the present church was constructed in 1871.

The first parochial school opened in 1863 with classes held in the basement of the church. After the new church was built, the original church was converted into a two-room school and Sisters' residence. The present brick school was opened in October, 1905. Mary Help of Christian School continues to form youngsters pre-school through eighth grade. Volunteers staff the Parish School of Religion for those who attend public school.

The material and spiritual growth of the parish has been fostered by parishioners working through organizations such as the Council of Catholic Women, which marked its centennial in 1994. Knights of Columbus Council 3790, which was chartered in 1954, continues to be of service to the church, school, and community. Mary Help of Christian outreach extends beyond parish boundaries through support of the local food pantry and the Adorers of the Blood of Christ ministry in Bolivia.

Four men from Mary Help of Christians Parish have been ordained to the priesthood, including Missionary Oblate of Mary Immaculate Father Allen Maes, and Father Jeffrey Moore, a priest of the Diocese of Lugano, Switzerland, as well as the late Father Robert Braun, OMI, and the late Father Leo Irose. Sixteen women have also dedicated their lives in service to the Church in religious life.

Since 1892, six priests have guided the parish with their vision and hard work. The present pastor of Mary Help of Christians is Father Eugene Wojcik. As the Belleville Diocese celebrates its 125th anniversary, Mary Help of Christians will mark 170 years as a Catholic parish. With over 400 families, the community cherishes its rich history while looking forward to the future opportunities to witness the Gospel through sacramental life, the parish school, parish school of religion, the Rite of Christian Initiation for Adults, ministry to the nursing homes and shut-ins, and web ministry, and others too numerous to mention here.

Immaculate Conception

COLUMBIA, ILLINOIS

Founded 1846

Pope Gregory XVI, who established the Diocese of Chicago in 1831, died on June 1, 1846.

■ Although the Catholic history of the Columbia area may be traced to 1673 when Father Jacques Marquette, the Jesuit missionary, traveled past the site of the present-day community on his exploration of the Mississippi River, the history of Immaculate Conception Parish began with the arrival of German immigrants in the late eighteenth and early nineteenth centuries into what would become Monroe County. By the early 1840s, the number of Catholics in the Columbia area had increased significantly, although there were only eight priests in all of southern Illinois at the time.

In was in 1846 that the Sixth Provincial Council of Baltimore petitioned the Holy See and asked that Mary, under the title of the Immaculate Conception, be designated "Patroness of the United States." This petition was granted, and it was only fitting that the new Catholic parish founded that same year in Columbia should be dedicated to Mary, the Immaculate Conception. From these founding days in 1846, through the time of the assignment of our first resident pastor, Father Arnold Pinkers, in 1857, to the second decade of the twenty-first century and the current pastor, Msgr. Carl Scherrer, the faith community of Immaculate Conception in Columbia has always been guided by the example of Mary, our Blessed Mother, who first said "Yes" to God.

Throughout its 165-year history, saying "Yes" to God has meant many things to the people of Immaculate Conception Parish, including, among other accomplishments: the construction of three church buildings; the founding of a Catholic elementary school in 1853; the creation of the Altar Society in 1859, the first parish organization; establishment of the St. Vincent de Paul Society in 1933 and the Holy Name Society in 1955; several additions to the school, including the construction of a new parish center in 1987; the establishment of an education endowment fund in 1977, reported to be the first in the Belleville Diocese; the establishment of a Parish School of Religion program; and the development of a Rite of Christian Initiation of Adults program.

Today, the faith community of Immaculate Conception looks to the future with anticipation of the construction of a new church to serve the needs of the growing community, currently numbering over 1,400 families. On June 24, 2011, Bishop Edward K. Braxton joined the members of Immaculate Conception Parish for a groundbreaking ceremony for the new church which will include space for offices, meeting rooms, quilting room and large social center on the lower level. Project completion is estimated for November 2012.

Following the example of their patroness, Columbia Catholics continue to say "Yes" to God's call in many diverse ways. While dynamic Sunday liturgical celebrations remain the center of parish life, spirituality is also expressed through a variety of parish ministries. In addition to providing an outstanding Catholic elementary school and an excellent Parish School of Religion to form children in the faith, the parish is proud of an active Immaculate Conception Youth organization. Other important ministries include a very active St. Vincent de Paul Society and a strong Knights of Columbus council, a Social Concerns Committee, and growing Eucharist Adoration and Prayer Shawl ministries.

For years, Immaculate Conception has sponsored a sister parish, St. Raymond, in Guatemala, while many parishioners participate in the Christian Foundation for Children and Aging program by sponsoring a child or elderly person living in poverty in a less developed part of the world. Recently the parish adopted the "ACTS Retreat" program.

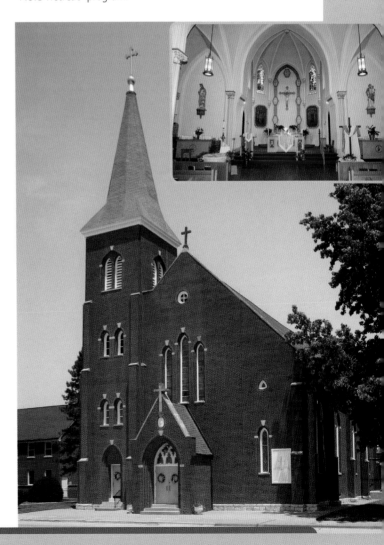

St. Mary Divine Maternity

ELLIS GROVE, ILLINOIS

Founded 1944

The historic Monte Cassino Monastery in Italy was destroyed in World War II bombings in 1944.

■ A small group of devoted Catholics, who lived at Reily Lake, made a sometimes dangerous crossing on a railroad trestle bridge and then a four-mile walk to St. Leo Church in Modoc. They had no church of their own until Father Francis Tecklenburg, pastor of St. Boniface Church, Evansville, was called to the bedside of a dying Catholic woman in 1932 and learned about this small band of Catholic families. With the permission of Bishop Henry Althoff, Father Tecklenburg organized this small group, rented a room above the Roots Store for five dollars a month and established a mission church attached to St. Leo with Father Joseph Pico as the pastor. For the next ten years, this mission church was attached to the Modoc parish, then Saint Pius V Church in Walsh, back to Modoc and then to Saint Mary Help of Christian Church in Chester.

In 1942, the mission was placed in the loving care of Father Joseph R. Sense, the new pastor of Saint Pius V Church in Walsh. The congregation continued to grow and moved to a new location, a deserted tavern at Fort Gage, just two miles south of Reily Lake. Through the hard work by Father Sense and his parishioners, this most unlikely site was converted into a house of worship. On December 14, 1950, the mission church

became large enough to become a parish, and Father Sense was assigned as resident pastor. Due to numerous flooding over the years, the Fort Gage location was not ideal. In 1957, the parish purchased six acres of land, which included an abandoned tavern, at the corner of Route 3 and Fort Kaskaskia Road (now known as Shawneetown Trail). Once again, a former tavern was remodeled into a church and residence for Father Sense.

Forty years later, shortly before Father Sense's death on May 29, 1990, Msgr. Bernard Sullivan was appointed administrator, and Father David Corrigan, S.J., as Sacramental Minister. Father Sense's bequest to his parish family made his dream of a new and permanent church for them a reality. The first celebration of the Eucharist in the new St. Mary Divine Maternity Church took place on Christmas Eve, 1992. Bishop James P. Keleher dedicated the church on January 24, 1993.

In July 1996, Bishop Wilton Gregory appointed Deacon Omer E. (Al) DuBois as Parish Life Coordinator. With his retirement, Bishop Edward K. Braxton appointed Father Benjamin Stern as administrator of St. Mary's on July 12, 2011.

St. Boniface

EVANSVILLE, ILLINOIS

Founded 1860

St. John Neumann died in Philadelphia on January 5, 1860.

■ The history of St. Boniface Parish spans over 150 years and recounts the story of the predominantly German immigrants, who made their new home on the banks of the Kaskaskia River. These dedicated men and women made faith the center of their lives.

Records indicate that small groups of Catholics gathered whenever a traveling priest arrived to administer the Sacraments. In 1860, thirty-eight families built St. Joseph Church, home of the first Catholic congregation in Evansville. After a fire destroyed that building, the cornerstone for a new church was laid in May 1867. This church was dedicated to the martyred missionary of the German people, Saint Boniface.

The mission statement of St. Boniface Parish reads: "We, the followers of Jesus gathered at St. Boniface Parish, will renew our faith in the Gospel and the life of our parish by inviting members to enthusiastic participation in ministering to the people of the parish and the larger church."

This mission statement is carried out in a variety of ways from visiting the aged and homebound to sharing the faith with grade school children through the St. Boniface Parish School of Religion. The Stewardship Committee has initiated food and monetary collections as well as toy drives that benefit the needy throughout Randolph County. This committee also inspires parishioners to serve in liturgical ministries, in faith development, in parish organizations and in areas of social concern.

The deep devotion and faith of St. Boniface Parish has been passed down through the generations. This rich and lively faith is evident from the number of vocations coming from the Evansville Catholic community. Since 1860 until the present day, thirty-one vocations of priests and sisters, a brother and a permanent deacon have come forth from St. Boniface Parish.

Parishioners demonstrate a strong devotion to the Rosary, which is recited before daily Mass. A sizeable number of parishioners gather for First Friday Mass during which the

Sacrament of the Anointing of the Sick is also celebrated. The sick are then prayed for during the Adoration of the Blessed Sacrament and Benediction, which follow this Mass. The Way of the Cross, an integral part of our Lenten worship, brings old and young alike to St. Boniface Church.

From quilting and picnics to ministry to the homebound, and parish organizations, activities at St. Boniface Parish strive to help each individual experience Christ's presence. This parish is centered on Christ, who has given the Spirit to share His teachings and become His true disciples. Father Benjamin Stern serves as pastor.

141

St. Augustine of Canterbury

HECKER, ILLINOIS

Founded 1824

James Monroe served as President of the United States.

■ Saint Augustine Parish was born in the hearts and minds of English Catholic settlers years before it was founded in 1824. These men and women brought a strong Catholic faith from their native Lancashire, England and they expressed that great faith in their worship and in the values which they sought to pass on to their children.

In the years between 1816 and 1824, twelve families moved to the Winstanley Settlement, on the present boundary of Monroe and St. Clair counties. The leader of the group was Thomas Winstanley, a devout Catholic. Other important early settlers were the Threlfalls, Gregsons, Newshams, Bambers, and Thomas Coop. The site of the Winstanley Settlement is marked by a monument at the current Saint Augustine Cemetery.

At first, Mass was offered in the Winstanley home on rare occasions by a visiting priest. In 1824, the settlers built a log church, choosing Saint Augustine of Canterbury, the Apostle of England,

as their patron. From 1833 to 1838, Father Vital van Cloostere of Prairie du Rocher said Mass once a month in the log church.

On March 5, 1834, a grant of sixty acres in Monroe and St. Clair counties was made to Bishop Rosati of St. Louis, from Edward and Mary Newsham and John and Catherine Winstanley, to be used solely and forever for St. Augustine of Canterbury Parish. A new stone church was completed in 1837 and consecrated by Bishop Rosati on November 11, 1838. It is reported to be the first consecrated church in Illinois.

Even though there was opposition from some of the parishioners, a third stone church was built in the village of Hecker, then known as Freedom, a few miles east of the Winstanley Settlement. The church was dedicated by Bishop John Janssen of Belleville on October 14, 1894. It is the current parish church which pastors and parishioners have continued to maintain and update to provide a place for worship.

The importance of the education of the parish children in the Catholic faith can be seen in the energy expended on providing Catholic schools in the parish. From the old log church, to a brick school at the Winstanley Settlement, to two school buildings in Hecker, the last of which was dedicated by Bishop Althoff in 1930, St. Augustine parishioners have shown their continuing dedication to Catholic education. For many years, the Poor Handmaids of Jesus Christ staffed St. Augustine of Canterbury School. Even though the school closed in 1997, St. Augustine parishioners continue to work together to raise funds to support the area Catholic schools in which Hecker children are educated.

Saint Augustine Parish has been blessed with six vocations to the priesthood and three men have professed their vows as religious brothers. Twenty women of the parish have become sisters. Msgr. Donald Eichenseer credits his parents, teachers, and his pastor, Rev. Joseph Frey, who was a role model for him, with helping him discern his calling. Brother Tom Ruhmann, OMI, was inspired by his teacher, Sister Marjaleen, PHJC.

St. Augustine Parish has had thirty-four pastors and administrators. The most recent pastor, Father Robert Gore, died on January 20, 2011. Father Von Deeke is the administrator of the Hecker Catholic community. St. Augustine Parish today continues to worship God and to educate children in the faith as their forefathers did. The parish reaches out in service to the community through the Hecker Emergency Fund and the Saint Vincent de Paul Society.

Immaculate Conception

KASKASKIA, ILLINOIS

Founded 1675

Jesus, the Sacred Heart, appeared to Visitation Sister,
St. Margaret Mary Alacoque in 1675 at Paray-le-Monial, France.

When the Diocese of Belleville was established in 1887, the Catholic Church among the Kaskaskias had been engaged in the works of evangelization and mercy for 212 years! When Pere Jacques Marquette gave honor to the Immaculate Conception of Mary at the original mission among the Kaskaskians in 1675, he began a long tradition of caring, spirituality, and devotion.

Pere Marquette's Immaculate Conception Mission moved south to present-day Randolph County in 1703 and it has been under the jurisdiction of the original Diocese of Quebec, the Archdiocese of Baltimore, Maryland (1789), the Diocese of Bardstown, Kentucky (1808), the Diocese of St. Louis (1826), Diocese of Chicago (1843), the Diocese of Quincy (1853); the Diocese of Alton (1857) and now the Diocese of Belleville since 1887.

Eight Visitation nuns arrived in Kaskaskia in 1833 to establish an academy for girls, the first in Illinois. Colonel Pierre Menard, first lieutenant-governor of Illinois, and William Morrison, merchant, were the patrons who helped fund the construction of the academy's four-story brick convent. The Kaskaskia mission gave the Church some of its earliest Illinois vocations, before the Visitation Sisters moved to St. Louis in 1844. Cornelia Hailman of Kaskaskia, in the first graduating class of the academy, entered the Visitation Convent and was known as Sister Aloysia. Four other Sisters made their professions at the academy. One of these, a native of Kaskaskia, Genevieve Brigid Kavanaugh, became Sister Mary Leonard.

Other religious vocations from Kaskaskia include Mary Turpin of Kaskaskia who became Sister St. Martha after she entered the New Orleans Ursuline Novitiate in 1749, the first American-born Ursuline; Marie Elizabeth Hedwigen DeRousse, born 1872, became the much beloved teacher Sister Celestine of the Adorers of the Blood of Christ Convent at Ruma. Nellie Cecelia Hartman, born 1910, entered the Benedictine Novitiate at Clyde, Missouri. She served her congregation as the architect for new convents.

It should be noted that Marie Rouensa, daughter of the chief of the Kaskaskias, begged to devote her life to Christ, but was persuaded by her father to marry. Through her influence, most of the native Americans became practicing Catholics. She was buried under her pew in church in 1725, a high honor for a woman of that time. The historic church is also the final resting place of two Jesuit missionaries, Father Gabriel Marest and Father Jean Mermet, were moved from the old chapel to the new church in 1727. Also, Blaise Barutel, churchwarden, who took charge of Immaculate Conception when the priests were away and Patron Antoine Buyat are also honored with burial in the church.

Another early inhabitant of Kaskaskia, Chief Jean Baptiste Ducoigne with his Kaskaskian warriors served as scouts and couriers for the colonial forces during the Revolutionary War. Through Chief Ducoigne's negotiations with President Thomas Jefferson for the tribal lands, the U. S. Government built a chapel, dedicated to St. Joseph, on the Indian reservation four miles above French Kaskaskia.

Immaculate Conception Church houses a hand-carved walnut altar, statues, reliquaries, and station frames dating to the early eighteenth century and a 750-pound bronze bell sent to the church in 1741 by King Louis XV and delivered by the Buyat family. For many years, it was the only bell in the Illinois country. Know as the Liberty Bell of the West, this bell rang when George Rogers Clark captured Kaskaskia from the British in 1778, and again when Lewis and Clark came to recruit and order supplies.

Kaskaskia Church also owns and preserves the first courthouse in Randolph County, where the circuit lawyer and future president Abraham Lincoln practiced law.

These historic sites and objects and parish records attract visitors from all over and provide Immaculate Conception parishioners an opportunity to show them traditional southern Illinois hospitality. A French-Indian Festive Ceremony is held each year at the Feast Day of the Immaculate Conception of Mary on December 8. The congregation gives thanks for all its blessings, and the many clergy, religious, and laity who have assisted on this 337-year journey.

Messenger Photo by Liz Quirin

Immaculate Conception

MADONNAVILLE, ILLINOIS

Founded 1838

Martin Van Buren was president of the United States in 1838.

■ Immaculate Conception Catholic Church, Madonnaville, traces its origins to the early missionary days of the neighboring parishes of Waterloo, Prairie du Rocher and the former parish at Harrisonville. In 1838, the Adelsberger family built a large log church in the area, where pioneer priest Father Patrick McCabe would visit once a month. The old St. Francis Xavier Catholic Church near Harrisonville was moved to James Mills or the James Settlement where it was renamed. Early records indicate that between 1850 and 1855, the priest at the Waterloo parish came over once a month and on the holidays to the James Settlement for mass. In 1861, the parish had its first resident pastor, Reverend Louis Hissen, who changed the name James Settlement to Madonnaville, in honor of the Blessed Virgin Mary. On Christmas Day in 1863, the parish was placed under the patronage of the Blessed Virgin Mary under the title of the Immaculate Conception.

The directory of the former Alton Diocese in 1880 listed the parish with the Reverend J. W. Gifford as the priest in charge. Father Longinus Quitter said the last mass at the James Settlement log church. The present church dates for the mid-nineteenth century and is built of hand-cut native stone. Numerous priests have served the parishioners at Madonnaville including Fathers Charles Hellrung, Edwin Hustedde, John Baptist Ssebitosi, Jose K. Jacob, SMMM, Stan Konieczny as associate pastor, to mention

but a few. Father Osang Idagbo, C.M., a Vincentian priest from the Nigerian Province is the current administrator while Father Dale Maxfield serves as associate pastor.

Since the establishment of the parish, there have been a number of vocations to the priesthood and the religious life. The parish has produced two priests, two religious brothers, and about 20 religious sisters. Sister Christine Wierschem was the first American girl to enter the Convent of the Adorers of the Precious Blood at Ruma. This was on January 10, 1878. Vocations to the priesthood and religious life are still being encouraged in the parish.

The Eucharist is the center of parish activities. Parishioners gather weekly and on some solemnities for the celebration of the Eucharist and also to strengthen their bond as a family. The parish also takes part in the Divine Mercy devotions which are held annually on the Sunday after Easter, Divine Mercy Sunday. These spiritual activities help to foster the unity of the parishioners.

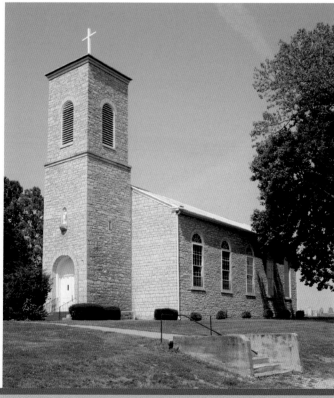

St. Leo the Great

MODOC, ILLINOIS

Founded 1846

The Cathedral of St. Peter celebrated its golden jubilee.

■ On the edge of the bluffs, overlooking the Mississippi River, stands St. Leo the Great Catholic Church in rural Modoc, located eight miles east of historic Prairie du Rocher. While the parish was founded as a mission of St. Joseph Parish, Prairie du Rocher, in late 1892, the first Church was blessed and the first Mass was celebrated the following year. The first resident pastor did not arrive until 1907.

In 1961, St. Leo Parish reverted back to a mission status, with the parish priest living in St. Patrick Parish, Ruma. In July 2009, St. Leo came full circle when it returned to sharing Father Daniel Jurek, the pastor of St. Joseph Parish in Prairie du Rocher.

Originally, Modoc Catholics wanted to name their parish after the reigning pontiff, Pope Leo XIII, but that was not permitted. They did the next best thing, placing their faith community under the patronage of Pope St. Leo the Great, who labored constantly to protect the integrity of the Faith, to pursue truth and unity, and to fill people with love and humility.

Throughout its 119-year history, the Catholic Church of Modoc has striven to imitate the example of their patron in improving their relationship with God and one another; living a more balanced and complete faith-filled and moral life; deepening parish-familial connections, possessing a deep humility, and celebrating the sacramental life of the Church. The Sacraments are extremely important to the People of God of St. Leo, Modoc.

One priestly vocation and three women religious vocations have been nurtured at St. Leo Parish over the years. "The Chalice and Paten" program encourages parishioners to pray for vocations in their homes as they do so at St. Leo Church where every Sunday prayers for vocations are offered during the celebration of Eucharist.

The St. Leo Parish mission statement stresses service of neighbor. This is achieved through different activities such as toy, coat, clothing, and food drives. The parish also collects gifts for the homebound and for those in healthcare centers.

St. Joseph

PRAIRIE DU ROCHER, ILLINOIS

Founded 1721

St. John Nepomucene, martyr of the confessional, was beatified on May 31, 1721.

■ Prairie du Rocher -- "the meadow beneath the rocky bluff" -- is considered the oldest continuing settlement in the State of Illinois. In 1720, Fort Duc de Chartes was completed on the banks of the Mississippi River and named in honor of the regent of France. It served as the headquarters of the civil, military and marine government of the Illinois Territory. At the same time a village, Nouvelle Chartres, grew nearby. Settlers from Canada and France, confident of protection, arrived and clustered near the fort.

The focal point of this little French community was the parish church of St. Anne du Fort de Chartres. The first resident priests were Jesuit Fathers Joseph le Boullenger and Nicholas de Beaubois, who served the needs of the garrison, the settlers, the Indians, and the Blacks.

As early at 1722, inhabitants of St. Anne de Chartres left the village and moved to higher ground at the foot of the bluffs, which was the beginnings of Prairie du Rocher. The original settlement and first church building were located at the site of the present parish cemetery. By 1767, the mother-church of St. Anne du Fort de Chartres was abandoned by the inhabitants of the village, and St. Joseph Church became the continuation of the mother church for the inhabitants of Prairie du Rocher and the surrounding area.

The patron saints chosen for these early Catholic communities remain extremely relevant today. St. Anne is recognized as the mother of Mary; and St. Joseph is known through the Scriptures as the foster-father of Jesus and the protector of the Holy Family. It remains the prayer of the Prairie du Rocher Catholic community that their patrons will help the parents of the parish to excel in teaching their children the ways of life and faith.

St. Joseph Parish's 290-year history echoes in its mission statement: "We, as Catholics and members of St. Joseph Catholic Parish of Prairie du Rocher, are called to give witness of the Gospel of Jesus Christ through our worship and prayer, through our fostering of a community of faith, and through our service to our neighbors. We are centered in the Eucharist and are united in the Holy Spirit, who empowers us to nurture our individual spiritual growth while caring for one another with compassion and love."

Fifty-one pastors from the pioneer Jesuit missionaries to the present pastor, Father Daniel Jurek, continue Christ's command to teach the faith by word and example. The parish is centered in the Eucharist, united in the Holy Spirit and care for one another. This commitment to Christian charity has been most evident in recent history during the devastating floods of 1973 and 1993, when people from several states came to help save the parish and town.

St. Joseph parishioners enjoy a good relationship with the local Baptist church, sharing opportunities to worship and quilt, and work together on a summer Vacation Bible School. In other outreach, the parish collects gifts during Advent and Lent for homebound parishioners as well as those in long-term care facilities. A committee sends out cards to the military, the hospitalized, the homebound and those in long-term care.

Scripture classes are offered twice a month in the evening. Afternoons of prayer and recollection are held on the Sunday afternoon immediately prior to the beginning of Advent and Lent. A Youth Ministry group is in its formative stages in an effort to bring Jesus Christ to teens. Grade school children receive religious education during the school year on Tuesday mornings. They also assist at Sunday Masses on a monthly basis.

Two priestly and thirteen religious women vocations have been produced by St. Joseph Parish. The parish's Chalice and Paten Program allows parishioners to take home a chalice and paten for the coming week. These are placed prominence in the homes as a reminder to pray for vocations. Jesus Christ has commanded us to love our neighbor. Our mission statement says to serve our neighbor. We do that service in many different ways.

St. John the Baptist

Red Bud, Illinois

Founded 1858

The Blessed Mother appeared to Bernadette Soubirous at Lourdes France, in 1858.

The origins of the Catholic Church in Red Bud can be traced to a meeting of Catholic families with Bishop Henry Damian Junker of Alton on November 26, 1858. The Bishop celebrated a Mass in the home of George Hoeffelin, and encouraged him, along with James Roscow, Anton Huegle, Anton Yaeger and George Bessen to collect funds for the building of a church. Less than a year later, a modest brick church was constructed and the first Mass celebrated on Palm Sunday, 1859. Bishop Junker came to dedicate the Church on Sept. 28, 1862, under the patronage of St. John the Baptist. Father John Mohr was the first resident pastor from 1862 to 1868.

Handing on the faith to future generations was of utmost importance to these pioneer Catholic families who in 1866 built a parish school and it has continued to be a driving force for the parish throughout its entire history. Today, 145 years later, St. John the Baptist Catholic School's teachers, parents and parishioners continue to work tirelessly to provide a faith-based education for its youth.

The influence of the Adorers of the Blood of Christ from nearby Ruma, would remain evident for many years as they taught in the parish school from 1913 until 1996. The Sisters' presence extended into the community's healthcare as the pioneer Adorer Mother Clementine would respond to the needs of the Red Bud community with the construction in 1900 of the former St. Clement Hospital, which continued under the Sisters' sponsorship until 1996.

Catholic education and the presence of dynamic priests and religious sewed the seeds for nearly a dozen church vocations from the parish. Four native sons were ordained priests and seven women entered religious life. Today, through weekly petitions at Mass and talking with the students both in school and in the Parish School of Religion classes, vocations are still encouraged.

The ongoing awareness of stewardship -- time, talent, and treasure -- has been a theme lived out and built on all through the parish's history. St. John the Baptist parishioners are challenged to demonstrate the love of neighbor through active participation in the parish council, the school board, finance committee, the St. Anne Council of Catholic Women, the Knights of Columbus and the junior and senior high school youth groups. As one parishioner stated while working on the Christmas outreach program, "when there is a need, the folks always come through with flying colors."

As St. John the Baptist anticipates its 150th anniversary as a parish in conjunction with the Belleville Diocese's 125th, anniversary, it is evident that the faith, determination, and sacrifice, which have characterized St. John the Baptist parishioners then and now, continues to be the strength and vitality of this faith family with Father Dennis Schaefer as pastor.

After nearly 150 years, challenges both spiritual and financial demand continued attention. As the parish faces these challenges and opportunities, they continue to actively bring the presence of Christ to the community of Red Bud.

Our Lady of Good Counsel

RENAULT, ILLINOIS

Founded 1879

Our Lady appeared at Knock, Ireland, on August 21, 1879.

■ Though founded in 1879, Our Lady of Good Counsel Church, Renault, did not have a resident pastor until 1897. During those first eighteen years, it was a mission at various times of Tipton, Ruma, and Prairie du Rocher. The parish church was built in 1880; the rectory in 1897; and the parish hall in 1919. Over its 133-year history, twenty-seven men have served as pastor of Our Lady of Good Counsel, with Father Roger Karban serving the community since 1988.

The parish makeup no longer mirrors its rural roots and few parishioners actually farm. Though located in a beautiful rural setting, the majority of parishioners are employed in non-farm related occupations. Like most modern parishes, Our Lady of Good Counsel parishioners are united more by their faith and their parish's common goals than by the physical circumstances of their daily lives.

Our Lady of Good Counsel Parish meets material needs of the parish as well as creates and deepens the relationships on which this Christian community is built through annual parish picnics and fish frys. All who participate in these essential "fundraisers" eventually experience the joy of serving others against the background of becoming one with others.

A most meaningful endeavor involves the Advent Food Challenge with neighboring Holy Cross Lutheran in Renault. Since its inception in 1991, the two parishes have collected nearly thirty tons of food and supplies for area food pantries and have drawn closer together as Christian communities serving those in need. This activity has become a weekly practice in the two congregations.

As with every parish, the parish's most meaningful Christian experiences spring from the weekly celebrations of the Eucharist. Music, homilies and prayers are based in Scripture, and as much as possible, reflect the faith of the community's ancestors in the faith. The parish works to make everyone feel welcome and families with small children notice how child friendly the Church in Renault tries to be. Almost all baptisms take place during these celebrations of the Lord's Supper.

Our Lady of Good Counsel Parish hopes that, through the years, ways to better imitate Jesus might continue to surface, as the community remains confident, as the Apostle Paul teaches, that "if we die with him, we shall also live with him." (II Timothy 2:11)

St. Patrick

RUMA, ILLINOIS

Founded 1818

Pere Jean Marie Vianney, patron saint of priests,
was assigned to the small French village of Ars in 1818.

The Catholic community at Ruma had a very humble beginning in the home of Henry T. O'Hara in 1818 when Father Desmoulin, pastor at Kaskaskia, celebrated the first Mass at what was then called the O'Hara Settlement. Today's St. Patrick parish roster still contains the names of the founding families, including those nine or ten families of Irish, Anglo-Irish, and Scots who attended that first Mass.

Priests from Prairie du Rocher and Kaskaskia came to O'Hara Settlement regularly. Upon his death, Henry O'Hara willed 100 acres of land to be used for church purposes and in 1827, the first St. Patrick Church, a log structure, was built. At that time the parish was part of the St. Louis Diocese and Bishop Rosati commissioned Father Donatien Olivier, pastor at Prairie du Rocher, to bless the new church at the O'Hara Settlement. The records indicate that in May 1831 the first class of 48 children and adults, including some from the English Settlement – now St. Augustine's in Hecker, were confirmed by Bishop Rosati.

St. Patrick's holds the singular honor of being the oldest English speaking parish in the State of Illinois. The contemporary mission statement of St. Patrick Parish echoes the spirit of the early Ruma pioneers: "St. Patrick's Parish mission is to share the Eucharist and the Gospel of Jesus Christ, to develop and encourage a community of faith, compassion, reconciliation and prayer. All are welcome."

The parish makes a monthly financial and sometimes physical commitment to someone in need – food banks, international charities, local families with an emergency need, educational projects and continued support for the parish relief fund. Devotion to the Blessed Mother remains strong within the parish with rosary every Sunday morning prior to Mass and several prayer days hosted by parish members in their homes. Members of the parish offer their time and commitment as teachers for our children's religious education and to adults traveling their faith journey. Father Clyde Grogan is the administrator of St. Patrick Parish.

Also unique to the Catholic Community at Ruma is the presence of the Adorers of the Blood of Christ, formerly known as the Sister Adorers of the Most Precious Blood whose Ruma Center is just across the front lawn from the parish complex. The Sisters established their motherhouse in 1876 in an abandoned academy built by St. Patrick's and later sold to the Alton Diocese and then to the Sisters. This community of religious women has been an integral part of St. Patrick Parish since their arrival. Ruma pastors have served as the convent chaplain for many of those years and the parish community is present and welcomed at the liturgical celebrations at the convent including regular mass attendance and special celebrations.

The Ruma parish has been blessed with many vocations to the religious life over its long history – 2 priests, two brothers and fifteen sisters. Sisters Mary Dorothy Simpson and Angelita Myerscough both became Provincial Superiors for the Adorers of the Blood of Christ. Sister Angelita was a founding member of the Leadership Council for Religious Leaders (LCWR), an international organization for consecrated women religious. Sister Beata Vinson was the co-founder of a Franciscan community in Maryville, Missouri, and was its first superior.

Our Lady of Lourdes

SPARTA, ILLINOIS

Founded 1897

St. Thérèse of Lisieux the "Little Flower" died on September 30, 1897.

■ The roots of Our Lady of Lourdes Parish, Sparta, can be traced to Kaskaskia, Illinois and St. Genevieve, Missouri. The first Catholic families in Sparta included the Wrights, Coles, Lindels, Boyles, Garragans, Dodges and Bartholomews. They were served by priests from Kaskaskia, Chester, Red Bud, Waterloo and East St. Louis who offered Mass in private homes. The first priest to visit the settlement and to offer Mass was Father Frederick Metzger, probably during the time of his pastorate at Kaskaskia, 1873 to 1880.

In the year 1892, the original church property was purchased for $1,000 through the generosity of W. R. Borders and a school building known as the Old Academy was converted into a church, which served the small congregation until 1962. There were 46 families who composed the congregation; 12 black families and 34 white families who were of Irish and German descent. The mission of Sparta continued to be served by pastors of neighboring parishes and on February 20, 1897, the mission was attached to St. Mary's Parish, East St. Louis. On July 29, 1897 ground was broken for a new rectory, a two-storey frame building which served as the rectory until 1962, and was later used as a religious education center until 1973 when it was razed after the construction of the present parish center.

The first entry in the baptismal register is dated May 19, 1895 and signed by Father Peter H. Jansen, who served the mission for approximately two years. Father Thomas Bannan became the first resident pastor when the mission was raised to the status of a parish on September 26, 1897. Improvements continued into the turn of the century including the installation of a new bell which was blessed in honor of Our Lady of Lourdes by Bishop John Janssen. The present Church and Rectory were built in 1962 during the pastorate of Father Raymond Malec.

A significant milestone in the history of the parish was reached on October 18, 1980, when J. Richard Downen was ordained to the permanent Diaconate. The parish continues to pray for additional vocations to the priesthood and religious life from the Sparta parish. Father Lawrence Mariasoosai, OMI, the present administrator of Our Lady of Lourdes was appointed on March 1, 2004.

St. Patrick

TIPTON, ILLINOIS

Founded 1850

The Trappist Monastery of Our Lady of Gethsemani was founded in Kentucky in 1850.

■ The peaceful, community of Tipton was founded by Irish immigrants in the 1840's. It was originally named Tipperary Town and then Tip Town, which finally was shortened to Tipton. With family names like Walsh, Kelley, and Dougherty, St. Patrick was the obvious choice as the patron of the church. The original St. Patrick Church was built in 1850, but it was not until 1869 that a resident pastor, Father Patrick Dee, was appointed. The present church was built in 1864.

Many descendants of the first settlers still make up the congregation, though there are a large number of parishioners of German descent present, also. St. Patrick Parish now consists of ninety families, with many younger families as parishioners. The parish has been under the care of, Father Jose Jacobs, SSM, for six years.

St. Patrick Parish embraces different ways to grow in our faith. Recently, the parish hosted a week-long Mission with excellent attendance by the parish family as well as other churches. Members of St. Patrick's Youth Group help conduct Sunday School classes for the little ones. Father Jacobs has held a Bible Study class to help parishioners become more aware of the meaning of the Apostle's Creed, and what it really means to be a Catholic and Christian.

The parish family rallies to support two annual fundraisers: a Wurstmarkt in the fall and a chicken dinner and auction in the summer. Many parishioners feel strongly about the need to help people and communities in need of financial or spiritual assistance. A Social Outreach Committee, along with many parishioner volunteers, has been working regularly at a soup kitchen in St. Louis. They also conduct food drives for the poor, and visiting at a nearby nursing home to bring cheer to "adopted" elderly people who have no relatives.

While under the protection of St. Patrick, the Tipton parish has a strong devotion to the Blessed Mother. During the months of May and October, the parishioners pray the Rosary before Sunday Mass. In October, parishioners gather for a lovely "living Rosary." Eucharist and meals are taken to the homebound and others, who cannot attend Mass. Special prayer services are held for those who are sick. Tipton gave the Church a number of priests and women religious earlier in its history. Now, the community prays for vocations every Sunday before Mass.

Seven Dolors of the Blessed Virgin

VALMEYER, ILLINOIS

Founded 1921

The Octave of Prayer for Christian Unity
was proposed in the United States in 1921.

■ Noah's ark might be an apt image to describe the perseverance of the parish of the Seven Dolors (Sorrows) of the Blessed Virgin Parish in Valmeyer. Popularly known as St. Mary Parish, this faith community survives despite frequent floodings of its western boundary, the mighty Mississippi River.

St. Mary Parish was established on March 24, 1921 as a mission attached to the former St. Francis of Assisi Parish in nearby Harrisonville. Lots were purchased at a cost of $1,200.00 and a frame church was constructed for a total cost of $3,500.00. Father Havey offered the first evening mass in St. Mary on All Saints' Day. Six years later, Father Anthony Keepes and the School Sisters of Notre Dame established the first religious education school in the Belleville Diocese here.

On May 24, 1943, the Mississippi River crested at 38.9 feet, forcing the congregation to flee to higher ground. The cleanup was barely completed when on April 30, 1944, the river crested at 39.0 feet, causing another evacuation. On June 26, 1946, the Mississippi crested at 40.2 feet, once again leaving behind muck and mud to be shoveled out of the white frame church and rectory.

On Mother's Day, 1993, a marble sculpture from Italy of the patron saint Seven Dolors of the Blessed Virgin was dedicated. Less than three months later, on August 3, 1993, this statue stood brave and strong in the church yard as once again the

Mississippi River devastated the little frame church. Volunteers from throughout Monroe County helped move the furnishings of the church, rectory, and parish center to higher ground. The last Mass at the original St. Mary Church was on Sunday, July 11. The levee break on August 3 brought 6.5 feet of water and swift currents into St. Mary Church crushing the hopes of continuing Eucharist celebrations in the white frame structure.

The late Father Edwin Hustedde, pastor, kept the Valmeyer congregation from being scattered. First, the met at Immaculate Conception Church, Madonnaville, and then moved to the library at Gibault High School. In January 1995, a fire destroyed the library, along with the organ, assorted furniture and various supplies belonging to St. Mary. Masses were celebrated in trailers until the parish moved into in the new St. Mary Church in the relocated Valmeyer on Christmas Eve, 1995.

As a testament to the dedication, faith and resolve of generations of parishioners at St. Mary in Valmeyer, a strong, growing Catholic community thrives high in the bluffs overlooking the homes of their ancestors. Historic artifacts from the parish's past below the bluffs have been incorporated in the new worship space in the relocated town. Perhaps most notable of these are the Italian marble statue of Our Lady of Sorrows which stands on a pedestal welcoming visitors and the original bell from St. Francis of Assisi Church, Harrisonville, which now rings in the bell tower. Vincentian Father Urban Osuji is the pastor.

St. Pius V

WALSH, ILLINOIS

Founded 1905

The former St. Adalbert Parish, East St. Louis and the former
St. Raphael Parish, Mounds, were also opened in 1905.

■ The first Catholic settlers of St. Pius V Parish were Ederers, Hennrichs and Storks, who came to Randolph County from Germany in the early nineteenth century and who worshipped in Chester and Kaskaskia. On May 2, 1905, Lawrence Stork, Sr., Michael Klein and Henry Zitt, St. contacted Father John B. Schlotmann about forming a congregation in the hamlet of Walsh. The parish first began gathering together in May 1905 after Father Schlotmann obtained the approval of Bishop John J. Janssen and secured a donation of land from John Schulein for the new church and cemetery.

Originally, from August 31, 1905 until September 30, 1910, the present day parish was mission of Our Lady of Lourdes, Sparta, and the Bishop assigned Father William Van Delft to minister to the Catholic community at Walsh. The church and its congregation were placed under the patronage of St. Pius V, the sixteenth century pope who enacted the reforms of the Council of Trent. On August 12, 1906 the Holy Sacrifice of the Mass was offered for the first time in Walsh with the liturgical appointments loaned by the church in Sparta.

On September 3, 1906, St. Pius V Church was solemnly dedicated with sermons preached in both English and German. A picnic celebrated the occasion and the Bishop and priests were hosted by Mr. and Mrs. Peter Pautler. The first Baptism was Ulysses Keiffer on August 26, 1906. A society for married ladies was formed on October 7, 1906. On February 15, the first marriage of Leon Arnold and Nettie Walker was performed and on May 26, 1907, the parish held First Communion Services with fourteen youths. The first Confirmation was on June 18, 1907 with a class of thirty-five. Before the Mass on this day, Bishop Janssen solemnly blessed the church bell in honor of St. Peter, the Apostle. A parochial school was built in 1908 with a seating capacity of thirty-four. Catholic students attended the school for six years.

On September 30, 1910, Father Joseph Voll became the first resident pastor. In 1990, the parish was clustered with St. Boniface, Evansville. From June 2009, Father Lawrence Mariasoosai, OMI, was assigned to this parish along with Our Lady of Lourdes, Sparta. The accomplishments of the parish result from the generous efforts of pastors, ministers and parishioners. Volunteerism is what holds this parish together.

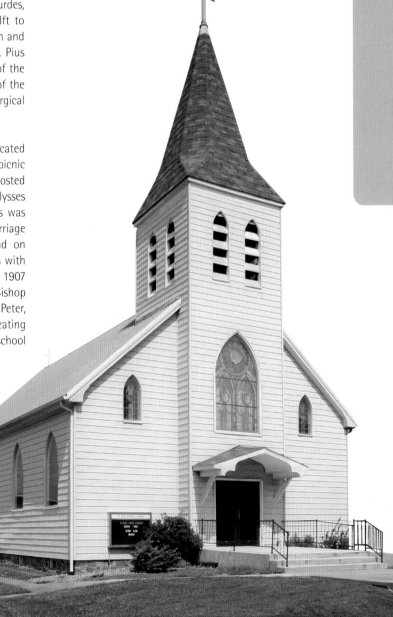

Sts. Peter and Paul

WATERLOO, ILLINOIS

Founded 1843

Charles Dickens first published "A Christmas Carol" on December 18, 1843.

■ The mission statement of Sts. Peter and Paul Church, Waterloo, identifies the parish as a "welcoming and giving community." The statement reads, "As members of Sts. Peter and Paul Parish in Waterloo, Illinois, we will strive to become the bearers of God's Word to each other and to members of our community through faith development at all age levels. We commit to be an active, welcoming, and giving parish community that will be open to change as needed for growth in our parish. We encourage active participation throughout the parish. We commit to strive to grow in the love of God and to be the best community we can be."

It is most appropriate, then, that the parish traces its beginnings to the Sacrament of Baptism, welcoming new members into the Church. On May 7, 1843, the first Catholic baptisms were recorded by Father Patrick McCabe, an itinerant priest from Ireland who opened the records of probably a dozen parishes in southern Illinois. Those were the first entries in the parish register. At that time, the patron of the parish was St. Francis of Assisi.

The first parish church building was built in 1852. It had to be extended due to the growth of the community. It was dedicated in 1862 by Bishop Henry Damian Juncker, then Bishop of Alton, who placed the parish under the patronage of Sts. Peter and Paul. The current church building was dedicated on November 27, 1883 by Bishop Peter J. Baltes who had served as pastor of the parish from 1853 to 1855.

Over 160 years after those initial entries in the parish register, the Sts. Peter and Paul Parish pastoral plan focuses on three essential aspects of parish life: evangelization, service, and stewardship. Active and non-active parishioners are helped to attain a fuller understanding of their faith. Evangelization is also carried out through an adult faith formation program, which includes the Rite of Christian Initiation of Adults. A unique program for seniors at Sts. Peter and Paul is OASIS, Older Adults Sharing In Service.

Young Catholics are formed through Sts. Peter and Paul School and the Parish School of Religion which has such a large enrollment that classes are held both at the parish school and Gibault Catholic High School! The parish celebrates a monthly youth mass and catechetical session along with other youth ministry activities.

The local conference of the Society of St. Vincent de Paul coordinates assistance for the less fortunate. The Stewardship Committee strives to recognize the unique giftedness of each member and calls each member to share those gifts as much as they are able with the Church.

Prayer plays a prominent role in Sts. Peter and Paul Parish. Each week, devotions to Our Lady of Perpetual Help follow the Tuesday morning Mass. An active prayer chain involves numerous parishioners in praying for the needs of fellow parishioners, their relatives and friends, and also for the needs of the universal Church. The Rosary is a part of parish devotions especially in the months of May and October and the Waterloo parish offers adoration of the Blessed Sacrament and benediction every month.

Seven parishioners have become priests and forty-eight women have entered religious life. One parishioner is currently studying for the permanent diaconate for the Diocese of Belleville. Vocations to the priesthood and religious life are highly encouraged through prayer and frequent talks to our youths especially by Father Osang Igdabo, CM, parish administrator, Father Dale Maxfield, parochial vicar, and Deacon Doug Boyer.

Adorers of the Blood of Christ

At Ruma, Illinois

since 1876

■ The Ruma Convent address of "Two Pioneer Lane" reflects the spirit of the early immigrant Adorers of the Blood of Christ (ASC) who first arrived there 135 years ago. The site, now within the Belleville Diocese, began as St. Patrick College in 1867. It was sold in 1871 to Bishop Peter Joseph Baltes, who in turn sold what had become Sacred Heart College to Mother Clementine Zerr and the Adorers in 1876.

Mother Clementine was a woman of great faith, hope and love. She walked the six miles from the Red Bud train station to Ruma and another mile to the vacant former diocesan seminary to view for the first time what would become a home and sacred ground for hundreds of future Adorers. Just thirteen days later on July 6, 1876, 11 sisters and novices loaded up the convent wagon in Piopolis, their residence since 1870, and moved to Ruma.

That first year the "German Sisters" survived by sheer grit and the Irish goodness of Catholic neighbors. The Sisters had few possessions to clean the abandoned site, plant gardens or plow fields. Area priests took bets if these women could make a go of a property that had twice before failed.

In 1887, when the Belleville Diocese was formed, Ruma Sisters staffed schools in Chester, O'Fallon, Bartelso, Madonnaville, St. Rose, Millstadt, Freeburg, Pinckneyville, Piopolis, Mt. Carmel, Ridgway, Centreville, Murphysboro and Evansville, Ill. St. Teresa Academy (East St. Louis, 1894) and St. Clement Hospital (Red Bud, 1900) were significant early ministries they served with pride. By 1887, the original 26 acres owned by the Adorers at Ruma had grown to 80 acres.

One hundred years later, at the Belleville Diocese's centennial in 1987, some 178 of the 342 Ruma Province Adorers were now living in 28 convents throughout southern Illinois, with 52 Sisters at Red Bud and 54 at Ruma. Mother Clementine might have been amazed to see the added acreage for crops and livestock, the original building completely renovated and the major building additions of the 1920s and 1960s to accommodate increased vocations. She would have rejoiced to hear how area high school girls had received a quality Catholic education and how postulants, novices and junior Sisters had received a quality college education there. She would have praised God that the "Center of Peace" was being used to foster spiritual growth for men, women and youth. She would have supported how the Sisters' responded to the turmoil in Central America by declaring sanctuary and taking in families and to the farm crisis of the mid-1980s by becoming eco-friendly and advocates for justice. She would have prayed by the Sisters' graves in the beautiful Ruma Convent Cemetery. She would have pondered how much had changed but how much was still the same.

The pioneer ASCs had adapted well to the language and customs of southern Illinois. Today we Adorers stand on their shoulders! Mother Clementine trusted deeply in God's providence, blended the active and contemplative life and took risks. We are her daughters!

Imbued with the spirituality of the Blood of Christ and steeped in the charism of our foundress, St. Maria De Mattias, the Adorers of the Blood of Christ of the U.S. Region continue the legacy. Today, 32 percent of the ASCs are vocations from the Belleville Diocese and 33 percent of the Sisters live in the Belleville Diocese. Like St. Maria and Mother Clementine, Adorers remain identified by their distinctively symbolic religious symbol: a traditional heart-and-cross necklace. And like their foundresses, they continue striving to meet the needs of the People of God.

-- An Adorer, who played a significant role in the history of the Belleville Diocese, was **Mother Clementine Zerr** (1832-1906). A native of the Black Forest area of Baden, Germany, the former Barbara Zerr entered the Adorers of the Blood of Christ in 1851. She arrived in the United States in 1873, among the last fifty Adorers who fled Bismarck's draconian Kulturkampf. She came to southern Illinois, where she led her Sisters in opening schools and hospitals throughout the territory of the future Belleville Diocese. There were 52 local communities when Mother Clementine died in 1906.

Missionary Oblates of Mary Immaculate

AT BELLEVILLE, ILLINOIS

since 1924

■ Interestingly, one might say the Missionary Oblates of Mary Immaculate came to the Belleville Diocese as a result of World War I. In October 1914, a group of German Oblate missionaries, working in Ceylon (now Sri Lanka), were interned in a prison camp by the British. They were later transferred to Australia. Prevented from returning to Germany, they ended up coming to the U.S..

Meanwhile, a number of German Oblates, who had been working in Canada, had come to the U.S. and were ministering in the upper Midwest. They were joined by some of the Oblates who had come from Australia. This was the nucleus of what was to become the Central U.S. Province of the Oblates.

The key to founding a province at that time was to establish a permanent mission house. Cairo, Illinois, was suggested as a possible location. On their way to investigate that possibility, two Oblates were diverted at the suggestion of a priest friend in St. Louis to see Bishop Hnery Althoff in Belleville. The Bishop was most welcoming and offered them the possibility of establishing both a mission house and a retreat house on property owned by the diocese, provided the Oblates staff and operate a college for the diocese.

What was then known as St. Henry's College began to operate with 13 students on October 4, 1926. Over the years St. Henry's thrived as a complete minor seminary, offering four years high school and two years college to candidates for both the diocesan priesthood and the Oblates. To their credit the staff was conscientious insuring there would be no discrimination or rivalry among the students.

In the early 1940's, during World War II, Father Paul Schulte, OMI, a German national, was confined to living at the seminary. Once a missionary in the Arctic where he was known as the "flying priest," Father Schulte introduced devotion of Our Lady of the Snows at St. Henry's. The original Shrine of Our Lady of the Snows was in a corner of the seminary chapel and consisted of a simple painting, which included Father Schulte with his plane bringing Holy Communion to an Eskimo family.

Promoted by the Missionary Association of Mary Immaculate, the devotion grew to the extent it became advisable to separate the devotion from the seminary. In 1957, 80 acres were purchased on the outskirts of Belleville. From there the Shrine has continued to grow.

In 1946, planning for a retreat house began. A cooperative effort by the diocese and the Oblates resulted in the building of King's House, which opened in 1951.

From the earliest years of their presence the Oblates have assisted in various ministries of \the diocese. They provided teachers to assist the staff at Assumption and Althoff High Schools. On a much broader and more sustained basis, Oblates have assisted in the parochial ministry of the diocese, by supplying week-end help to numerous parishes. On occasion Oblates have filled in where needed as pastors or administrators. Among parishes served in that way at various times are: St. Henry's, Belleville; St. Leo, Modoc; Immaculate Conception, Centreville; St. Philip's, East St. Louis; St. Pancratius, Fayetteville; Our Lady of Lourdes, Sparta; Immaculate Conception, Kaskaskia.

Historically, one of the blessings the Oblate congregation has enjoyed is that virtually everywhere the Oblates went they were blessed with so-called native vocations. That has held true for the Oblates who came to the Belleville diocese. Many young men from the diocese came to St. Henry's Seminary and eventually became Oblate brothers and priests.

Oblates working in the Belleville diocese have sought to live up to the exhortation of their founder, St. Eugene de Mazenod. On his deathbed St. Eugene encouraged his spiritual sons to exercise charity among themselves and beyond that to be zealous in seeking to win souls for Christ.

157

A native of the Belleville Diocese, **Father Edwin Guild,** OMI, (1906-1995) is considered the founder of the National Shrine of Our Lady of the Snows in Belleville. Born and raised in rural Illinois, at Tamms and Wetaug respectively, Edwin Guild was ordained an Oblate priest by Bishop Henry Althoff at the Cathedral in Belleville and celebrated his first Mass at St. Mary Church, Belleville. Working at St. Henry Seminary, Father Guild became familiar with the devotion to Our Lady of the Snows and as provincial he purchased the site of the present Shrine, with appropriate permission, in 1958, and construction began in 1960.

The National Shrine of Our Lady of the Snows is one of the largest outdoor shrines in North America. On 200 landscaped acres, visitors pray and reflect at devotional areas suuch as the outdoor altar and amphitheatre, Our Lady of Lourdes Grotto, Our Lady of Guadalupe Hill, the half-mile Way of the Cross. The Shrine hosts a variety of adult spirituality programs, an annual novena, and a Christmas Way of Lights, which includes 1.7 million holiday lights.

Poor Clare Monastery of Our Lady of Mercy

AT BELLEVILLE, ILLINOIS

since 1986

■ Acting on the suggestion of a member of the Diocese, Carol Reigle, Bishop James P. Keleher invited the Poor Clares of Roswell, New Mexico, to found a monastery in the Belleville Diocese in February 1985. "We are basically a rural diocese in southern Illinois. We have many dedicated priests and religious ministering to over 125,000 people. And the people here are beautiful with a deep and abiding faith. The presence of the Poor Clares in our Diocese would add a new dimension to the witness we give to Jesus through our service," Bishop Keleher explained in the letter of invitation to Mother Mary Francis, PCC.

In just over a year, the Holy See granted permission for the foundation and on June 6, 1986, the six foundresses of the Poor Clare Monastery in Belleville arrived at their temporary home on the ground of the Diocesan Pastoral Center. The Sisters were housed in the convent of the former St. John's Orphanage. A seven-foot cedar fence provided temporary enclosure for the cloistered nuns. The founding Poor Clares came from Quebec, Canada, and News Mexico, Michigan, Arizona, and New York. They were later joined by others from Iowa, Indiana, Massachusetts, and another from Quebec.

Ground was broken for a permanent monastery on the grounds of the former St. Henry Preparatory Seminary on May 1, 1988. The Missionary Oblates of Mary Immaculate donated the site which is on North 60th Street in the west end of Belleville. The chapel was dedicated and the monastery was blessed in ceremonies on December 8, 1989. At the Mass of Dedication, Bishop Keleher imposed the papal enclosure, indicating that the contemplative vocation is so precious to the Church that it is subject immediately to the Holy Father. The enclosure also notes that the cloistered monastery is a special place, "guarded by God."

The vocation of the Poor Clares is to pray for the world. Since arriving in the Belleville Diocese, the Sisters note that they have never missed praying in common a single hour of the Divine Office, the Prayer of the Church. They have not missed Matins or the Night office in the wee hours when most of Belleville is sound asleep. The Monastery chapel is open for daily Mass and Eucharistic adoration during daylight hours. The Sisters also host an annual novena leading up to the feast of their foundress, St. Clare of Assisi, August 11.

Adjacent to the Monastery of Our Lady of Mercy is a residence for Oblates of Mary Immaculate, many of whom are retired, and a residence for Adorers of the Blood of Christ engaged in ministry in the area.

On August 27, 2011, the first abbess of Our Lady of Mercy Monastery, **Mother Mary Therese Tremblay,** PCC, celebrated her 60th anniversary in religious life. Before entering the monastery, the future Poor Clare built a porch on her family home at age twelve. Youthful skills, honed over the decades, came into play in the foundation of the Our Lady of Grace Monastery.

Mother Mary Therese explained that the Poor Clares themselves finished most of the interior of their monastic living quarters in order to maintain Franciscan simplicity and to make the visionary cruciform monastery more affordable. The Sisters installed flooring. Mother Mary Therese built cabinets and cupboards from materials that were recycled from the renovations at the Hincke-Sense Residence. The Sisters planted 300 trees in their enclosure on the grounds of the former St. Henry Preparatory Seminary. "It was not just building a house. It was beginning to live a community life. And through it all, we were always at prayer," Mother explained.

Other Religious Congregations Serving The People of God in the Belleville Diocese

CARMELITES OF MARY IMMACULATE

CONGREGATION OF THE MISSION-- VINCENTIANS

CONGREGATION OF THE RESURRECTION

CORDI-MARIAN SISTERS

DAUGHTERS OF CHARITY OF ST. VINCENT DE PAUL

DOMINICAN CONGREGATION OF OUR LADY OF THE ROSARY

FELICIAN SISTERS

FRANCISCAN SISTERS OF OUR LADY OF PERPETUAL HELP

HOLY CROSS SISTERS

HOSPITAL SISTERS OF ST. FRANCIS -- USA

JESUITS OF THE MISSOURI PROVINCE

MARIANIST PRIESTS AND BROTHERS

ORDER OF FRIARS MINOR -- FRANCISCANS

ORDERS OF THE MOST HOLY TRINITY

POOR HANDMAIDS OF JESUS CHRIST

SCHOOL SISTERS OF NOTRE DAME

SERVANTS OF THE HOLY HEART OF MARY

SISTERS OF PROVIDENCE OF ST. MARY-OF-THE-WOODS

SISTERS OF ST. FRANCIS OF CLINTON IOWA

SONS OF MARY MOTHER OF MERCY

URSULINE SISTERS OF MOUNT ST. JOSEPH

Catholic Secondary Education in the Diocese

ALTHOFF CATHOLIC HIGH SCHOOL
Belleville, Illinois
Founded: 1964
David Harris, Principal
"We are called by Jesus Christ to educate young people, through the Catholic tradition, to lead successful faith-filled lives."

MATER DEI CATHOLIC HIGH SCHOOL
Breese, Illinois
Founded: 1956
Dennis Litteken, Principal
"Mater Dei, a Catholic, diocesan regional high school, nurtures the spiritual, moral, intellectual, emotional and social growth of young men and women. In a caring environment, respectful of individual differences, her comprehensive program educates, fosters faith and develops gospel values."

GIBAULT CATHOLIC HIGH SCHOOL
Waterloo, Illinois
Founded: 1966
Russell Hart, Principal
"Gibault Catholic High School, a Catholic educational community, celebrates the dignity and uniqueness of every person, cultivates lifelong learning and the pursuit of excellence, fosters faith, inspires commitment to service and justice, and works to develop a life giving relationship to the world."

Bishop Braxton visits St. James School in Millstadt and gives a student a chance to try on his zucchetto during the visit.

Continuing the Healing Presence of Jesus

ST. ELIZABETH HOSPITAL
Belleville, Illinois
Hospital Sisters Health System

ST. JOSEPH HOSPITAL
Breese, Illinois
Hospital Sisters Health System

ST. MARY'S GOOD SAMARITAN HOSPITAL
Centralia, Illinois
St. Mary's Good Samaritan, Inc.

GOOD SAMARITAN REGIONAL HEALTH CENTER
Mount Vernon, Illinois
St. Mary's Good Samaritan, Inc.

ST. JOSEPH HOSPITAL
Murphysboro, Illinois
Southern Illinois Healthcare

160